Howard Webb was born in Rotherham in 1971, and became a Premier League referee in 2003. He went on to take charge of some of the biggest matches in football, including the FA Cup final, Champions League final and World Cup final. He retired from the game after the 2014 World Cup and now works as a pundit for BT Sport, offering his views and opinions on the world of refereeing. He also had a consultancy role in Saudi Arabia, training a new generation of match officials. He is currently working in the USA to deliver Video Assistant Refereeing (VAR) to MLS.

Joanne Lake, who collaborated with Howard Webb on this memoir, is a Stockport-based ghostwriter whose first book, *I'm Not Really Here* (the story of ex-Manchester City footballer Paul Lake) became a *Sunday Times* bestseller. Twitter: @joanne_lake

# *The* Man in the Middle

## THE AUTOBIOGRAPHY OF THE WORLD CUP FINAL REFEREE


**Howard Webb**

with Joanne Lake

SIMON & SCHUSTER

London · New York · Sydney · Toronto · New Delhi

A CBS COMPANY

First published in Great Britain by Simon & Schuster UK Ltd, 2016
This paperback edition published by Simon & Schuster UK Ltd, 2017
A CBS COMPANY

1 3 5 7 9 10 8 6 4 2

Simon & Schuster UK Ltd
1st Floor
222 Gray's Inn Road
London WC1X 8HB

www.simonandschuster.co.uk

Simon & Schuster Australia, Sydney
Simon & Schuster India, New Delhi

The author and publishers have made all reasonable efforts
to contact copyright-holders for permission, and apologise
for any omissions or errors in the form of credits given.
Corrections may be made to future printings.

A CIP catalogue record for this book
is available from the British Library.

ISBN: 978-1-4711-5997-8
Ebook ISBN: 978-1-4711-5996-1

Typeset and designed in the UK by M Rules
Printed in the UK by CPI Group (UK) Ltd, Croydon, CR0 4YY

MIX
Paper from
responsible sources
FSC   FSC® C020471
www.fsc.org

Simon & Schuster UK Ltd are committed to sourcing paper
that is made from wood grown in sustainable forests and support the Forest
Stewardship Council, the leading international forest certification organisation.
Our books displaying the FSC logo are printed on FSC certified paper.

*To my dad: my mentor, my coach,*
*my fiercest critic, my biggest supporter, my chauffeur*
*and my best friend. This one's for you.*

# CONTENTS

# PROLOGUE:

# Webb, England

It's 5.55 p.m. on Thursday 8 July 2010, and I'm sitting in a meeting room at Kievits Kroon, the Pretoria country retreat that's been the FIFA match officials' World Cup base camp for the past six weeks. The nine remaining referees' teams are gathered together for the most important announcement of the tournament which will see, in five minutes' time, one lucky trio being awarded Sunday's 2010 World Cup final in Johannesburg. The conversation in the room is friendly enough – we've all become quite close as the weeks have passed – but the rivalry, unsurprisingly, is intense.

I'm flanked by my assistant referees (Darren Cann on my right and Mike Mullarkey on my left, as our Ant and Dec-like superstition dictates), both of whom are calmness personified. I, however, am a fidgety bag of nerves as the minutes tick by, tapping the floor with my foot, squirming about in my chair and popping Tic Tacs like they're going out of fashion. I also happen to be desperate for a pee, but I daren't leave the room at this late stage for fear of getting locked in the toilet. Daft, I know, but I don't want anything to jeopardise this most crucial of days.

'You all right, Howard?' asks Darren as my tics and twitches go into overdrive.

'Yeah, I'm fine,' I reply, clasping my clammy hands round the back of my head and glancing anxiously at the clock on the wall, invoking positive thoughts as the minute hand edges slowly to the top.

'I just need to know, mate. I just need to know.'

Exacerbating my nerviness is the fact that the lads and I feel that we are definitely in with a shout for Sunday's final. The tournament has treated us well so far: we've won plaudits for our handling of Spain v Switzerland, Slovakia v Italy and Brazil v Chile in the previous rounds and we've survived a pretty brutal cull which has seen twenty officials' teams being sent home at various stages. Some have been told by an uncompromising FIFA to pack their bags due to substandard fitness levels, others as the result of unfortunate errors.

The Uruguayan, Jorge Larrionda, for example, has been given his marching orders after controversially failing to award Frank Lampard's over-the-line goal against Germany, thus denying England the equaliser that could have kept them in the World Cup. Roberto Rosetti, the eminent Italian referee, has been disregarded for the final stages after allowing Carlos Tévez's offside goal to stand during a tense contest between Mexico and Argentina. It's all been very cut-throat.

I, like all England fans, am totally gutted that Fabio Capello's men are no longer in the mix, despite the fact that their exit may have actually accelerated my progress (I wouldn't have been able to preside over any latter-stage England games, of course).

What's taken me aback, though, is that some people at home now seem to be transferring their patriotic loyalties to us, effectively pinning their 'England Expects' hopes on to a 38-year-old ref from Rotherham, a linesman from Norwich and another from Exeter. William Hill bookmakers are quoting odds of 5-4 that we'll land Sunday's plum job, and the national media has run stories alongside my photograph, bigging up our World Cup final chances and proclaiming that *ENGLAND CAN RULE THE WORLD*. As a Premier League ref of seven years' standing, I'm not generally used to attracting a groundswell of public support but hey, I'm not complaining.

So, while we're not taking anything for granted, Darren, Mike and I know we've got a decent chance. Since our arrival in Pretoria our tight-knit little unit has worked ridiculously hard, both on and off the pitch. We've maintained our fitness levels, we've projected the right attitude, we've integrated well with the other officials and, without being arse-lickers, we've forged good relationships with the all-important FIFA committee. Deep down, we believe that we're a worthy selection for the flagship game. We think we deserve it.

The final being an all-European Spain-versus-Holland affair definitely helps our cause. FIFA favours 'continent neutrality', whereby refs have a better chance of an appointment if both teams hail from your home continent (other than your own country, naturally) or if both teams belong to another, thus reducing any accusations of bias. Mixed continent finals can be an issue: had Uruguay overcome Holland and reached the final against Spain, for instance, that may well have reduced our chances and pissed on our European chips.

Also weighed in our favour is the fact that the two officials' teams who presided over the semis are unlikely to progress to the final, as that isn't generally the done thing in FIFA-land. So, realistically, we reckon we've got a one-in-seven chance.

My main rival for the final is Benito Archundia, a highly competent, well-respected Mexican referee who oversaw the 2006 Germany v Italy World Cup semi-final in Dortmund. Based on our recent performances and our levels of expertise, the English and Mexican contingents are probably on an equal footing. Benito, as it happens, is sitting directly in front of me in the Kievits Kroon meeting room, looking decidedly more cool and composed than his edgy English counterpart.

At precisely 6.00 p.m., a FIFA committee representative from Algeria, Belaïd Lacarne, sweeps in, and the low hum of chatter peters into silence.

The first announcement, he solemnly informs us, will be the appointment for Match 63, the third-place game between Uruguay and Germany in Port Elizabeth. It is, of course, a great match to officiate – though not on a par with the razzmatazz of the opening game or a gung-ho semi-final – but I know full well that if I hear my name called out I'll be crestfallen. On the other hand, if I *don't* get a name check in the next few seconds, I might end up going home with nothing. It's like some *Who Wants To Be A Referee?* quiz show presented by an Algerian Chris Tarrant.

'Match 63, Uruguay versus Germany,' pronounces Mr Lacarne, 'will be refereed by Archundia, Mexico.'

My head goes a bit woozy at the realisation that my closest competitor is out of the reckoning. I lean forward and tap Benito on the shoulder to wish him well; he turns round and gives me a friendly smile, albeit one tinged with disappointment.

So it's now all or nothing for me and the lads. My heart's pounding. My bladder's bursting. My restless legs are almost Riverdancing. The three of us exchange fleeting glances as the unsmiling FIFA official casts down his eyes at his sheet of paper. I pop another Tic Tac.

'Match 64, Spain versus Netherlands,' he declares, lifting his gaze and scanning the room, 'will be refereed by Webb, England.'

*Oh my GOD. We've got it.*

Darren and Mike simultaneously grip my left and right thigh. A surge of adrenalin courses through my body and a rush of blood gurgles towards my head. The staidness of the occasion doesn't lend itself to me leaping up, punching the air and yelling 'FUCKIN' YEAAAAAAAH!!!', so I just stay rooted to my chair, tensed up like a steel girder, suppressing the urge to grin like an idiot.

*I'm reffing the World Cup final*, yelps a voice in my head. *I'M REFFING THE WORLD CUP FINAL.*

There follows a restrained ripple of polite applause, before a member of FIFA's technical team, Jean-Paul Brigger, takes to the floor. For the next hour he meticulously outlines the suggested tactical approaches to both games, replaying video clips of the final four teams' tournament highlights.

I'm trying my damnedest to concentrate on his presentation, but all the while I can feel my mobile phone vibrating in my tracksuit pocket. The news of our appointment has obviously broken in the UK, and I afford myself a private little smile as I visualise an ecstatic Webb clan running round a front room in Rotherham.

'Dad's doing the final! Dad's doing the final!' I picture the kids squealing as they jump up and down on the sofa, sporting their England kits.

Before long, the meeting comes to an official close and, after hotfooting it to the gents for a world record pee, I finally allow myself to relax and enjoy the moment. My fellow referees line up to offer their congratulations, the likes of Viktor Kassai from Hungary, Ravshan Irmatov from Uzbekistan and Frank De Bleeckere from Belgium doling out handshakes, back-slaps and bear hugs. There exists a genuine warmth and affection between us all, which I massively appreciate; my colleagues here in South Africa are the only people who will know exactly how much this appointment means to me, and just how hard I've grafted to achieve it.

And, with Darren and Mike by my side, I step out of the building and into the cool night air, my emotions swirling with pride, relief and excitement.

# CHAPTER 1

# Big Girl's Blouse

It was in December 1989, on the Sunday before Christmas, that I took charge of my first ever game as a referee. I'd been selected to officiate a Rotherham and District Centenary Junior League Under-11s match near the village of Orgreave, a mile or so away from my home in Brinsworth.

I'd qualified as a ref just three days previously and, to be frank, was crapping myself. While I'd passed my exams with flying colours and had spent my Saturday night revising the laws of the game, putting it all into practice was an entirely different proposition. I was nervous as hell.

Not helping matters was the fact that I looked like a right muppet. Having not yet bought my own kit, I'd had to resort to borrowing my dad's refereeing outfit, a shiny nylon monstrosity that comprised a shapeless black shirt with white detachable collar and cuffs, a pair of matching, baggy under-the-knee shorts and some ribbed black socks with big white turnovers. Visualise the least cool outfit that an image-conscious 18-year-old could possibly wear, and you get the picture.

*I look like Stanley friggin' Matthews*, I thought to myself as I trudged up the path that led from the wooden cabin-style changing rooms to the pitch.

My heart sank further as I approached the playing surface. Not only was it on an incline, the wintry conditions had rendered it boggy and uneven, with patchy, flattened grass and flaking, greyish-white lines. As both sides huddled together to hear their respective coaches' team talks, I felt myself shudder, partly through cold, partly through trepidation.

*I've never reffed on a real football field before*, whimpered a voice in my head. *I don't know where to run, where to look, how to get in position, how to even blow my bloody whistle properly …*

Helping to calm my nerves was my dad, who offered some wise words from the touchline.

'Be confident, keep control, and stay calm, Howard. Don't worry so much, or else you'll get too worked up,' he said. 'You'll be all right, son, I promise you.'

His fatherly advice was spot on, of course. I needn't have fretted so much after all. The game, which was just half-an-hour each way, went as well as it could have and – according to Dad – I did OK, all things considered. The fact that I received five warm, genuine handshakes after the final whistle was a good sign, he reckoned; an accurate barometer by which to gauge my refereeing debut.

Casting their long shadows over the pitch that day were the chimneys and cooling towers of the disused British Steel coking plant. Just five years earlier, in June 1984, this huge, soot-blackened furnace had been the scene of the notorious Battle of Orgreave, a violent confrontation between thousands of striking South Yorkshire mineworkers and baton-wielding riot police.

That year, much of the national news agenda had been dominated by the miners' strike, as well as the conflict's two main adversaries, Prime Minister Margaret Thatcher and National

Union of Mineworkers' president Arthur Scargill. Inflammatory headlines like *NO SURRENDER* and *MINE FÜHRER* screamed from tabloid front pages, and BBC and ITN reporters were frequently dispatched to picket lines from Nottinghamshire to Northumberland. Alarming allegations would emerge from both sides of the divide, whether it was hostile strikers lobbing rocks at police lines, or officers burning tenners in front of the protesting miners.

I was a 13-year-old schoolboy at the time and, when rumours abounded one morning that things were kicking off big-time at Orgreave, a mate and I sneaked out of the school gates during our lunch break and cycled over to the village on our Raleigh Grifters. By the time we'd scrambled up an embankment to find the best vantage point, the fighting had been and gone. The air was still heavy with menace, however, with plenty of miners, police and camera crews still milling about.

To a thrill-seeking teenager who didn't fully understand the incendiary political landscape, these dramatic events were ghoulishly fascinating. After all, it wasn't every day that you found the national news slap bang on your doorstep.

'Damn, we've missed it. S'pose we'd better head back,' I muttered, hopeful that we'd be able to creep into double maths unnoticed.

The strike had a profound effect on the local Rotherham community, since everybody in the town either knew or was related to a miner or a copper (some families even contained both). It was certainly a massive deal in the Webb household. My dad Billy had been a collier, like his father before him, and was just 15 years old when he'd first descended the Silverwood pit, only a matter of days after leaving school.

He went on to spend the best part of a decade toiling underground, finally quitting in 1966 after two tragic accidents within a fortnight had killed ten of his workmates. The trauma of having to dig out his best pal, buried alive under tons of rubble following a roof collapse, was the final straw. The job may have been well paid, and the camaraderie may have been top-notch, but the risks were too high for a man with a family to consider.

'I think I've had enough, Sylvia,' he'd tearfully announced to my mum that evening, resigned to the fact that his mining days were over.

Dad embarked upon a career in sales, becoming a regional rep for Wall's in the mid-1980s and delivering the firm's various meat products to shops and retailers across South Yorkshire. During the miners' strike he'd regularly stop off at Orgreave, where he'd fling open the doors of his Wall's transit van, slide out a tray of freshly baked pork pies and hand them out to his former colleagues on the picket line.

Throughout my childhood, my dad had spent a significant chunk of his weekends on a football pitch, refereeing a variety of local fixtures. He'd decided to take up the whistle in 1969, albeit by default. The Sunday League team that he played for would often find themselves lacking a ref – usually due to a no-show, a cock-up with the allocation, or a general shortage of bodies – and, to enable the match to take place, Dad would step in and save the day. His larger-than-life character, his no-nonsense approach and his big booming voice proved ideal qualities for officiating, and following encouragement from teammates and spectators, he decided to get properly qualified.

Billy Webb went on to build a decent reputation as a firm-but-fair man in the middle. He won the local Referee of the Year award five times on the bounce and progressed through the rankings of amateur and semi-professional divisions, finally reaching Yorkshire League level. I regularly accompanied Dad when he was on duty, journeying to pitches and grounds across northern England and lugging his heavy kitbag from car boot to changing room. Every Friday night I'd clean his boots for a quid, too, lining up the dubbin and brushes and using old copies of the *Yorkshire Post* to protect the kitchen floor.

Prior to the game I'd watch from the sidelines as he'd beckon both teams over, take them to one side and dish out his pre-match pep talk, the wording of which remained unchanged.

'Right lads, you know what I'm all about, and one thing I don't want to hear on this pitch today is foul and abusive language,' he'd warn, wagging his finger. 'I don't care if it's to me, your teammate, your opponent or t'cows in t' field, I won't tolerate it.'

Sometimes I'd get out my notebook and scribble down the match statistics as I watched the action unfold, timing all the major incidents with my Casio watch, logging any red or yellow cards and pencilling in player ratings. When I got home I'd scamper up to my bedroom, grab my football scrapbook and write up a mini-match report. I was a proper little statto.

Dad's refereeing status meant that he was also asked to take up linesman duties at FA Conference and reserve league matches. This would entail travelling to some of the biggest grounds in the north and the Midlands, including the likes of Maine Road, Old Trafford and Villa Park.

I remember my mate Matthew Page and I once accompanying Dad to the City Ground in the early 1980s, since he'd been invited to run the line for a Pontin's League reserve game. Nottingham Forest were still basking in the glory of their amazing back-to-back European Cup triumphs, and theirs was a stadium that I'd always wanted to visit. There was lots of excited chatter as we approached Nottingham, having made the hour-long journey down the M1 in Dad's bronze Austin Princess.

It was thrilling enough for Matt and me to enter the first-team dressing rooms but, as Dad got changed into his ref's kit, in walked none other than the great Brian Clough. Sporting his trademark uniform of green jersey and black jogging pants, he'd come to extend his welcome to the officials.

'Just let me know if you need anything, gents,' he'd said, smiling as he took turns to shake the hands of my star-struck dad and his colleagues. 'Hope all goes well for you tonight.'

Dad was deeply impressed by this show of kindness and humility, and couldn't quite believe that one of football's most revered managers had taken the time to say hello to a lowly linesman from Rotherham. And things got even better, because Mr Clough ended up sitting next to Matt and me for the duration of the match, chatting animatedly to us about our favourite players and matches as Dad patrolled his line.

Being a member of the Rotherham Refereeing Association had its advantages for my dad, most notably the annual lottery for a pair of FA Cup final tickets. In May 1980, a few days before Terry Neill's Arsenal were due to line up against John Lyall's West Ham United, the slip of paper bearing the name B. WEBB was pulled from the hat.

He came home cock-a-hoop that night, proudly brandishing the coveted tickets as he walked through the front door. Naturally, I was desperate as hell to go to Wembley, but so was my elder sister Joanne. Claire, my younger sibling, was only seven years old so was deemed too young for the trip.

'You'd better draw lots, Billy,' advised Mum. 'It's the fairest way, isn't it?'

Joanne won the day, and I promptly burst into tears. In fact, I kicked up such a fuss, slamming doors and stomping up and down the stairs, that in the end my sister backed down.

'Oh, let him go, for God's sake,' she said, whipping the ticket from her back pocket and angrily slamming it on to the dining room table. I didn't argue with her, of course. I just shamelessly swiped up the ticket before running to my bedroom and proudly pinning it on to my noticeboard. I was going to Wembley – yes, Wembley! – and for the next few days, I could think of and talk about nothing else.

The following Saturday we travelled from Rotherham to London on an early morning coach, Dad insisting that we took along a cumbersome folding stool to help me get the best view of the match action. We arrived in north London with lots of time to spare, taking the opportunity to marvel at the iconic twin towers and to saunter down a Wembley Way swarming with flags and teeming with cockney accents. I used my pocket money to buy a giant rosette from the first souvenir seller I saw, who happened to be of the West Ham variety. I had no allegiance that day, but immediately took a shine to its bold claret and blue colours.

After passing through the turnstiles we found a prime position at the front of the East Stand (which, incidentally, was full of Arsenal fans, many of them scowling at the rosette affixed to my anorak). Dad nestled our well-travelled stool next to the main tunnel wall, enabling me to step up and view the vast pitch in all its glory – albeit through fencing – while soaking up the legendary Wembley atmosphere.

But, as Dad was to learn, taking an eight-year-old to an FA Cup final wasn't without its hazards. As referee George Courtney led both sets of players on to the pitch – and just as the decibel level was reaching a deafening crescendo – Dad felt a tug at his coat.

'I need the toilet,' I whispered.

'You what, son?' he replied distractedly, craning his neck as the players began to line up for the national anthem.

'I need to go to the toilet, Dad.'

'Chuffin' hell, Howard ...'

Exasperated at my appalling timing (we'd been standing there for the best part of two hours) and conscious that a return trip to the loo would take us at least 20 minutes, he suggested I pee against the nearby wall so that neither of us missed any action. No one would notice, he assured me.

'But Dad, I need a big job,' came my corking conversation stopper.

His face was a picture. I bet he'd wished he'd taken my sister after all. Within moments, however, he was asking a friendly steward if I could possibly be dropped over the wall, ushered through the East Stand tunnel and taken to a nearby toilet. Luckily this bloke obliged, leading me down oak-panelled corridors to some plush executive loos before delivering me back to a very grateful parent a few minutes later (and a few ounces lighter). It's a story that, some 40 years later, is gleefully regaled to all and sundry.

'... and, after the game, did our Howard rave on about Trevor Brooking's winner, eh? Did he wax lyrical about Phil Parkes' heroics in goal?' Dad will ask some unsuspecting friend or neighbour as I'm cringing in a corner. 'Did he 'eck. All that lad could talk about for days on end was doing a poo in the posh toilets at Wembley ...'

Not strictly true, of course, as there were plenty of on-field incidents to discuss with my schoolmates the following Monday, including the controversy involving West Ham's Paul Allen that would, ironically, change the course of refereeing.

At just 17 years old, Allen was the youngest player to figure in an FA Cup final, and it looked like a fairy-tale scenario was on the cards when, with two minutes to go, he found himself one-on-one with Pat Jennings in the Arsenal goal.

'Go on, lad, go on!' my dad had bellowed, willing on the youngster and no doubt needling the surrounding Arsenal fans.

The advancing Willie Young had other ideas, though. The Gunners' centre half slide-tackled Allen and dragged him to the ground, his cynical foul denying the teenager an obvious goal-scoring opportunity and causing howls of derision from the Hammers contingent.

As it happened, George Courtney was correct to show the Scot a yellow card that afternoon since, at that time, the laws didn't permit dismissals in such circumstances. However, the ensuing outcry sparked a debate and forced the International FA Board into changing the laws. Eight years later, red cards for so-called 'professional fouls' would become the norm.

That same season, Dad had also started to take me along to Millmoor to see his beloved Rotherham United. Situated on the fringes of the town centre, it was a typically old-fashioned, lower league stadium with a capacity of 15,000. After parking up the car, the pair of us would amble up Masbrough Street, chatting ten-to-the-dozen about the match ahead, the pungent smell of tobacco, pies and stale beer hitting us as we neared the ground.

While there was a small seated area in the main stand, the vast majority of the ground was standing. Dad and I always preferred to watch from the terraces. In those days you could change your vantage point as the match progressed, depending on the direction of play. As the game kicked off, Dad and I would find ourselves a prime spot at the front of the Main Stand, towards the Railway End, before upping sticks at half-time and merging with the more raucous, hardcore supporters in the Tivoli End (so named after the cinema it had once backed on to). It was access all areas, really; the match-day stewards wouldn't bat an eyelid if fans sat on walls with their legs dangling over advertising hoardings, or spreadeagled themselves atop the home dugout's concrete roof.

If it was a chilly day, Dad would give me 20p to buy him a half-time Bovril from the pitch-side refreshment trolley. The old fella manning the stainless steel urn would often fill the plastic cup right to the top; this meant that, by the time I'd dragged myself up seventy-odd steps and fought my way through tight knots of fans, half a cupful of scalding, stinking beef stock had slopped all over my left hand.

'Cheers, Howard, lad,' my dad would say, unperturbed, as I sullenly handed over his drink, my woollen Rotherham United glove stained a deep shade of brown.

My fledgling support for Rotherham coincided with one of the club's most memorable seasons. The Millers became the toast of the town in May 1981 when they secured the Division Three championship, mounting a hugely entertaining campaign and pipping South Yorkshire rivals Barnsley to the title. That victorious team, led by manager Ian Porterfield, was widely regarded as the greatest ever Millers side and certainly made a massive impression on me. My bedroom walls would soon become plastered with pictures and posters torn from my growing stack of match-day programmes, and there was nothing I liked more than discussing the virtues of my promotion-winning idols.

Performing heroics in goal that season was Ray Mountford, who went on to make nearly 150 appearances for the club. Operating in front of him were John Breckin, a local lad and a top-drawer left back, and Gerry Forrest, perhaps the most cultured defender to have sported the red and white shirt. Man-mountains Paul Stancliffe and John Green expertly patrolled our central defence behind the midfield duo of Liverpool-born John Seasman – a player of great skill and finesse – and Mick Gooding, a combative, tough-tackling Geordie.

Spearheading Rotherham's strike force was Ronnie Moore,

the scorer of 23 goals that season and a Millers legend in the making. Partnering Ronnie up front was the inimitable Rodney Fern who, in my opinion, was the most accomplished finisher to ever grace Millmoor. Fern was one of those old-school players who, with his bald patch, sideburns and Mexican 'tache, looked like his teammates' great uncle. But what a footballer. It was his winning goal against Plymouth Argyle that finally secured our promotion, prompting thousands of fans (including me) to invade the pitch and nick a big chunk of Millmoor turf.

But my favourite Rotherham player of all time, no question, was a pint-sized right-winger called Tony Towner, who'd arrived from Millwall with Seasman in the summer of 1980. Nicknamed 'Tiger', he was renowned in football circles for not wearing shin pads, and was one those tricky and tenacious players who, whenever he dribbled with the ball or skipped past a defender, would create a huge buzz around the stadium.

He was also the origin of my favourite chant – a tuneful 'Tony Towner, is one in a million, one in a million to me, to me' – which Dad and I would belt out at full volume from the Tivoli End. I hero-worshipped Tony 'Tiger' Towner more than any other Rotherham first-teamer; during school holidays I'd often lurk outside Millmoor wearing my favourite blue and yellow away kit, waiting for the great man himself to sign my autograph book.

The following campaign witnessed two of the most celebrated results in Millers' history. With new manager Emlyn Hughes now at the helm – Porterfield had controversially jumped ship to Sheffield United in the close season – we hammered Chelsea 6-0 at our place in October 1981, before trouncing them 4-1 at Stamford Bridge the following spring.

'A 10-1 aggregate against one of the biggest clubs in England,' my jubilant dad had yelled, pumping his fist as the *Final Score* teleprinter confirmed our away-day scoreline. 'Who'd have thought it, eh, son?'

Disappointingly, though, despite this upsurge in form and reputation, most kids in my school doggedly refused to support their nearest team. That season, there were only about three Rotherham United fans in my year at Brinsworth Comprehensive; a couple of classmates followed fourth-tier Sheffield United but most opted to support the starrier, glitzier Sheffield Wednesday who, in 1984, would earn promotion to the First Division under the stewardship of boss Howard Wilkinson.

As far as I was concerned, the future of small, community clubs like Rotherham United relied on local support which, in our area, was often found wanting. As a consequence, over the years I would cultivate an intense dislike of Wednesday, something that, rightly or wrongly, I found hard to shake off.

Occasionally my dad would have refereeing duties on a Saturday afternoon and, whenever that was the case, my elder sister would take me to Millmoor instead. Joanne was four years my senior, with a sensible head on her shoulders, so was fully entrusted to protect me and to keep me safe. My mum's only caveat was that I couldn't watch matches against Leeds United, Millwall or Chelsea; they were strictly out of bounds.

'I'm not having you getting caught up with all those hooligans,' she'd say, her concerns a reflection of the fierce reputation that followed some travelling fans in the 1980s. Crowd violence at Millmoor wasn't just confined to the usual suspects, though; as a kid I remember being taken aback by the sight of knife-wielding Hull City fans kicking off in the stands.

In my mid-teens I was finally allowed to attend games on my own and, relishing this newfound freedom, chose to travel to away fixtures on the official RUFC supporters' club bus. I trekked up and down the country to an assortment of grounds – from Cambridge to Carlisle and from Blackpool to Brentford – and, over the space of five seasons, managed to tick off sixty-plus league stadiums from the master list of ninety-two.

Life as an away-day fan wasn't always the most joyous of experiences, though. My mates and I became accustomed to being treated more like criminals than customers, whether it was police escorts herding us off the bus and frogmarching us to turnstiles, or donkey-jacketed blokes shoving half-time cans of Coke and tepid meat pies though little hatches cut into the metal fencing. Granted, Millmoor was never the most salubrious of grounds, but some of the venues I visited were absolute shitholes in comparison, with their glass-strewn coach parks and overflowing urinals.

Once, during an away trip to Exeter City, I remember our bus being stopped by the police on a motorway slip road, a few miles from the ground. As they performed the obligatory search for alcohol, one copper told us how desperate he was for us to beat the Grecians that day.

'That'll mean they'll get relegated, see,' he explained in his Devon burr as he rummaged through my holdall. 'Then there'll hardly be any away fans to deal with, and we won't have to waste our time doing *this* every week …'

It was on the way home from this particular match, on Saturday 15 April 1989, that news of the Hillsborough tragedy in Sheffield began to break. We'd heard snippets of information via blokes listening to their transistor radios, but during the interval a Tannoy announcement informed supporters that the FA Cup semi-final between Liverpool and Nottingham Forest had been abandoned.

As we headed home on the coach and listened to Radio 2's *Sports Report*, it became increasingly evident that a huge disaster had taken place, with many casualties. Hillsborough was local to us – the ground is only eight miles away from Rotherham – and many of my fellow supporters had known people who'd gone to the game. With that in mind, the coach stopped off at Exeter services, allowing Rotherham fans to join the huge queue for the payphone to check that their family and friends were safe. The atmosphere on the coach home remained sombre as news of the tragic events filtered through.

When I wasn't following the Millers, my spare time would be spent running around local football pitches or watching games on telly. Like most young lads, I loved my TV footy, and I would sit on the sofa for hours consuming a diet of *On The Ball* with Brian Moore, *Football Focus* with Bob Wilson, *Midweek Sports Special*, *Sportsnight*, *Match of the Day*, *Saint & Greavsie* … you name it, I watched it. I'm ashamed to admit, however, that it was years before I realised that both of the Jimmies – Greaves and Hill – had been players in their own right. I just thought they were really good TV personalities-cum-presenters who happened to know loads about football. My dad soon put me straight, though, filling me in about their illustrious careers with Tottenham and Fulham respectively.

I remember bouncing up and down on the sofa when Rotherham flickered onto our 32-inch Pioneer one Saturday night in September 1980, the highlights of our match at Sheffield United being broadcast on Yorkshire TV's *The Big Match*. We won 2-1 at Bramall Lane, with the goal-poaching Richard Finney knocking in the winner.

The annual TV feast dished up on FA Cup final day was also a major event in our house. Along with the Grand National and both Wimbledon singles finals, it was the highlight of my British sporting calendar. I'd take my place on the sofa from nine o'clock – ensuring I drew the curtains to prevent the sun reflecting on the glass screen – and from breakfast to teatime I'd be glued to the telly. I wouldn't miss a minute of the coverage, from the player interviews on the team coach to the euphoric post-match celebrations.

My mum, fully aware that her husband and kids would be parked in front of the box all day, did her bit to enhance this special occasion by bringing in trays of party food and fizzy drinks. It was the only day of the year that we were allowed to eat our lunch on a picnic table in the front room; a proper treat.

'Don't be spilling anything on my lounge carpet,' she'd say as she poured Tizer into our plastic beakers.

Arsenal v Ipswich, in May 1978, was the first final I recall watching. I supported the latter that day, primarily because Bobby Robson's boys were considered underdogs, but also because I was drawn to a side that contained brilliant England and Scotland internationals like Mick Mills, John Wark and Paul Mariner. The 1979 final between Arsenal and Manchester United – memorable for Alan Sunderland's last-gasp winner for the Gunners – was one of the most enthralling matches I'd ever seen.

But it was the Tottenham Hotspur v Manchester City showdown in 1981 that really inspired me. A frenetic, end-to-end thriller, I was mesmerised by the talent on show, from Spurs' Osvaldo Ardiles and Ricky Villa to City's Joe Corrigan and Tommy Hutchison. I remember Dad also pointing out that the referee, Keith Hackett, was not only one of the youngest refs to oversee an FA Cup final, but was also a Sheffield lad, born-and-bred.

The match got me properly buzzing, and as soon as the final whistle blew I forfeited my usual dose of *Jim'll Fix It* to go outside with my football, kicking it against the brick wall until dusk set in.

*

Like thousands of northern, working-class schoolboys, I harboured dreams of becoming a professional footballer. I spent hours honing my skills on various streets in Brinsworth, or playing rowdy five-a-sides in the fields opposite my house. The *Kevin Keegan Soccer Skills* book was my bible. I'd pore over it in my bedroom when I was supposed to be doing homework, absorbing King Kev's advice about passing with the outside of my foot or maintaining the perfect keepy-uppy. I also treasured my copy of *The Football Grounds of England and Wales* by Simon Inglis, and would devour all the facts and figures I could about my favourite stadiums.

Once I'd finished reading I'd drag out the Subbuteo game from under my bed, staging my own Hamburg v Rotherham United European Cup showdown (granted, the box stated Arsenal when I bought it from Woolworths, but our red and white kits were virtually identical).

I turned out to be a half-decent footballer at school, as it happened. With my tall, stocky frame – I was the biggest lad in my year – I performed best as a central or right-sided defender and relished Whiston Juniors' weekly tussles with other local schools. Also, as captain of our team (and a Rotherham fan to boot), I was once handpicked by our PE teacher to present a thank-you gift to Ronnie Moore and John Breckin when they'd attended our school assembly.

'I want to be a footballer like you two,' I announced to my Millmoor heroes, who seemed like giants to me as I stared up at them, awestruck. 'I'm going to have trials and get myself a contract at a really big club,' I added, as I shook their hands and passed over their present.

'Not short of confidence are you, lad?' came big Ronnie's reply, as he winked knowingly at his teammate.

Between Under-11 and Under-16 level I also played for Bethel

Rovers, a local side that became one of Rotherham's many nursery teams. We were supplied with our own United kit – manufactured by Patrick – and would train in the gym at Millmoor every Monday, before playing our matches on Sunday afternoons. My youth team's Rotherham affiliations meant that we were drafted in as ball boys at home games, too. You can only imagine how thrilling it was for me to scamper along the Tivoli End perimeter, lobbing errant balls back to Bobby Mimms or Nigel Johnson.

I made good progress with Bethel. I found that I could read the game, could intercept passes, and could put in a well-timed tackle (I was one of those 'thinking footballers', apparently). The part of my game that required attention, according to my coaches, was my physicality. Ever fearful of knocks and injuries, I hated getting stuck in and tended to shy away from crunching tackles. Unusually for someone so tall, I was also pretty crap in the air and would dread going up for headers.

My strong will to win stood me in good stead but, on the flip side, I could be a really poor loser and regularly lost my rag on the pitch. I remember once falling out with my mate Christopher Jackson during a game – maybe he'd misplaced a pass – and kicking him not once, but twice up the backside. The second time he'd put his hand there to cushion the impact and I ended up breaking his finger. Mum and Dad weren't best pleased.

That said, during my teenage years I never once got cautioned or dismissed on the field of play. I probably ought to have been on a couple of occasions – bloody refs, eh – but I generally managed to control myself.

When I was about 13, Bethel Rovers' manager stepped down from his position and my dad, who'd always taken a great interest in team affairs, assumed the reins. It was around that time that, much to my dismay, some of my early maturing teammates had begun to overtake me in terms of physique. I'd always been the

beefiest kid in the squad, but suddenly I found myself in a situation where lads with muscles and moustaches were starting to
tower over me. I recall my spirits sagging as I realised that a young
Bethel trialist – a fellow right-back – was streets ahead of me in
all areas: bigger, faster, stronger.

I lost my regular place for a year or so, only regaining it when
I had my own growth spurt and finally caught up with my contemporaries. Dad would often have a pop at me from the
sidelines, though, moaning that, considering my size, I was still far
too timid for my own good.

'How can a strapping lad like you be so soft, Howard?' he'd ask
in the car afterwards, shaking his head. 'When you and their
centre forward went up for that header, there was only one player
who was going to win it, and it wasn't you.'

I could always guarantee what Dad was going to say next, and
I'd just sit there in the passenger seat, awaiting the inevitable. 'A
big girl's blouse, that's what you are,' he'd boom in his heavy
Rotherham accent. '*A big girl's blouse …*'

It was a phrase that he used often, and one to which my mum
took great exception. She also hated the fact that Dad would
frequently substitute me during these matches, possibly more
than was necessary. Being the team coach, he didn't want to be
accused of any bias towards his son, so would have no qualms in
hauling me off the pitch at half-time, even if it wasn't merited.
This hard-headedness caused no end of marital strife.

'Dad subbed me again, Mum …' I'd whine when I returned
home, my eyes brimming with tears as I threw my shin pads on
to the kitchen table, '… *and* he called me a big girl's blouse …'

Mum couldn't bear seeing her only son so upset. Her murder-
ous stare as my dad came through the back door, laden with a
bagful of dirty football kits, conveyed more than words ever could.

*

In hindsight, I was crazy to think I could ever have made it as a professional footballer. I was miles away, in so many respects, and simply didn't have enough talent to make the grade. When my time with Bethel Rovers came to a natural end, I reached the sad conclusion that my chances of becoming the next John Breckin or Gerry Forrest were non-existent.

Not long after this realisation, my dad posed the question that would change the course of my life, 'Why don't you take up the whistle?' he'd suggested one sunny afternoon as we'd sat chatting in the back garden. 'I've had a good career out of refereeing, Howard, and I've loved every minute, so why not give it a go?' he grinned, as I raised my eyebrows.

'You never know, son, you might even like it.'

In all honesty, despite my dad's involvement with the local refereeing association, I'd never contemplated following in his footsteps. Playing for Bethel and watching Rotherham had been my main passions and, like many of my teammates, I'd tended to see referees as bald old men running around in baggy black kits. However, once I'd given my dad's words some serious thought, I began to warm to the idea of officiating. Refereeing needed an injection of younger blood, I reckoned and, not only that, it would keep me fit and would provide me with a bit of extra cash.

Within weeks I'd made up my mind, and had enrolled myself on to a refereeing course in Rotherham. Unbeknown to me, I'd taken the first step on a long and extraordinary journey.

The Rotherham Referees' Association course lasted six weeks and took place in the British Steel Training Centre, a 1970s office building based on Sheffield Road. Our tutor, Alan Young, was a wiry, forty-something guy who worked as a long-distance coach driver by day and a part-time ref at the weekend.

'... so, if you'd all like to turn to page one of your *Laws of the Game* book, we may as well begin ...' he said, placing a sheet of acetate on to the overhead projector's platen glass and flicking the light switch to illuminate its handwritten contents on to the white wall.

## LAW 1: THE FIELD OF PLAY

I nudged the lad sitting next to me. 'Bloody hell, it's like being at school again,' I whispered.

'I know,' he smiled, scanning the room of a dozen middle-aged men, 'and I bet you're the youngest pupil here.'

The trainee ref sharing my desk was a lad in his late twenties called Paul Canadine, and that autumn evening marked the beginning of a long friendship. We had lots in common did Paul and I, and down the line we'd find our professional paths crossing on many occasions.

The course, as Paul and I would discover, was largely theoretical and extremely intense: most of the teaching centred around the FA's law book and Alan's acetates, without any explanatory videos, clips or films for us to watch and learn from. Each week we'd rattle through at least three of the 17 regulations – *Law 4: Players' Equipment, Law 5: The Referee, Law 6: The Assistant Referee*, and so on.

Like an old schoolmaster, Alan would recite all the technicalities that we needed to absorb. 'The touchline has to be a minimum of one hundred yards long, and the goal line a minimum of fifty yards,' he'd declare while we scribbled notes in our exercise books, 'and all white lines must be of the same width, which is not more than five inches ...'

Some laws were more complex than others. Not surprisingly a

whole evening had to be devoted to the most intricate – and most interesting – of the lot: *Law 12: Fouls and Misconduct*. The detail involved in deciphering player offences and referee sanctions was exhaustive, and I remember going home that night and grilling my dad about indirect free kicks and ungentlemanly conduct.

At times we were also asked to take part in role play scenarios with Alan and a fellow Referee Association instructor, the idea being to mock up a typical match-day situation. I remember sitting in the classroom, having to pretend to wield a yellow card at a portly bloke in his sixties, using the specific procedure we'd been taught.

'Frank's unhappy with your decision to award a free kick against him, and is going to tell you in no uncertain terms,' said Alan. 'Howard, I want you to draw upon what you've learned and react to this dissent accordingly.'

Frank seemed the least likely person to unleash a tirade of abuse, but he had a right good go, edging menacingly close and aggressively jabbing his finger. I stepped towards him, suppressing the grin that was threatening to appear and assumed the straight face of an unyielding referee.

'I am cautioning you for dissent. What is your name?' I said sternly, pencilling FRANK BLOGGS in my referee's notebook. 'I must advise you,' I continued, fixing him with a steely stare and trying desperately to remember the mantra I'd been taught, 'that if you commit a further cautionable offence you will be dismissed from the field of play.'

And then, with an authoritative flourish of my yellow card, foul-mouthed Frank was well and truly booked.

'That's the idea, Howard,' smiled Alan.

The course culminated in a straightforward written exam which, we'd been informed, had a pass mark of 70 per cent. We were given our results that same day, and I was thrilled to discover that I'd scored 95 per cent; at least that month-and-a-half of toilsome study had been worthwhile. My pal Paul had graduated with flying colours, too.

'Well done, mate,' I said, patting him on the back when I caught up with him outside the training centre.

Then Alan the tutor collared me, advising me to get my hands on a black kit from Sugg Sport in Sheffield (Mum and Dad would end up buying it me for Christmas) and to send off for my own Acme Thunderer stainless steel whistle.

'All the best for the future, Howard,' he said, shaking my hand. 'Hope refereeing treats you well.'

So it was official: I could now call myself a Class 3 status referee, albeit one who'd never patrolled a pitch and was yet to blow a whistle in anger. I felt excited but daunted, eager but nervous. I can only compare it to knowing your *Highway Code* from cover to cover but not having a clue how to drive a car.

# CHAPTER 2

# The Referee's A Banker

While no match for the Madchester scene located 40 miles down the A57, Sheffield's nightlife wasn't too bad for a lad in his late teens. My social outings tended to revolve round The Leadmill, a live music venue in the south of the city, once described by the *NME* as 'combining the thrift and intimacy of a working men's club with the leisure processor of a Haçienda'. Right you are, then.

Me and my old school pals would head down there most Friday and Saturday nights, chatting about that weekend's football (they were all Wednesdayites, sadly), swigging from bottles of Stella and watching bands-of-the-moment like Inspiral Carpets, the Wonder Stuff and Pulp (the latter's frontman Jarvis Cocker being a Sheffield lad, of course). Sometimes, for a change, we'd take in gigs at the Town and Country Club in Leeds or Nottingham's Rock City, hopping on to the train with carrier bags of cans for the short journey north or south.

Occasionally, when we were too hammered to know better, we'd find ourselves staggering into a city centre 'nitespot' called Cairo Jax, formerly known as Romeo and Juliet's. It was one of those 1980s-style two-in-one clubs where you'd have the choice of two rooms: one would blast out poppy chart-toppers (imagine Stock Aitken Waterman on a loop) while the other would churn out soul and dance tunes, a better option for those attempting – and in my case failing – to go on the pull. Following chuck-out time we'd invariably end up emptying out our pockets in a local kebab joint or curry house.

Once I began refereeing, however, I had to try to curb these Saturday night excesses. Being newly qualified meant that my appointments would generally comprise Sunday kids' games, so I couldn't really turn up with a raging hangover and reeking of Lamb Jalfrezi.

Transferring all the theory of my refereeing exams on to the pitch was tough and, as I'd expected, it took a good few matches in the Rotherham Centenary Junior League for me to relax into my new role. Like most novices, I felt extremely nervous and self-conscious in those early days, especially when I needed to raise my voice or brandish a card while being scrutinised by players and spectators alike.

'You need to project, Howard, project,' implored my dad after one particular game. Very easy for him to say; his Brian Blessed-like boom could be heard from one goalmouth to another.

As the months went by, however, the more assured and less fretful I became. Each final whistle would be accompanied with a sigh of relief that I'd got through another game, as well as a sense of satisfaction that I'd gained more vital on-the-job experience. Slowly but surely I began to feel more comfortable in my role, applying the laws just like I'd been taught, communicating as best I could with players and coaches and, ultimately, having the courage of my convictions when it came to difficult decisions.

I tried to be pragmatic, too; while mistakes during games

would be inevitable, and always regrettable, agonising over them for the rest of the weekend could be counter-productive. I had to view human error as part of a huge learning curve, and not to let it hold me back or knock my confidence. By the end of my first season, in summer 1990, I was able to walk on to the pitch with a smile on my face and a spring in my step, a far cry from the edgy, self-doubting lad who'd tiptoed on to that waterlogged pitch at Orgreave.

What they hadn't taught us at referee school, however, was how to best handle junior league parents. There were no tutorials about coping with mouthy, misbehaving grown-ups who could be an absolute nightmare for newly qualified refs.

As a rule of thumb, the younger the team's age group, the more parents you'd find lining the pitch. Under-12s games that I reffed, for example, would attract hordes of mums and dads whose kids still needed an element of support and supervision. With the older-age sides, however, you'd notice that the parental involvement seemed to dip markedly. No doubt their single-minded, independence-craving teenagers reckoned they were old enough to look after themselves, and the last thing they wanted was uncool, uncouth family members showing them up on the touchline.

Thankfully, most of the football mums and dads I encountered were unfailingly fair and friendly. There did exist, however, a minority of parents who made my job a misery. First up were the extra-competitive brigade who, if they thought your decision had unfairly penalised their lads' team, would gladly offer their opinion.

'Are your eyes painted on or what, ref?' I'd hear as I ran past or, occasionally, something a little more insulting.

What used to really piss me off, however, was the know-it-alls who'd take it upon themselves to loudly call decisions during play.

Referees operating at junior level rarely had a linesman to assist them, which meant I'd have to multitask and effectively run the line myself. Some onlookers probably thought they were doing me a favour with their screeches of 'Offside!' or 'Penalty!', but such actions could be hugely destructive to the game.

These foghorn fathers would often stop these poor kids in their tracks, puzzled as to whether they should be heeding their dad's yell in their left ear or the ref's whistle in their right.

'D'you mind keeping quiet while the game's on, mate?' I'd ask Bigmouth Brian from Brinsworth. 'You're confusing your lad, you're stopping the flow of the game, and you're not helping me one bit.'

'Sorry, ref, it just looked like he'd brought him down from this angle. Won't happen again.'

Most parents in that scenario, like Brian, would hold their hands up and apologise. Not everyone was so respectful, however, as I'd discover to my cost during that first season.

I'd been overseeing an Under-13s game at Herringthorpe playing fields and my attention had been drawn to a troublemaker on the sidelines. This fella was a total nuisance, swearing like a trooper – effin' this, effin' that – and, at one point, even exhorting his petrified-looking son to break an opponent's leg. All completely inappropriate, of course, especially within a junior setting.

When I spotted him trying to take a swipe at the away team's manager (there were no Respect campaign cordons in those days) I decided to stop the game and nip things in the bud. This idiot needed to be told. I slowly walked towards him, my heart racing, my knees wobbling.

'Excuse me, pal, but—'

'You take another step towards me, lad,' he snarled, like a pit bull, 'and I'll fucking rip your fucking head off.'

Despite the impulse to run whimpering to the car park, I knew that I was at the point of no return. I took another stride forward and steeled myself for a right royal battering. Just as he was drawing back his fist, another hefty parent intervened to restrain him, thank God. Had he not, I think I'd have been sporting a couple of black eyes to match my ref's kit.

The man was calmed down and led away, and I was able to resume the match. This incident had badly shaken me up, though. Here was I, a rookie ref, being threatened by a bloke old enough to be my dad, in the middle of a local kids' football match. Unbelievable. Another one to put down to experience.

For a year or so, my weekends were totally monopolised by football. I was still watching Rotherham on Saturdays, both home and away, and most Sundays were spent playing for a local side in the morning, followed by reffing a junior league game in the afternoon.

Henry Boot FC was the somewhat unusual name of the side I turned out for (in recognition of the local construction firm who sponsored our kit and donated a Portakabin for us to get changed in). I'm not saying that my once-promising football career was in terminal decline, but I'm confident that Leeds United's talent scouts weren't fighting among themselves to watch a team with a weird name flailing around the lower reaches of the Rotherham and District Sunday League.

However, in the summer of 1992 I found myself at a crossroads, with an important decision to make. My refereeing was progressing nicely, and various people-in-the-know were suggesting that, if I played my cards right, I could have a decent career ahead of me.

'You're a natural, Howard,' said my dad's brother, Uncle Frank, when he was up visiting from Kent one weekend. He'd done some reffing in his time, too – it was something of a family trait – and I greatly valued his opinion. 'If you put the work in, son, I think you've got a really good chance to move up those ranks,' he added.

I was well aware that, if I was going to improve and develop as a referee, I'd have to experience some higher level senior league matches. I needed to add some extra fixtures to my schedule, ideally two on a Saturday and two on a Sunday.

'Get your match practice in now while your fitness is good and your legs are still fresh,' said Dad, who by now was in the twilight of his refereeing career. 'Cram everything in while you've got youth on your side.'

After some thought, I made the decision to put all my eggs in one basket and concentrate on refereeing at weekends. Inevitably, this meant me having to give up watching Rotherham United and playing for Henry Boot. Forsaking the latter was an easy decision to make. While I relished our rowdy Sunday morning run outs, there was always a risk of injury at that level and I didn't want any broken arms or sprained ankles to jeopardise my progress.

Having to sacrifice my beloved Rotherham was a massive wrench, though. Following the Millers home and away had been a huge part of my life for over a decade, and I knew I was going to really miss that match-day buzz, from the camaraderie in the Tivoli End to the chants on the supporters' coach. I'd still take in the occasional midweek game at Millmoor, of course, but to me it felt like the end of an era.

The Rotherham and District Association League comprised forty-eight open age clubs in South Yorkshire. Many were affili- ated with the pubs and social clubs that dotted the area, from Sunnyside Working Men's Club FC to The Joker FC, and from Park Hotel FC to Three Magpies FC.

Some venues were better than others, it has to be said. Arriving at two o'clock to find a warm, dry clubhouse where you could get changed and have a cuppa was always a bonus, but they were few and far between. At most grounds you couldn't find a kettle or a cubicle for love nor money. I became accustomed to hurriedly pulling on my ref's gear at the side of my Peugeot 205 or behind a suitably wide-trunked tree, trying to avoid eye contact with any passing dog walkers.

Togged up in kit and boots, I'd then head over for the obligatory pre-match pitch inspection, checking for puddles, divots, broken glass and, inevitably, dog muck.

'This surface isn't playable until all that crap's off the grass,' I'd say to both team managers, who'd return five minutes later armed with long branches they'd found in the nearby woods. They'd then embark on a game of dog shit hockey, expertly guiding the offending turds over the touchlines before deftly flicking them into the bushes.

Rules and regulations at that time decreed that teams were obliged to offer referees the services of their own linesmen. They'd help out with the bread-and-butter decisions over 90 minutes – flagging when the ball went over the touchline or the byline, generally – and weren't expected to adjudge fouls or offsides. Despite these quasi-officials being more trouble than they were worth, us referees were encouraged to accept any such offers.

'You'll be pleased to know we've got a lino to help you today, ref,' a manager would say, pointing out a Selwyn Froggitt lookalike with a fag in one hand and a flag in the other.

'Geoff's still a bit pissed from last night, and his knee's been giving him some gyp, but I'm sure he'll be fine,' he'd add as I smiled through gritted teeth.

Geoff and his ilk were more of a hindrance than a help. Out of the corner of your eye you'd see them idly watching the match and chatting to their mates, rather than monitoring their lines and, when they did shake themselves into action, it would be to stick up their flag and shriek 'Offside!' five seconds after a false appeal by their own team. A quiet word in the ear was often in order.

'Appreciate you're trying to help, Geoff, but no need to give me offsides,' I'd say, trying to hide my irritation. 'Just look out for the ins and outs, corner kicks and goal kicks, pal. You judge the line and I'll do the rest, all right?'

These gentle admonishments would rarely go down well, particularly as they were dished out by a lad three decades their junior – and they'd sometimes throw their flags down in disgust, grumbling about that ungrateful bloody jumped-up ref. I recall one aggrieved linesman angrily snapping his in half during a match, hissing 'What's the flamin' point, then?' before stomping off to the clubhouse like a toddler having a tantrum.

Joining the biased and bevvied linesman were some bent managers, too. Most clubs at that time didn't have a pot to piss in, and there were plenty of shell-suited skinflints who'd try to scarper without paying my astronomical fee of £8. It was comical, really. My dad's sterling advice, which I adhered to for longer than you'd think, was to keep hold of the match ball until money changed hands.

'Make sure you grab it at full time, son, and don't let go of it until they cough up,' he'd say. 'That ball's your currency.'

By this stage I was combining my refereeing with a proper day job. Following a decent set of O levels in June 1987, I'd stayed on to study for four A levels at Brinsworth Comprehensive but, after a few weeks, had made the decision to quit the sixth form and jack in school for good. I wasn't particularly enjoying the lessons and, to be honest, my head had been turned by the lure of the wider world. I'd started to feel reined-in at school, and felt this urge to spread my wings, to find out more about life outside the classroom. In hindsight, it was one of the daftest decisions I ever made – I'll forever regret turning my back on academia – but I was young, I was stubborn and I had plans.

Since childhood I'd quite liked the idea of joining the South Yorkshire Police force. My parents had always encouraged me, too. This may appear incongruous in light of Dad's allegiances during the miners' strike, but he too had harboured youthful ambitions of being a copper. He also knew that there were plenty of decent bobbies doing great work in our local community, and thought it would be a good profession for me to go into.

I needed to be eighteen before I could apply, though, so had to find myself a full-time job in the interim. A good friend of Dad's was the manager of the Yorkshire Bank in nearby Mexborough and, following a brief interview with him, I was offered an entry-level role at the Rotherham branch, on the corner of Frederick Street. As part of the deal I'd also have to complete a full course of banking exams, attending twice-weekly evening classes at Sheffield College.

My Rotherham pals found my new job status highly amusing. 'The referee's a banker, the referee's a banker!' chanted one when I told him my news.

As it happened, my first day at work – Monday 25 January 1988 – brought me into contact with my future wife, Kay, who was a member of the admin team. We wouldn't become an item for another three years – she had a long-term boyfriend – but I remember being immediately drawn to this friendly, fun-loving and vivacious blonde who, from day one, took this wet-behind-the-ears new boy under her wing. The world of banking was all a bit bewildering to me and, before the branch opened at 9.15 a.m., she'd regularly sit down beside me and go through my workload.

'I'll help you get up to speed, Howard,' she'd say as she sifted through an in-tray groaning with paperwork. 'You really don't want to be falling behind.'

I spent most of my working day sitting at the customer counter, attending to the banking requirements of the good folk of Rotherham. My regular clientele included a few sweet old ladies clutching savings books who'd specifically request to be served by me.

'I'm waiting for young Howard,' they'd coo, dithering behind the rope cordon until I was free and Happy To Help.

This came in handy sometimes. Whenever any renowned pain-in-the-arse customers walked in, I'd cunningly stall for time, engaging in rambling conversations about *Emmerdale Farm* or that nice Alan Titchmarsh with one of my OAP admirers so that Mr Angry from Aldwarke could question his standing order with some other hapless colleague.

The way things panned out, what was supposed to be a temporary stopgap at the bank turned into a five-year stretch. When I eventually turned eighteen I'd decided to defer my application to South Yorkshire Police, reaching the sensible conclusion that perhaps I wasn't as streetwise as I'd thought, and that I probably needed to acquire more life and work skills to maximise my chances of success.

Before long, however, the daily grind of the bank had started to drag me down. While it was a busy, bustling environment (this was before online or automated banking, so queues would snake round the building all day), my nine-to-five existence had become drearily humdrum and, consequently, I'd begun to feel trapped and hemmed in. Also, the fact that I'd joined without an A level to my name – more fool me – meant that I had to attend night school instead of day release, and had to self-fund my textbooks. While all this bred resentment towards the firm, deep down I knew much of it was of my own making.

As it transpired, I played a large part in paving the way for my own exit. Just before Christmas 1992, the company had produced a batch of Yorkshire Bank diaries for staff to hand out to customers. During a coffee and mince pie break, I'd nabbed one off the pile before absent-mindedly leafing through its pages.

Etched in gold lettering on the inside cover was a list of Yorkshire Bank's core principles. 'We value the development of our people' it proclaimed. *Like hell you do*, I thought, so I promptly picked up a pen and scribbled WHAT A LOAD OF BOLLOCKS next to it in big block capitals. 'We work hard for local businesses' was printed underneath, which just begged for my WHEN WE CAN BE ARSED riposte. Beginning to enjoy this boredom-busting biro rebellion, I then doodled a wiggly arrow pointing to 'Yorkshire Bank: We care for our customers', adding COMPLETE BULLSHIT in 3-D lettering, alongside a few scrawled WANKERS and KNOBHEADS for good measure.

I can only think I was then distracted by a colleague because, instead of binning it, that defaced diary somehow ended up back on the customer pile.

'Would you like one of these, Marjorie? Free to our most valued clients ...' I heard myself saying ten minutes later, blithely handing the topmost diary to one of my favourite senior citizen groupies.

Poor old Marjorie was back at the counter the next day, diary in hand, utterly confused by the coarse graffiti that had caused her to cough up a Mint Imperial on the bus back to Catcliffe. I was hauled into the bank manager's office – he'd recognised my spindly handwriting – and, after apologising profusely, had to explain that this childish act was born of frustration. As we sat glaring at each other from either side of a mahogany desk, both he and I knew that my banking days were numbered.

*

My refereeing, meanwhile, continued apace. I'd won the Rotherham Sunday League's Most Promising Referee of the Year award in 1991, and was pictured in the *Rotherham Advertiser* alongside my dad who'd won two similar gongs of his own that year.

'We treat the players with respect and always give one hundred per cent at whatever level,' my dad was quoted as saying when asked about the secret of the Webbs' success.

'And we're both six-footers so we don't get many arguments.'

I soon progressed through to the Whitbread-sponsored Sheffield and Hallamshire County Senior League, before being promoted on to the assistant referees list of the semi-professional Northern Counties East League. It was great to have the chance to travel further afield; before I'd just been confined to Rotherham and its outskirts, but I was now being appointed to fixtures throughout Yorkshire as well as the bordering counties of Lincolnshire, Nottinghamshire, Derbyshire and Humberside, refereeing teams like North Ferriby United, Hucknall Town and Stocksbridge Park Steels.

I had the pleasure of visiting many scenic venues, some with fantastic backdrops: Pontefract Collieries FC, for example, overlooked the famous flat racing circuit and Tadcaster Albion FC was nestled in the grounds of John Smith's brewery, the heady aroma of hops often drifting across the pitch.

And with these larger scale outfits came upgraded facilities too, including modern clubhouses with luxuries like tea bags and toilet roll. But it was the people allied to these clubs who impressed me most. On my travels I met countless chairmen, presidents, secretaries and salt-of-the-earth supporters whose passion for local football was nothing short of inspirational.

At that time, it was compulsory for officials to referee one week and perform linesman duties the next. Not only that, we had to run the line at the level above that in which we reffed. So, for example, if you were 'in the middle' for the County Senior League, you'd assume the assistant referee's job in the higher-ranked Northern Counties East League. Similarly, further up the scale, if you reffed at Conference level you'd line for the Football League. And, finally, when you reached the Football League middle, you'd cease linesman duties altogether and would devote all your time to refereeing.

Surprisingly enough, I'd not been given proper instructions about how to line during my referee course in Rotherham. Alan the tutor had never sat us down to explain the nuances and intricacies of this specialist role and, as a result, my first flag-waving experience – at Barker's Park, Kimberworth, not long after I'd qualified – proved to be a total embarrassment.

As the match had kicked off I'd got myself into the zone – or so I thought – focusing intently on the action and attentively following the direction of play. After a couple of minutes, though, I'd noticed the opposite linesman furiously shouting and gesticulating.

'What the hell are you doing, Howard?' he'd yelled, stopping me in my tracks with my flag aloft. 'This is *my* half, you daft sod! Stay on your own patch, eh!'

The assembled spectators found it hilarious, but I was totally mortified. Despite witnessing my dad running the line on numerous occasions, I simply hadn't twigged that linesmen were confined to their own respective halves, and certainly weren't expected to gallop along the whole length of the pitch. From that day on, I embarked upon a personal crusade to brush up on my lining skills – and avoid any more stupid blunders – by speaking to masters of their trade. This included my dad, who'd run the line at National Conference level.

'Emotionally, Howard, it's all about keeping calm, maintaining your concentration and holding your nerve,' he'd explain. 'Physically, it's about your agility, your speed off the mark.'

Not only that, he told me, while making key, time-pressured decisions I'd also have to cope with lots of barracking from the sidelines.

While I absorbed his advice, and paid extra attention to the linesmen I subsequently worked with, deep down I knew I'd never win any prizes for assistant refereeing. My sturdy physique meant that I wasn't as nimble as some of my colleagues and, as far as I was concerned, running up and down in a straight line with a flag could never compare with the buzz of refereeing.

Moreover, while I never underestimated the importance of good lining, I was ever mindful that my skills in the middle held the key to my progression. Indeed, the entire promotional structure from the local Rotherham Association League to the national Football League was built on our prowess in the middle of the pitch rather than our proficiency on the touchline. In a nutshell, you could be a completely useless linesman, but if you impressed as a ref and were subsequently promoted, you'd automatically step up a league as an assistant too, regardless.

Conversely, if you happened to be demoted due to substandard refereeing, that would downgrade your linesman status too. So you could be the finest assistant in the league, flagging up fouls and offsides better than anybody else, but if your refereeing wasn't up to scratch it would fundamentally affect your progression as a whole. Some would argue that it wasn't the fairest system in the world but, as they say, rules are rules. Luckily for me, refereeing was my forte.

That said, in those early days there were always teething troubles to overcome. Ron Skidmore, one of my assessors at the Sheffield and Hallamshire County FA – and a long-time supporter of mine – alluded to a couple of minor issues in an assessment following a game at Maltby. He managed to get in a dig about my dad's expanding belly, too.

'You've got an annoying habit of pulling up your shorts, Howard,' he wrote. 'If you need some stronger elastic, see your mother. If you need to put some weight on, see your father.'

In July 1993, at the age of twenty-two, I was finally able to bid farewell to my colleagues at the bank as, much to my delight, I'd finally been accepted into South Yorkshire Police, albeit a few years later than planned.

The one workmate I didn't have to part company with was Kay. After she'd split up with her boyfriend, we'd started to see a bit more of each other, and what had started as the occasional game of tennis or post-work drink evolved into a more serious relationship. In March 1992, following eight months together as a couple, Kay and I finally got engaged. We'd been in Stratford-upon-Avon when I'd got down on bended knee, presenting her with a fancy box stuffed with pink confetti and, somewhere among it all, a diamond ring.

The police application process had commenced a year before I left the bank, culminating in a tough, two-day selection interview at Police HQ in Sheffield. Twenty hopefuls had been met there by Sergeant Ruth Pears who'd left us under no illusions as to the demands of the next 48 hours. 'We'll only be recruiting the very best candidates today, ladies and gents,' she'd said. 'You've all done well to get here in the first place, but it's only the cream of the crop who'll be successful tomorrow afternoon.'

We proceeded to be subjected to a series of physical and psychological tasks, incorporating a gruelling fitness assessment, a *Krypton Factor*-style observation test and a *Question Time*-style current affairs debate. After a number of eliminations, only four of us remained for the final stage, a set of white-knuckle, one-to-one interviews in which we were grilled about our strengths, weaknesses and aspirations. Judging by the expressions on the faces of my fellow candidates afterwards, I wasn't the only one to be left emotionally exhausted.

As we waited in a side room, nervously chatting among ourselves, in breezed Inspector Mick Venables. 'Congratulations,' he grinned. 'I'm happy to tell you you've all passed. Welcome to South Yorkshire Police.'

Feeling absolutely ecstatic – and utterly gobsmacked that I'd got into the police at my first attempt – I phoned in the good news to Mum and Dad. It still counts as one of the proudest moments of my life.

Fast-forward a couple of weeks and I'd returned to HQ to take the official police oath, pledging 'to serve the Queen in the office of constable, with fairness, integrity, diligence and impartiality.'

The formalities over, I was then handed my new black uniform. I can clearly remember trying it on for the first time, my smile broadening as I caught my reflection in the mirror, my shoulder bearing my brand new collar number: PC2799.

Life as a police constable with South Yorkshire Police began for me on Monday 16 May 1993, at the force's A1 sub-division, based in Doncaster town centre. I loved being stationed in Donny; in fact, I'd go as far as to say that it was probably the happiest time of my working life. Not only were we operating in the busiest district in South Yorkshire, we were, in our minds, part of the finest team of officers in the force. 'The Premier League of policing,' we used jokingly to refer to ourselves. I went on to strike up a great friendship with my detective inspector, Dick Venables (brother of the aforementioned Mick) who – as well as being a top bloke – happened to be a Rotherham United fan and a local referee.

I spent my first 18 months on foot patrol in the town centre. Initially I was accompanied by a tutor, PC Iain Robb, to help me learn the ropes, but after a few weeks I was granted full independence. I was bursting with pride when I first pounded the pavements alone, wearing my pristine uniform and sporting my bobby's helmet. Here was someone who'd been cooped up in a stuffy old bank for five years, who was now doing a job he'd coveted for ages, and who'd been given the freedom of his own patch.

There was never a dull moment in Doncaster, either. Whenever I wasn't responding to emergencies, I could conduct my own crime research or investigate suspicious activities, poking my nose into this, casting my eye over that, having a word with him or her. It felt right down my street, in so many ways.

I didn't forget my first day on the beat in a hurry, either. Early that morning, I'd noticed this big, scruffy guy in his twenties staggering through the main shopping area, catcalling passing shoppers and schoolkids and generally making a nuisance of himself.

Clearly wired on drugs, alcohol or both, this lad wasn't responding to my gentle requests to curb his crude behaviour, and was becoming increasingly aggressive. 'Mate, I think you need to sit down here, hand me that can and calm yourself down a bit,' I said, attempting to guide his burly frame towards a nearby bench. 'You're scaring the good people of Donny.'

'Fuck off, you shithouse,' came his slurred reply as he brushed off the hand that I'd firmly placed on his shoulder, before trying to make a run for it.

While I'd just undertaken many weeks of rigorous police training, I'd never expected to be making an arrest on my own during the first hour of my first day on independent patrol. Ideally I should have shouted for back-up before I chased him, grabbed him and read him his rights, but this guy needed restraining, and quick.

What ensued was one of the biggest fights I ever had as a copper. My nemesis wasn't having any of it, kicking me, clawing at me and spitting in my face. As our ruck progressed, Doncaster's finest congregated around us, some cheering us on like it was a

*World of Sport* wrestling bout, others helpfully shouting 'Leave him alone, you piggy bastard ...'

All the restraint techniques that I'd practised just a week earlier went straight out of the window and I ended up having to sit on the lad while wedging my elbow in his face to keep him quiet. Within a couple of minutes, a pair of colleagues had arrived as back up, and our miscreant was apprehended.

'A nice baptism of fire for you, Howard,' smiled the female officer as she bundled him, yelling and flailing, into the police van.

Coming from a secure, loving background – and never having mixed with crooks or criminals of any sort – life on the beat came as a culture shock to me. My default position had always been to see the good in people before the bad; it took some time to rid myself of this ingrained naivety and acknowledge that the world contained some wrong 'uns.

As a rookie PC I still had my gullible moments, though. I remember being called to a closed garage forecourt in the early hours, its windows smashed and its alarms blaring. As I arrived on the scene I saw a bloke skulking off with blood pouring from a gash on his arm. I approached him, only for him to tell me that he'd been on his way home from the pub, had got caught short and had leaned against the garage window while having a pee.

'The glass gave way, mate, and I cut my arm, see,' he said dolefully as I stood there, totally buying into this cock-and-bull story. 'Can I go home now so I—'

Before he could finish his sentence – and before I could pat the cheeky scamp on the head and tell him to run along – another copper raced into the forecourt, *The Sweeney*-style, took one look at this bloodied reprobate, handcuffed him immediately and arrested him for suspicion of burglary. I felt like a right tit.

*Get a grip, Howard*, hissed a voice in my head. *Don't be so bleedin' green*.

I toughened up quickly, though, none more so than when faced with a firearm for the first time. I'd been partnered up with a driver colleague, PC Adie Crawley, when our radio alerted us to an armed robbery at the Yorkshire Electricity Board shop in Doncaster. We raced over to the premises on Silver Street, blues and twos in full effect, but the offender had already made his getaway, in a Ford Escort.

'Shit! Follow the bastard!' shouted Adie, screeching his tyres and slamming his accelerator while I radioed for the armed response unit. We joined the pursuit through a nearby housing estate, the gunman recklessly waving his pistol out of the driver's window the whole time. I'll be honest, I was shitting my pants.

Much to our frustration, we lost track of him somewhere among the maze of dead ends and cul-de-sacs.

'Time to search sheds, Howard,' declared Adie, and we began to skulk down alleyways and backyards, creaking open a succession of rotten and rickety doors. Without any warning, our offender burst from an outhouse, screaming and brandishing his gun in our faces. The most frightening moment of my career, bar none. I'd seen action like this on *The Bill*, but to experience it at first hand was terrifying.

'Don't do anything stupid,' warned my colleague, his voice trembling as we slowly backed off. 'Just put the gun down, right now ...'

Suddenly, two red laser dots appeared on his chest. With impeccable timing, South Yorkshire Police's armed response unit had arrived on the scene, the sights of their automatic weapons trained on their prey within seconds.

'Look down at your chest, look down, look down!' I hollered, at which the man realised the state of play and dropped his pistol. Thank God.

In our district, however, knife crime was much more prevalent than gun crime. On a cold, blustery New Year's Eve my patrol had been called to a variety of domestic assaults, including an incident involving a teenage girl running amok with a huge carving knife.

'I'm gonna kill him, I'm gonna kill him, I'm gonna fuckin' kill him …' she ranted as we jumped out of the car.

It transpired that her boyfriend had attacked her father in the house and had since fled into the night. Our presence wasn't exactly welcomed, however, and despite being told to drop the weapon, the girl began to lurch towards us, her face skewed with rage. When she got within a couple of metres I took a sharp intake of breath and made a quick decision.

'I'm getting the CS spray,' I whispered to my colleague, nervously reaching in my pocket for the canister (I'd only recently been on a CS spray course, and it was the first time I'd used it). I gave it a vigorous shake and a long squirt, but a nanosecond before maximum impact, a gust of wintry wind blasted in my direction. This changed the course of the airborne crystals, which promptly hit me straight in the face.

So there I was, totally blinded, with a deranged teenager waving a carving knife in my face. I remember stumbling to the other side of the road to hide behind a car, tears streaming down my cheeks while backup colleagues with fully functioning eyes took over.

Admittedly that wasn't my finest hour, but it was a blip in what was turning out to be a pretty successful PC posting for me. I'd like to think that I was a diligent and fair-minded copper who, whether I was based at the station or walking the beat, did my best to serve and protect the local community. I must have been on the right lines because in 1995, having successfully completed my police probation, I was called into the office of my inspector, Mick Wheldon.

'Listen, Howard, I've been thinking, and I reckon you've got the potential to become a sergeant,' he said, before suggesting that I tackle the exam course straight away. 'It's hard work, I'll be honest with you,' he added, 'but I'll do all I can to help you through.'

For the next six months I studied every night, burning the midnight oil and getting up to speed with the four key areas of study: general police duties, evidence and procedure, traffic and law. In January 1997 I qualified as a sergeant and, sporting my new stripes on my right shoulder, began acting up in my new role at Doncaster station.

The more experienced I became, the more I was able to apply my policing principles to the football field. I don't think it was a coincidence that many of the referees I met were coppers or teachers, adept at managing discipline, resolving conflict and enforcing rules and regulations. While I couldn't take any extendable batons, CS spray, handcuffs or Alsatians on to the field of play – much as I'd have sometimes liked to – there were other tools of my trade that I could utilise.

For me, more than anything, my police work gave me the mettle to make quick decisions within tight time frames. It gave me the self-control to keep calm and composed when my heart was beating out of my chest. It gave me the wisdom to analyse what was in front of me and to take action without dithering, whether it was arresting someone on the street for thieving, or dismissing someone from the pitch for elbowing.

On a sunny day in July 1995, at Whiston Parish Church, Kay and I got married, surrounded by our nearest and dearest. Acting as best man that day was my cousin Adam who, at just 13 months my junior, was the closest thing to a brother I'd ever had. In his speech he mentioned our shared love of football, and how we'd argued about who was the best England goalie – being a Spurs fan he was always firmly in the Clemence camp, whereas I was resolutely Team Shilton.

Kay and I spent a low-key honeymoon in Cornwall, before returning home to start our new life together in Brinsworth. Three years later, much to our delight, our household would welcome another occupant. Hollie Webb was born on 30 June 1998, on the very same day that England came up against Argentina in the World Cup finals in France. I vividly remember watching the first half of the match in Rotherham District General Hospital – with my beautiful new-born daughter by my side – and catching the second half at my mum and dad's.

'Our Hollie's not the only person kicking and screaming today, is she?' laughed Mum as the red-carded David Beckham, fresh from lashing out at Diego Simeone, exited the pitch in St Etienne.

# CHAPTER 3

# You're Bald, And You Know You Are

I was in my early twenties when I started to go thin on top and, for about three or four years, determinedly clung on to what was left of my increasingly wispy, unruly mop. Each morning I'd spend ages smoothing it down with gels and sprays, only for it to stick up like a feather duster when I took off my police helmet or ran around a blustery football pitch.

However, after the eighty-third joker had asked me if I'd come to work on a motorbike, I decided enough was enough and that, like it or not, it was all getting shorn off. In any case, I couldn't bear the prospect of shedding even more hair, revealing a larger bald patch and, as a consequence, looking like the oldest cop – or ref – in town. This decision certainly wasn't a ruse to look hard, as was later levelled at me in police and football circles; if anything, it was an attempt to stay young.

Despite feeling like I was stark naked when I first walked out of the barbers, I soon got used to my shaven-headed appearance. 'I really like it,' said my wife when I'd returned home that afternoon feeling slightly nervous about her reaction.

On Tuesday 27 August 1996 – not long after I'd gone for the chop – Kay was among the crowd at Burnley FC's Turf Moor. Six-and-a-half years after my refereeing debut, I'd finally made it to the Football League as a linesman. Kay rarely attended games – she couldn't bear hearing fans hurling insults at me – but even she knew what this Burnley v Shrewsbury Town fixture meant to me. I'd been a Football League aficionado for nearly two decades, visiting nearly seventy grounds as a teenager, and here I was, sporting the official badge on my shirt, carrying my yellow flag, playing an active role in the game I'd loved since boyhood.

My dad had also experienced life in the Football League, albeit a few years earlier. One morning, in January 1985, I'd been the talk of my classroom when I'd proudly announced his appointment as fourth official at Millmoor that night (in those days you were just termed a 'reserve official') and I remember how thrilled I'd felt for him. He'd spent years watching Rotherham United from the terraces, and had finally been handed the chance to get involved on a match day, taking up a position in the main stand and sporting an official Umbro tracksuit.

Kay probably felt a similar pang of pride as she watched me emerge from the Turf Moor tunnel that summer's evening, following behind the referee, Bill Burns from Scarborough.

Running the league line was a daunting prospect. Unlike the Pontin's reserve games that I sporadically oversaw, these matches seriously mattered. While reserve ties could be fairly competitive, they were generally used as trial games for up-and-coming youngsters or run-outs for senior players returning from injury. As such, no one was hugely bothered whether their side won, lost or drew.

Professional league matches like Burnley v Shrewsbury were a different proposition though. The stakes were huge. All it took was one dodgy offside decision to pre-empt a defeat, which could in turn induce relegation or promotion and which, via some awful domino effect, could be to the detriment of a club's staff, finances and support base. I knew this all too well – I'd followed an erratic, yo-yoing team all my life – and I never took my role and its ramifications lightly.

This debut also saw the first airing of the 1996-97 season referee's kit. Like most footballers, we keenly anticipated the arrival of the new season's gear, and would look forward to its delivery at the end of July. That year's effort, produced by Umbro, was a notable exception. It was awful. The random white splats down the side of the shirt made it look like we'd been crapped on by a family of loose-bowelled pigeons, and it was immediately christened the 'birdshit kit'.

Worse still, due to some supply issues, Umbro informed us that they hadn't made enough kits to go round. That meant that, for the next few weeks, I had to share one XL birdshit shirt with a fellow ref, Rob Pashley, who lived in a village called Clowne, near Chesterfield (an apt place name for a referee, some might say). So, once he'd finished his game and had washed his sweaty top, I'd then have to make the 40-mile round trip to Derbyshire to collect it.

'Here you go, mate,' Rob would sigh as he handed over the freshly laundered shirt.

'Bet Graham Poll and Dermot Gallagher never have to bloody do this ...'

Occasionally I'd be tasked with an early-round FA Cup tie and, in November 1997, I ran the line for Scunthorpe United v Scarborough. In the visitors' midfield was Ian Snodin, a fellow Rotherhamite who'd previously starred for Everton and Leeds United, among others.

In the second half, I disallowed a Scarborough goal for offside.

Snodin wasn't having any of it, though, and ran over to tear a strip off me, telling me in no uncertain terms that his teammate's strike was legit. He was almost foaming at the mouth, was Ian, calling me all sorts and waving his hands in my face. By this time I'd had enough, and I could feel my hackles rising. I waited for him to shut up before squaring up to him, my nose just inches from his.

'FUCK OFF, IAN,' I shouted, as he recoiled in shock at this potty-mouthed linesman.

Not only was this highly unprofessional behaviour, it was massively out of character. I rarely lost my cool on the touchline – it wasn't my style at all – but that afternoon I properly snapped. To be fair, I'd never taken kindly to players who'd quite happily trash officials but who couldn't stomach a taste of their own medicine.

After the final whistle, Snodin stormed into the dressing room, demanding to speak with the referee, Alan Wilkie. 'I want to make a complaint about your linesman's bad language,' he growled, jabbing his finger in my direction. 'He told me to fuck off.'

Wilkie shot me a concerned look. 'OK, Howard, this is a pretty serious allegation. D'you want to give your version of events?'

By this time, I'd had a few minutes to get my story straight. Clever comebacks and funny one-liners weren't my speciality – I'd never be as sharp-witted as refs like Neil Midgley and John Key – so I instead rattled off my account in my most serious, officious police sergeant tones. This only served to further infuriate my adversary.

'The ball was played forward, Alan. There was an offside decision, and I raised my flag. Then Mr Snodin came over and verbally challenged my decision.'

Wilkie nodded. 'Go on, Howard …'

'I waited until he'd calmed down, and then just simply stated "He was a foot off, Ian."'

At this, Snodin almost spontaneously combusted, accusing me of being a liar, a cheat and a piss-taker. When Wilkie conceded that he couldn't take any action without substantial evidence, the player stomped off, slamming the door so hard the dressing room shook.

The summer of 1998 proved to be an eventful one for me. In May I was thrilled to discover that I'd been promoted to the Nationwide Conference referees list, and as such would be officiating matches within a catchment stretching from Morecambe in the north to Welling in the south. My first game – at Hednesford Town in the West Midlands – was a proper rude awakening. I soon realised that life wasn't going to be easy in this fast-paced league of hardy players and crunching tackles.

I was handed officiating responsibilities for the FA Trophy, too. A hard-fought, hotly contested competition that catered for lower tier sides, it presented me with one of the most challenging matches I've ever refereed. The tie took place at Droylsden FC, located on the eastern fringes of Manchester, with Derbyshire side Belper FC as their opponents.

Let's just say that it was an unmitigated disaster from beginning to end. Lining up for Droylsden were some of the most menacing Mancs I'd ever seen – with a sprinkling of Scousers – who proceeded to maraud around the pitch, kicking lumps out of their rivals, swearing like troopers and laughing in the face of the quivering wreck with the whistle.

Within minutes of kick-off, I lost total control and all semblance of respect. It became one of those games – all refs have had them – where my performance slowly, painfully and publicly nosedived. I was out of my depth, and once I'd blown the final whistle I couldn't exit the pitch quickly enough.

Any hopes of sweeping this horror-show under the carpet were dashed when Roger Dilkes – a well-known referee who'd been among the crowd – was quoted in that night's *Manchester*

*Evening News*, suggesting that my officiating hadn't been good enough. That hurt, it really did.

Usually I'd try to avoid dwelling on particularly shitty performances, but that match gave me cold sweats and sleepless nights for weeks. Once I'd picked myself up, however, I made a pledge to learn from the whole dismal experience. For the rest of the season, whenever I felt like I was losing my grip, I'd mentally reference the Droylsden debacle to get myself back on track. I still break out in hives whenever I pass road signs for that place, though.

The more I reffed, however, the thicker my skin became. In November 1998 – after yet another tricky FA Trophy game – I remember Doncaster Rovers' new chairman, John Ryan, issuing a venomous bollocking to me because I'd sent a player off during their 2-0 defeat to Frickley Athletic (not their finest hour, it must be said). We get along fine now, but we were at serious loggerheads that day.

I also received stick from another unlikely source that afternoon. Jeremy Clarkson, no less, was at Belle Vue with a camera crew in tow, filming a tongue-in-cheek piece about Doncaster (the 'Town of Dreams', he mockingly dubbed it) for his eponymous BBC1 show. Although he hailed from a nearby village, Tickhill, he'd never been to a match before – no shock there, then – and, that Saturday, lowered himself to speak to some die-hard supporters before joining them in the stands.

The footage showed Donny supporters singing their usual anti-Rotherham chants, before the camera panned across the pitch and focused on yours truly. Clarkson laughingly pointed out that the ref was himself from Rotherham, and then drew upon on that world-famous sense of humour of his. 'GET YER HAIR CUT,' he yelled as I jogged past the centre circle, while a chant of 'you're bald, and you know you are' rose up from the home fans.

\*

One of my appointed Premier League reserve games – Newcastle United v Aston Villa – took me to Kingston Park, the home of Newcastle Falcons, where the Magpies played their reserve team matches. I actually got lost on the way there – this was long before the days of sat-nav – and had to call a local referee, Clive Oliver, who kindly met me at the Metro Centre to escort me to the ground. Sitting in the passenger seat that evening was his 13-year-old son Michael, a would-be referee who, later down the line, I'd get to know very well.

They both stayed to watch the game, which I remember as being a pretty straightforward 90 minutes with few incidents. Two reckless tackles had gone in – both cautionable offences – but I'd decided to keep the yellow cards at bay as I'd felt I was controlling the game well and was allowing it to flow nicely.

It was while having a post-match drink in the lounge that the legendary Bobby Robson, United's manager and former England supremo, made a beeline for me. Being so ingrained at the club, his was a regular presence at reserve games.

'Hello, Bobby,' I smiled, shaking his hand and trying to mask the fact that I was totally awestruck.

'Well done tonight, ref, I thought you did all right,' he said. 'But I'd like to offer you a word of advice if I may.'

'Of course,' I replied. 'Go ahead.'

'If you want to get to the top, lad, you've got to do the job properly,' he simply said, giving me a friendly wink before returning to his tea and biscuits.

I knew exactly what he was implying and, and as I stood there, I mentally kicked myself. I should have cautioned both players for those forceful tackles. Two yellow cards were in order, regardless of the fact that I'd thought I was managing the game well. At that elite level, clubs expected referees to show some steel and apply the laws consistently. I'd been too damned nice that evening, and had let myself down.

The match assessor's mark was a disappointing six out of ten, which effectively cost me promotion that year. Bobby had taught me a valuable lesson, though. If I wanted to progress I had to be ruthless and clinical when necessary, even if it wasn't my default position.

It was an opinion shared a few years later by another esteemed north-easterner, the legendary referee George Courtney, during a pep talk about being strong when it mattered. 'To succeed as a ref, Howard, you've got to be prepared to be a bastard, but without being a c***.'

In May 1998 – around the same time I was promoted to the national Conference and Premier League reserves – I received an unexpected letter from the FA informing me that I'd been appointed as an assistant referee in the Premier League. While I'd been attracting decent ratings on the Football League line, I hadn't factored in this development at all.

Hearing the same news was my old pal Paul Canadine, who I'd met on my first day of referee training, and who'd since followed a similar path to mine. *REFS ON THE RIGHT LINES* was the headline in the *Rotherham Advertiser*, next to a photo of us sporting the birdshit kit, holding up our flags and smiling broadly.

To me this was a fabulous development, since I knew I'd learn so much from working alongside the best refs in the business. I'd spent the past few years admiring Graham Poll, Paul Durkin and Jeff Winter from afar, and now I had the chance to join forces with them on the pitch.

My top-flight debut, Newcastle United v Charlton Athletic on Saturday 15 August 1998, got off to an inauspicious start. Like a fool, I'd mistimed my journey and had hit the holiday traffic crawling up the A1, swaying caravans and all. I eventually arrived at St James' Park at 1.20 p.m., with just ten minutes to spare before the start of the pre-match schedule. Being the last official to roll up to the dressing room, stressed, sweaty and with a heat rash creeping up my neck, wasn't exactly the height of professionalism. In fact, it was appalling preparation on my part.

That day's referee, Dermot Gallagher, didn't utter a word to me before kick-off, apart from his standard pre-match instruction which he delivered to his team of officials. Whether he was (quite rightly) irritated by my tardiness, or just getting in the zone for the first game of the season, I don't know. He was, in fairness, coming back from an injury that he'd sustained during Euro 96 – at St James' Park itself – so doubtless had much on his mind. I do remember feeling slightly put out that he'd not felt the need to give his young debutant linesman a pep talk, but, looking back, I was probably being over-sensitive.

As for the match itself, I spent most of the 90 minutes willing the ball to stay at the other end, thus limiting my chances of ballsing things up. I was aware that, by making a mistake as a lino, you didn't only ruin your own day but the ref's as well, and I didn't want to give Dermot any more reason to take issue with me. The game went OK from our point of view, though, finishing 0–0 with a pretty clear-cut 25th-minute dismissal of Richard Rufus.

It was only when the match ended that the significance of the occasion hit me. Just three years previously I'd been exiting the pitch at Selby Town in the Northern Counties East League. Yet here I was, on a sunny Saturday, at one of England's finest grounds, shaking hands with household names like John Barnes, Gary Speed and Alan Shearer.

'Welcome to the Premier League,' smiled Dermot when I entered the dressing room, putting his arm round me. *You've changed your tune, Dermot,* I thought. *You could have done that before the game, when I was on bloody tenterhooks …*

Observing top-class referees from the sidelines taught me that, despite having different methods, techniques and procedures, the common denominator among them was the possession of a hugely strong character. To survive at this level, it seemed, you had to have a supersized personality, whether it was the calm and meticulous David Elleray – a traditional, old-school ref who approached his games with military precision – or the charismatic Paul Durkin, who charmed players and managers alike with his warmth and good-humour. I gained insight and inspiration from each and every one of them.

The most cocksure member of the group was undoubtedly Graham Poll, who I assisted more than any other referee; sixteen occasions in total. Depending on which side of the fence you occupied, Poll either had a strong persona that radiated confidence, or a raging ego that oozed arrogance. What was evident, however, was that this was an official at the summit of his powers who had an innate trust in his own ability. Unsurprisingly, in the summer of 2000 he'd be appointed as England's representative referee at the European Championships in Holland and Belgium.

Poll's self-assured brand of refereeing was showcased at the 1999-2000 Merseyside derby at Goodison Park, which also happened to be my final run on the Premier League line. With added time petering out, it seemed the game would end all-square at 0-0. However, in the final few seconds Liverpool goalie Sander Westerveld cleared the ball upfield, before striking Don Hutchison on the back which resulted in it looping towards goal. As the ball trickled towards the line, inches from securing a dramatic three points, Poll blew for full time. A less confident, more cautious referee might have added that extra second. But not Graham. That was him all over. He didn't give a monkeys.

While I was proud of my thirty appearances on the Premier League line, I knew I was miles away from making FIFA's assistant referee list. Life in the top flight had shown me that, while I gave it my all, I probably didn't have the analytical skills or the forensic attention to detail needed to be a first-class lino. However, being able to study leading referees at such close quarters had only whetted my appetite to follow in their footsteps.

Having made a decent fist of it in the Conference and Pontin's leagues, I knew I was in the running for a coveted refereeing berth with the Football League. This was confirmed when I was summoned to a formal interview at London's Lancaster Gate on 10 April 2000, before the five officials on the FA Review Board. This would include the organisation's chairman, Ron Barston, whose very name seemed to embody no-nonsense league football to a T.

I travelled down on the train from Sheffield that morning, with my dad coming along for moral support.

'Just be yourself, son,' he advised, 'but make sure you think before you speak. They'll know all about Howard the referee, but today I reckon they'll want to know more about Howard the person.'

He wasn't wrong. The panel posed a variety of questions, not all of them football-related. Being asked solemnly if I had a reliable and roadworthy car wrong-footed me slightly, I'll admit. Aware that a reply of 'No, gents, I've got a C-reg Metro with a broken aerial and a habit of conking out on the Snake Pass,' would scupper my big chance, I opted just to smile and nod.

A selection of fit-and-proper questions followed: what would I do if I heard a racist comment in the tunnel? How would I react if I spotted smoke coming from a factory fire behind a stand? When would extreme weather conditions cause me to abandon a match?

Then, in order to satisfy themselves that refereeing was Howard Webb's number-one priority, and that the league would always come first, they grilled me about my work-home-football balance. This I found easy to explain since, for better or for worse, football *did* take precedence at that stage in my life.

Put it this way, had Kay phoned me at the police station, asking me to knock off early because Hollie was screaming, and that she'd got a banging headache and needed to go to bed, my reply would have been along the lines of, 'Sorry love, but I'm really busy at work. Take an Anadin and put your feet up, you'll be all right.'

However, if the phone had rung two minutes later, and it had just happened to be the Football Conference appointments secretary saying they'd had a referee cry off a game that night, and could I leave work immediately to step in, I'd have been packing my kitbag and revving my engine before you could say Kidderminster Harriers. Sad, but true. In those days I put football before everything else, and that was certainly the message I conveyed to the men in blazers.

Later that afternoon, as Dad and I waited on a St Pancras platform for the Sheffield-bound train, we caught sight of Ron Barston, himself heading home to Leicester. He saw me, winked, and gave me a smiley thumbs-up.

'I reckon that's a good sign!' said Dad.

Sure enough, the following morning the official letter dropped on to my doormat, confirming my promotion to the National List. Out of the 27,000 working referees in the country, I was now ranked in the top seventy, and it felt brilliant. Even the considerable drop in income didn't dampen my delight; at that time officials earned £400 per game for running the Premier League line, but received a smaller purse of around £200 for refereeing the league middle. For me, however, striding out with a whistle and a ball under my arm at Colchester surpassed walking out with a yellow flag at Chelsea. That was my specialism, and I couldn't wait to get started.

I received many good luck messages, including a heartfelt letter from Premier League referee Alan Wilkie who, a few years earlier, had withstood that Ian Snodin rant.

'Cherish the moment, for no matter what riches become you, this is the definitive moment of your career,' he wrote. 'There will be many new twists and turns ahead. I am on the end of a phone if you need a chat or a shoulder to cry on.'

My first league game – Southend United v Brighton and Hove Albion – should have been on Saturday 12 August 2000. Kay, however, was heavily pregnant with our second child who, despite being due five days earlier, was resolutely refusing to budge. By the time Friday morning had arrived – and after hurry-along therapies of spicy curries and brisk walks had failed to work – I was starting to seriously fret. Selfish, I know, but my overriding thoughts were not of my bored, exhausted wife, but my big refereeing debut.

*C'mon, love*, I remember thinking. *Sort it out and get this baby born. I've been waiting all summer for this, passed my fitness test and everything ...*

By Friday lunchtime I had no other option but to ring Jim Ashworth, the league's appointments secretary. Southend was just too far away in the circumstances, I told him – I couldn't justify being 200 miles from home if Kay went into labour – and I asked to be excused. Our wonderful baby son, Jack, finally arrived on Monday 14 August, enabling my league debut – Darlington v Exeter City – to take place five days later.

My maiden season in the league seemed to progress really well, barring one troublesome Stoke City v Bournemouth fixture that had seen me banishing Potters' manager Gudjon Thordarson to the stands. I was gutted, therefore, to receive a letter in February informing me that, taking into account my assessment marks, I'd been placed in Band F – the lowest possible rank – for the following campaign. I was so convinced that there'd been a typing error that I actually went so far as to check my desktop computer keyboard to see how close the 'F' key was to 'B'.

Chats with my superiors confirmed that I hadn't been mistaken, however. Clearly, the transition from Conference to Football League had been much tougher than I'd thought, and there was still much ground to make up.

The final fixture of that campaign was Blackpool v Barnet. The game went OK, although I remember being somewhat distracted at half-time and full-time. Ronnie Moore's Rotherham United were simultaneously playing Brentford at home that Saturday, my team requiring a victory to promote us to the Championship.

After the match I immediately checked my phone, punching the air when I scrolled down to find that Alan Lee had nicked our winner. I celebrated the Millers' feat in true Blackpool style, standing on a windswept North Pier and wolfing down a tray of steaming fish and chips, washed down with a can of Coca-Cola.

As my league career progressed, the juggling act between my refereeing duties and my police work became increasingly difficult. On the one hand, I needed the financial security of full-time employment with the force – and I still harboured aspirations of becoming a high-ranking officer – but on the other hand I had my officiating prospects to consider.

Occasionally, my worlds of policing and football would merge. Back in June 1996, three years after I'd joined up, most of the South Yorkshire coppers were assigned to the Euro 96 tournament that had rolled into Sheffield. Hillsborough was host to several fixtures and, for the next four weeks, we were tasked with monitoring the crowds and manning the control rooms.

The city acted as the main hub for the Denmark squad – they were spotted playing croquet on the lawn of their hotel, apparently – and the streets were awash with thousands of fanatical, fun-seeking Danish fans. They endeared themselves to locals and landlords alike, many of the latter having to order in emergency supplies of fags and beer to meet the demand.

Occasionally I'd be drafted in to police home games at Doncaster Rovers or Sheffield United.

'Watch the crowd, not the game,' came the instruction from on high, but sometimes I just couldn't help myself. Once I got into trouble for a concentration lapse at Bramall Lane – during a lively Steel City derby – that led to me totally missing a flare that had been thrown from one stand to another.

'Where the hell did *that* come from?' crackled the message via my handheld radio. 'X-Ray Sierra Zero Five, who threw that flare?'

*Fuck knows*, I felt like replying, *but the ref's just played a bloody great advantage* ...

From my position in the aisles I'd witness lots of verbal abuse aimed at players. I remember Paddy Kenny patrolling his goalmouth when Hull City came to visit, and the away fans giving him so much stick, really offensive stuff. 'You fat bastard!' they chanted in unison, many of them with young children sat beside them. 'You Irish wanker!'

The Blades won 2-1 that day and, when the decisive goal went in, Kenny turned round to his detractors and made a 'two-one' gesture that incorporated a 'V' sign. Not a wise move to incite fans like that, of course, but the lad had been subjected to name calling for 90 minutes and it was his way of retribution, albeit misguided.

An hour later, back at the police station, we were met with twenty Hull City fans clamouring to report Kenny for his offensive actions. 'My kids shouldn't be witness to that,' one of them ranted, utterly oblivious to the irony of it all.

In June 2000, at the second attempt, I was promoted to a fully fledged sergeant with a new base at West Bar station in central Sheffield. We had a newly installed inspector too – Paul Wright – so a group of us thought it would be a good idea to have a summer's day out to York for some team bonding over a few drinks.

It was while we were sat in the sunshine – outside the King's Arms, on the banks of the River Ouse – that my beer-goggled self decided that the water looked quite appealing.

'Anyone for a dip?' I asked, before stripping off to my pants and diving in, followed by two equally sozzled constables. The Ouse wasn't exactly the cleanest river in those days, but the more we swam, the harder we laughed, swallowing gobfuls of water as we thrashed about.

Waiting for us at the other side, however, were some stony-faced counterparts from the North Yorkshire police, who, as we drunkenly clambered up the banks, threatened to arrest us for obstructing the waterway. 'You stupid bloody idiots,' barked one of the coppers. 'Have you never heard of Weil's Disease?'

He then began to lecture us about this life-threatening bacterial infection, contracted from waterborne rat's piss, that could bugger up your vital organs. That sobered me up a bit.

Within a couple of minutes Paul Wright had tottered over to intervene, explaining who we were – our interrogators weren't at all impressed that we were coppers – and eventually managing to get us off the hook.

'I'm their inshpector,' he'd slurred. 'I promish I'll dischipline them when we get back to Sheffield ...'

It wasn't the only time that work and alcohol hadn't mixed well. Once, the night before a Championship match between Wolves and Coventry, I'd managed to get myself a little bit too pissed. I'd been working at West Bar police station one Friday afternoon in December, with our staff Christmas get-together in the city centre scheduled for later that night.

'I'll have a couple of beers to be sociable,' I said as I swapped my uniform for my civvies, explaining to all and sundry that I had a match to referee the next day.

I ended up getting carried away with all the festivities – not a complete shock; I could be easily led in my younger days – and ended up drinking and partying beyond my usual midnight curfew. It was both irresponsible and unprofessional.

I left for the Midlands at 9.30 a.m. the next morning and I felt and looked like shite, my eyes bleary as hell and my head banging like a drum. I certainly wasn't in any fit state to officiate, but I didn't want to let everyone down by throwing in a last-minute no-show.

I distinctly remember blowing the whistle to get the captains together and thinking *FUCK ME, THAT'S LOUD* as its shrill *peeeeeep* pierced the fog between my ears.

Despite my pre-match unprofessionalism, the game went like clockwork. I can't remember a second of the action, but I just recall coming off the pitch, gasping for water, and thinking *how on earth did I pull that one off? Maybe I should get wrecked every Friday night …*

In 2002 my role as sergeant became even more involved. I was appointed to head up a Community Support Group in Tinsley, a deprived ward in Sheffield that had become increasingly lawless and that had virtually succumbed to gang rule. Locals were hardly able to catch a bus without it being stoned, send a letter without the postbox being torched, or go to the pub without the windows being put through. Hence the setting up of a CSG, comprising myself and four PCs, to combat crime and vandalism.

'We need to reclaim the area,' I'd said to my team as we launched the initiative. 'We owe it to the good people of Tinsley to root out the bad guys.'

Our work involved countless evening and night shifts, since that's when most misdemeanours occurred. Working in a small, targeted area with the aid of a police van and a Dragon Light torch, we'd do our utmost to disrupt the lives of those who were disrupting everyone else's, knocking on front doors, stopping and searching cars, and spot-checking various shops and pubs. We found the best use of resources was to target the criminal rather than the crime, so undercover surveillance was often key to our success.

The Tinsley CSG became a 'best practice' initiative, something that made me feel extremely proud. I was often asked to talk to neighbouring districts about its success, something that I always attributed to proper hands-on, old-fashioned policing.

'It's not rocket science,' I'd explain. 'If you put enough time and resources in one area, and you have cops with energy and enthusiasm who can engage with the community, you'll make a difference.'

It was commonplace for me to referee games on the back of a night shift. I'd do a Friday night in the city centre, for example, which could easily finish at 5 a.m. or 6 a.m. Then, after shoehorning in a couple of hours' sleep, I'd drive down south to officiate at Peterborough. Following the game, I'd bomb back up the A1, snatching another quick nap before heading back to the police station for a 10 p.m. start.

'Howard, you're going to make yourself ill,' Kay would say as I pulled myself from pillar to post. 'You can't go on like this for much longer.'

She made a good point; all this multitasking could get a bit ridiculous. Sometimes I'd referee midweek games, only for my concentration to be interrupted with police-related matters. *You'd better go easy on the added time*, I'd say to myself. *You're due on shift in a couple of hours …*

Conversely, refereeing could occasionally interfere with life down at the station, too. If I knew I was due to be officiating at Grimsby v Northampton at 3 p.m., but was timetabled for a Saturday morning stint of policing, I'd purposely turn off my radio at 9 a.m. and clock in for office-bound clerical duties. What I didn't need was a sudden death at 10 a.m. to tie me up for three hours, precipitating the nightmarish situation of having to wait for the arrival of the body recovery people just as the team sheets were being presented at Blundell Park.

I'd regularly fly by the seat of my pants. Once, following a spate of burglaries in Tinsley, the CSG devised a plan to go to ground in strategically placed locations in residents' back gardens. With the benefit of expert crime analysis, we were able to pinpoint where future thefts were likely to take place, and we earmarked a suitable Saturday evening – at 6 p.m. sharp – for the operation to go live.

That same day, however, I had an appointment as fourth official for Aston Villa v Derby County, and I knew there wasn't a cat in hell's chance of getting back in time. Due to the importance of the planned exercise, I'd have to be careful not to take the piss and annoy my superiors. I did the match as scheduled, hurtled back up the motorway like Nigel Mansell, parked up my car in Sheffield and crept into the targeted garden. I'd not missed any action, as it happened, and my PCs promised they wouldn't dob me in to my inspectors.

So, three hours after loitering near the dugout at a packed Villa Park, within shouting distance of Paul Merson and Steve Staunton, I found myself crouching under a laurel bush, lying in wait for burglars. My high-pressure day wasn't in vain, however, as we caught a local toerag in the act, trying to put in some old dear's back door with a garden spade. Result.

Many of my police colleagues liked the fact that they had a league referee in their midst, I think. They'd often collar me for a chat about my alter-ego, quizzing me about all the various managers and footballers that I'd encountered. 'So what's Neil Warnock like, then?' they'd ask, to which I'd reply, 'He's bloody hard work, if truth be told.'

I was regularly featured in the police staff magazine and, once I rose through the ranks to league level, began to attract a fair bit of media attention. The local press ran headlines like *DRIVERS GET THE YELLOW CARD* and *IT'S A FAIR COP, REF*, while the nationals opted for *LAYING DOWN THE LAW* and – my personal favourite – *THE HAND OF PLOD*.

Admittedly, there were a few less-than-sympathetic supervisors who were highly irritated with my police-referee job-juggling, but the vast majority – especially those with a passion for football – were very understanding. In fact, without their support, I don't think I'd have been able to make the progress that I did.

Getting hold of Premier League tickets (which I was able to do when I ran the line) didn't harm my cause, either; requesting a shift change from my supervisor would always be sweetened if I dangled a pair of VIP tickets for Anfield or Highbury as bait.

Sadly, this bargaining tool wasn't quite as effective when I moved over to the Football League. No disrespect, but presenting my superior with two Tuesday night tickets for Bury v Darlington didn't really have the same cachet. That particular career move may have been a positive development for me, but it certainly wasn't for them.

The decision to give all Premier League match officials full-time professional status, in 2001, went hand-in-hand with the creation of the Professional Game Match Officials Limited (PGMOL). This body, headed up by general manager Philip Don, was established to provide referees with high-quality training and support, enabling them to cope with the increasing demands of the game.

The following year, I began to receive advice and guidance from former referee Keith Hackett who, as the PGMOL's second in command, also had special responsibility for priming and developing young refs. It seemed that Keith had earmarked myself, Mark Clattenburg and a clutch of others as future members of the so-called Select Group of eighteen Premier League officials. I'd made gradual but impressive progress over the previous couple of seasons – moving through the refereeing ranking system and climbing from Band F to Band C – and he'd obviously spotted my potential.

I flourished under Keith's coaching that season. A great mentor and motivator – and with over twenty years of high-octane refereeing experience behind him, including that famous 1981 FA Cup final – he did his utmost to boost my confidence and performance. The fact that he was a fellow South Yorkshireman probably helped to strengthen our bond, too.

'It's all about self-belief, Howard,' he'd say whenever we met up for a coffee in Sheffield city centre. 'There are so many possibilities out there, and it's up to you to realise them.'

With his advice ringing in my ears, I had a blinding game at Pride Park for Derby County v Portsmouth, awarding a penalty to the latter from a great position as well as making a succession of assertive, instinctive decisions. Keith was watching from the stands that day and, following the final whistle, caught up with me in the dressing room.

'Judging from that display, Howard, I think you might be on your way to the Premier League,' he smiled, which meant the world to me, coming as it did from someone whose opinions I greatly respected.

My season went from strength to strength. That May, I found myself presiding over three play-off matches, starting with the first leg of the League Two semi-final tie between Cardiff City and Bristol City. My elation at the appointment was tempered, however, when I heard that both teams had contacted the Football League to query my credentials. Fair dos, I suppose; I'd only been reffing at that standard for three years, and I wasn't exactly a big name. Jim Ashworth had to intervene, informing their respective club secretaries that I was one of the top-performing guys that year, and assuring them that I'd do a decent job.

The match itself finished 1-0 to Cardiff and, thankfully, passed without controversy. I was completely enthralled with the atmosphere at Ninian Park. The stadium was heavy with tension, nerves and drama, and the awareness that one season's work was distilled into two legs of football was as unnerving as it was exciting. I appreciated how crucial and critical such games could be, and I knew that just one daft slip-up could forever define a club's future and a referee's career.

Four days later, I oversaw Reading v Wolverhampton Wanderers in another semi-final, this time in the Championship. Proceedings went well for me at the Madejski Stadium – the away side won this second leg 1-0, augmenting their aggregate score of 3-1 – and, just moments after the final whistle, my phone buzzed with a text.

'Outstanding, young man,' it read. 'See you next year.'

Its sender, much to my surprise, was Premier League referee Jeff Winter. I didn't know him very well at that stage – I'd only lined for a him a couple of times – but his kind-hearted sentiments really touched me.

The following evening took me to yet another semi-final play-off – Sheffield United v Nottingham Forest at Bramall Lane – yet this time I was attending in my capacity as police sergeant. I was supervising the notorious cell van, which comprised ten self-contained cubicles for any boozers or brawlers who required segregating.

I remember chatting to one rum 'un who needed calming down and, to make conversation, telling him about my previous night's run-out at Reading. I think he thought I was bullshitting him, to be honest. However, it was at that moment it dawned on me how bloody lucky I was that I had two areas of work that I cared so passionately about. Refereeing one night, policing the next; I was truly in my element.

Home life was great, too, since Kay was expecting our third child, a daughter. Like her brother, though, she was doing her best to scupper one of the most important games of my career. In mid-May I'd received the nod to officiate the final of the Division Two play-off between Cardiff and Queens Park Rangers on Sunday 25 May 2003 at the Millennium Stadium. Our baby was due on the 11th but, ten days later, the stubborn little minx was still a no-show. Both Kay and I were getting more vexed as time went on; she'd had enough of waiting around and I was shitting bricks that I'd miss the biggest game of my season. After some pleading and coaxing, however, a sympathetic obstetrician agreed to induce the birth, and the lovely Lucy was born three days before the match. Panic over.

The play-off, like my daughter, went to extra time, with Andy Campbell's match winner securing promotion for the Welshmen in their home city. It was one of the most electrifying football atmospheres that I'd ever experienced, and I'd managed to control things really well.

'How was that, then, Howard?' asked the great Jack Taylor when I'd caught up with him for a drink in a corporate lounge. Jack was England's most celebrated referee – he'd memorably presided over the 1974 World Cup final between Johan Cruyff's Holland and Franz Beckenbauer's West Germany – and was a hero of both mine and my father's. Following his retirement as a match official he'd worked as an ambassador for the Football League and, for a young ref like me, meeting him was always a pleasure and a privilege.

'It was absolutely bloody brilliant out there,' I grinned, feeling delighted that I'd coped with the big occasion, and knowing that I was good and ready for the next step up.

# CHAPTER 4

# You're Starting
# To Let Us Down, Ref

As I prepared for my transfer to the Premier League, my fitness regime went into overdrive. My physique had always been on the chunky side – I came from a 'big-boned' family, many of whom had struggled with their weight – but in the late 1990s it had become glaringly obvious that I needed to shed some excess kilos.

The turning point came while reffing my inaugural Pontin's League game, namely Derby County v Leicester City at the Baseball Ground. It was my first encounter with top-level pro-fessional footballers, and it was crystal clear that their fitness, power and pace were on a different scale. As these elite athletes zipped and zig-zagged round the pitch, I was horrified to find myself puffing, panting and struggling for breath. The longer the game went on, the more my legs ached, and the more my lungs heaved.

*Shit, I'm chasing this game,* I remember thinking as a wiry defender whipped past me with the ball. *I can't bloody keep up …*

This public humiliation shocked me into action. How could a big lump like me possibly represent a new breed of young, dynamic refs? I needed to get fitter and slimmer, and pronto.

I remember having a chat with Uriah Rennie, a Premier League referee and fellow South Yorkshireman who knew a thing or two about keeping in shape. He offered me some plain-speaking advice.

'At this level, Howard, you've got to get from A to B without even thinking about it,' he said. 'Good fitness should be a given. You need to be able to focus solely on your refereeing, not whether you're going to make it from one box to another without collapsing in a heap.'

He went on to explain how top-class officiating was all about maintaining integrity and projecting authority, something that could be so easily compromised if a ref was physically unfit.

'You're never going to compete with a 21-year-old striker, Howard, but if you want to take your job seriously you have to train hard.'

Aware of Uri's astute advice, and determined to transform my body shape, I kick-started my lard-to-lean health and fitness plan. First off I tackled my diet, eliminating snacks and junk food (including my addiction to potato crisps and dry roasted peanuts), curbing my beer intake and swerving the police canteen's legendary cooked breakfasts. Then I devised my own exercise regime, building up my strength via gym-based weight and resistance training as well as boosting my stamina with regular runs and cycles around the South Yorkshire hillsides.

The rewards were tenfold, and had psychological as well as physical ramifications. Within a few months I'd shed two stone, and my improved fitness levels had brought a new vim and vigour to my refereeing. The more I looked the part, the more my confidence grew. As a result, I found it considerably easier to connect with players and convincingly 'sell' my decisions. Measuring 6 foot 3 inches in my studs and weighing in at 94 kilos also meant that I was often the biggest person on the pitch, which – allied to the fact that I had age on my side – probably gave me more clout and credibility than some of the older, slighter referees.

By the time I reached Select Group level – and with the welcome support of top-notch physios and sports scientists – I found myself in peak condition, able to cover 10,000 metres per match without blowing out of my arse.

Premier League training was highly structured and incredibly prescriptive. Individualised, seven-day schedules would be emailed to us every Sunday night, comprising specific instructions relating to training days, recovery sessions and rest periods. All our activity – whether it was a high-intensity session or a low-impact strength and conditioning exercise – would be transmitted to a heart rate monitor, via a chest band. This virtual 'coach' was attached to you the whole time, whether you were officiating at a match, competing with colleagues at the Select Group HQ or training alone in a local park.

Every Monday morning we'd Bluetooth a week's worth of data over to the sports scientists, Matt Weston and Simon Breivik, who'd conduct all the necessary analysis and feedback. Their scientific approach made a huge difference to me, both emotionally and physically, enabling me to maintain an excellent level of fitness and well-being throughout my top-flight career.

'Bloody hell, are you in good shape or what?' I remember Middlesbrough manager Gareth Southgate once commenting when he'd spotted me walking around in my base layer, prior to a game.

While I was more than happy with my new physique, I never dreamed of matching the supreme fitness levels displayed by top-flight footballers. Lads in the Premier League sometimes got a raw deal compared with other sports professionals – I'd often hear comments suggesting they were lightweights as opposed to rugby stars or tennis players, for example – but I'd regularly see their superb athleticism at close hand.

While the likes of John Terry or Ryan Giggs would never be as powerful as Martin Johnson or Gareth Thomas, or as agile as Rafa Nadal or Roger Federer, they were unbelievably fit for purpose. Not only did they have to cover acres of ground on the pitch, they also had to tackle, and twist, and turn, and head, and pass. And all this while keeping their footballing brains on full alert for 90 minutes.

Very occasionally, Select Group referees were invited to take part in Premier League clubs' training sessions. I remember once being put through my paces with Sunderland's first team, and being astounded by the fitness levels on show. We'd finished off a gruelling cardiovascular session with some 40-metre shuttle runs and, despite me being in decent nick (on a refereeing scale, granted) every single member of the squad had made mincemeat out of me. Even Titus Bramble, one of the division's heftier defenders, had left me trailing in his wake. The only person I could hope to compete with was the Black Cats' coach, Steve Guppy.

'Mate, these lads are immense …' I'd panted, sprawling out on the training pitch as I attempted to get my breath back.

I'd been officially invited into the Premier League's Select Group in June 2003, following an informal chat over dinner with PGMOL supremos Philip Don and Keith Hackett. At the age of thirty-one I became one of the youngest referees to be appointed to English football's top tier, earning a basic salary of £65,000 per year plus performance-related bonuses.

'Great to have you on board, Howard,' said Philip, shaking my hand. 'Hope this is the start of a long and illustrious career for you.'

Also receiving a promotion was Peter Walton, a forty-something ref who'd impressed the powers-that-be by finishing top of the Football League ratings list. Missing out on this occasion was Mark Clattenburg, whose turn would come 12 months down the line.

My first get-together with my new colleagues – a pre-season boot camp week at Lilleshall – took place in July 2003. It didn't take me long to realise that that the Select Group was going to be a pretty challenging environment. I was already aware of some personality clashes within our unit – this had been glaringly obvious during my time on the Premier League line – but I'd not realised the true extent of the disharmony. While there'd always been an element of healthy rivalry in the Football League, we'd generally operated as individuals and rarely had the chance to hook up en masse.

The group, it became clear, was split into two distinct factions. In one camp belonged Graham Poll and his pals, namely Paul Durkin, Rob Styles, Mike Dean, Andy D'Urso and Graham Barber. They dubbed themselves 'The Red Wine Club', in light of the fact they liked to relax with a tipple (or two) while off-duty.

Occupying the other side of the fence was another circle of officials led by Middlesbrough ref Jeff Winter, who'd never hidden his intense dislike of Poll. Joining him were Mark Halsey – who shared Winter's sentiments – alongside Mike Riley, Neale Barry, Steve Bennett and Barry Knight. There existed a vague north-south divide among the group, too, with Poll's posse generally based in and around London and the Home Counties, and Winter's group predominantly hailing from the Midlands and the north.

Taking the middle ground, and often acting as peacemakers, were Alan Wiley, Dermot Gallagher, Matt Massias and Uriah Rennie. I suppose I became one of these intermediaries too, but gravitated more towards Winter's crew. Jeff had taken me and Peter under his wing for the first couple of seasons – his general gist had been 'stick with me and you'll be fine' – and he'd made us feel a little more involved and more welcome than Graham and his group.

The simmering tensions between the rival cliques would occasionally turn nasty, as it did during the following year's team-building week at an isolated Lake District cottage. What had been intended as an informal beer 'n' barbecue night in Cumbria almost descended into a version of *Fight Night* at the NEC, following a ruckus between Graham Poll and Mark Halsey.

There was no love lost between the pair, evidently, but the depth of the acrimony took me by surprise. Watching them trading personal insults and squaring up to each other was pretty unedifying, to say the least. These were well-regarded, well-paid Premier League referees acting like badly behaved schoolboys.

It was big Uriah Rennie who eventually stepped in, shouting 'Enough!' as he grabbed Poll and Halsey by the scruffs of their necks before dragging them apart. Peter and I, the relative newcomers, just sat there, wide-eyed and open-mouthed, aghast at what we were seeing. I remember thinking *Jesus Christ, what the hell have I let myself in for here?*

The formal Select Group get-togethers, organised by the PGMOL and scheduled every fortnight, were intense affairs. From Wednesday evening to Friday morning we'd base ourselves in Staverton Park, a hotel in deepest Northamptonshire, for a programme chock-full with technical training, fitness coaching and information sharing. Team-bonding tasks would be on the agenda, too, although these weren't always hugely effective within such a discordant environment.

Keith Hackett, however, who replaced Philip Don as PGMOL general manager in 2004, preferred us to work through problems together as a group, and tried to disregard the in-fighting. He attached great importance to assessing our video clips together, believing that, by sharing and reviewing our errors and oversights, we'd be aiding our development as elite referees.

Every time we attended Staverton, therefore, there'd be a video session in a conference room, with footage of recent refereeing decisions being projected on to a large screen. Keith would ask one of us to lead the meeting, giving this nominee carte blanche to hand-pick clips of his choosing.

Unsurprisingly, this often accounted for some bum-clenchingly awkward moments, since the group's social chasm meant that personal agendas could emerge if Rob Styles, for example, replayed unflattering clips featuring a rival like Jeff Winter, before dissecting his mishaps and blunders.

Ostensibly, these group reviews were designed to keep us on our toes and raise our game, knowing that any false moves might be pored over by our contemporaries the following week. In reality, though, they became counter-productive, merely acting as convenient vehicles for slating rivals and settling scores. Indeed, Hackett's PGMOL successor, Mike Riley, realised this shortcoming and would later scrap these intensely awkward sessions. Refereeing errors would continue to be identified and scrutinised, of course, but within more intimate, less public surroundings.

'Thank God for that,' I remember saying to Peter Walton when this decision was finally rubber stamped. 'At last, the end of the video nasties.'

All this back-stabbing and backbiting could get quite wearing.

While the Select Group was always going to be highly competitive – each of us were vying for the top matches, after all – I found it sad that some refs seemed to go out of their way to undermine and destabilise their colleagues.

Over the months I grew a thick skin, though, brushing aside the inevitable snidey comments that would come my way if, the previous Saturday, I'd misjudged that penalty shout or had discounted that clear-cut offside. Some of the more abrasive members of the Red Wine Club were certainly prepared to point out your errors.

'Come on, Howard,' they'd sneer. 'You've got to do better than that, for fuck's sake. You're letting us all down, pal …'

Other refs, like Mike Riley, would instead offer up some constructive criticism, putting their arm round you and talking things through. Mike was an interesting guy, in many respects; he may not have been the most outgoing person in the world, but if you ever felt down and needed someone to put your head back on straight, Riley was your man.

'I feel like shit after missing that red card, mate,' I'd moan following a particularly taxing game, and he'd gladly give me ten minutes of honest advice and reassurance. Mike had a knack of putting the spring back into your step, and I'd always emerge from our chats with a more positive mindset.

Prior to taking up my Premier League role, I'd decided to reduce my policing hours and go part-time. My bosses were as supportive as ever, but requested that I base myself in the control room rather than the community. This change of scenery may not have been ideal for me – I much preferred being at the coalface, not in the office – but I agreed to it nonetheless. I was just relieved that they were continuing to employ me, if I'm honest; I had no idea whether my Premier League career was going to take off – I'd known refs getting demoted after one season, or retiring unexpectedly through injury – and I still needed the safety net of my police work.

I became a sergeant in a department that dealt with jobs over the phone, handling crime reports and complaints from the public as well as despatching community officers to sort out various issues. Occasionally I'd manage to venture outdoors, organising ad hoc off-licence checks, for example, or promoting safe driving schemes. It wasn't the most exciting police work I ever did, and certainly wasn't what I'd joined the force to do, but it was a fair compromise. Something had to give in my professional life, and it happened to be the policing.

On the plus side, my part-time status meant that I was able to fulfil all my refereeing commitments without fretting about energy-sapping night shifts, crazy 4 a.m. dashes up the M1 or burglar stake-outs.

'So, no more hiding in back gardens for you then,' smiled a colleague when I reported for my first day in the Control Room.

I had to wait until October 2003 for my Premier League refereeing debut. As a new recruit I had to defer to my more experienced colleagues for the first few weeks, biding my time and blowing my whistle at various First Division stadiums in the interim. It was a pretty frustrating period.

*C'mon, guys, I'm ready now*, I remember thinking to myself. *Give me a chance, for Chrissakes ...*

On the afternoon of Monday 13 October I received the email informing me that I'd been appointed to Fulham v Wolves. The match would take place at Loftus Road, since Craven Cottage was still undergoing refurbishment to meet the all-seater requirements of the Taylor Report.

'Treat it like a normal game, Howard,' said Dad when I rang

him with my good news. 'You've done plenty of big matches, lad. Just go for it.'

I was nervous, of course – so much so that I didn't dare look at the FA Premier League badge on my shirt for fear of becoming overwhelmed – but the match itself went relatively smoothly, finishing goalless.

On the way home I stopped off at a service station on the M1 for a quick coffee. As I walked through the concourse I happened to pass some fans poring over the results in the hot-off-the-press *Football Pink*. What happened next was so daft, and so unlike me, really, but I just couldn't help myself. So proud did I feel, and so keen was I to spread my news, that I tapped one of these fellas on the shoulder and excitedly pointed at the Fulham fixture.

'I refereed that game today, lads,' I said, grinning like an idiot as the looks on their faces screamed MOVE AWAY FROM THE WEIRDO.

My second game saw a trip to the Reebok for Bolton Wanderers v Southampton, which proved to be another 0-0 stalemate. About five minutes into the game I remember the home side's captain, Kevin Nolan, sidling over to me.

'Ref, calm down, calm down,' he said condescendingly. 'You look really nervous, really edgy. I know it's only your second game, pal, but no need to shit yourself.'

Maybe I was a little tense, but I wasn't stupid. I knew full well that Nolan, perhaps put up by Wanderers' boss Sam Allardyce, was trying to unnerve and intimidate the rookie ref in the game's early stages. Big Sam would leave no stone unturned if it meant his team gaining a psychological advantage; to me, it all felt a bit too contrived to be an off-the-cuff remark from a player who wouldn't ordinarily know that it was the ref's second game.

Quite amazingly, the first five Premier League games I

officiated were 0-0 draws. A long run of blanks like this was virtually unheard of and, unsurprisingly, most of these fixtures were relegated to the lower reaches of the *Match of the Day* running order. This state of affairs became a slight concern for me, since a mundane no-score draw could be dodgy for a ref watching himself on Britain's favourite footy show. If there weren't any notable goals or incidents, Lineker, Hansen et al. would be more likely to pinpoint some debatable decision that might normally be overlooked.

'Thank Christ I didn't mess up today,' I said to Kay, relieved, as we watched the Southampton 0, Leicester City 0 highlights from the sofa that January.

I seriously began to worry that I'd put a hoodoo on my fixtures until, in February 2004, Wolves broke the deadlock by beating Fulham 2-1. When Paul Ince banged in his 20th-minute goal at Molineux I almost felt like celebrating with him myself.

So, as it happened, I had a fairly steady start to the season. In order to gradually bed me in, the PGMOL sensibly appointed me to a series of lower-profile games, interspersed with some Football League and cup matches. There were a couple of blips: I failed to give a clear penalty during Tottenham Hotspur v Newcastle United in March 2004 (my fault entirely – a proper rabbit-in-the-headlights moment) and, at St Mary's on the final day of the season, I awarded a controversial spot-kick to Aston Villa after harshly adjudging that Southampton's Danny Higginbotham had been guilty of pushing.

There may have been mitigating circumstances relating to the Spurs oversight, however. My cousin Adam – childhood buddy, best man at my wedding and a lifelong Tottenham fan – had sadly died the previous summer, succumbing to diabetes-related complications. The Webb family were devastated, particularly since he was only 30 years old when he passed away. Had Adam still been alive, he'd have been my VIP guest at White Hart Lane, and I think my heightened emotions might have subconsciously affected my concentration that afternoon.

Just prior to kick-off I stood in the centre circle and had a little private moment to myself.

'Thinking of you, mate,' I whispered, casting my mind back to us chasing a football in the back garden, both sporting our white Admiral England kits.

I received two tickets for every Premier League fixture that I refereed, one of which I'd always give to Dad. On a match day we'd travel to the ground together, but if I was particularly knackered afterwards he'd do the honours and drive the return leg home. On one occasion, however – on the way back from a tough old game at Millwall – he managed to fall asleep at the wheel.

I'd been trying to snooze since Newark, but had kept sensing that the car was swerving slightly off course.

'You OK there, Dad?' I'd asked, giving him a quick nudge to check that he was in control of his faculties. 'Not dropping off, are you?'

'Shurrup, I'm fine,' came his gruff reply. 'Go back to sleep.'

The next thing I knew we were in a ditch at the side of the A1 near Worksop.

'Bloody hell, man, you could've killed us,' I said as the fan belt whirred beneath us and steam rose up from the engine.

'I'm so sorry, son,' he gasped, looking all dazed and dishevelled. 'I must have nodded off ...'

Once the AA man had bailed us out, we were able to get back on the road and head home to Rotherham, this time with yours truly in the driver's seat.

That evening, as with most Saturdays, I dropped Dad off and

stayed for a quick catch-up cuppa with Mum. She'd maintain that she could always tell whether I'd had a good game or not, merely by the rhythm of the doorbell chime. If my footsteps up the driveway were followed with a jaunty *DING-DONG-DING-DONG-DIIIIIIING-DONNNNNNG* she'd breathe a sigh of relief, as it indicated that all had gone swimmingly, and that her boy was feeling happy with life. If she just heard a plain old *DING-DONG* her heart would sink as she knew she'd be opening the door to a son with face like a wet weekend in Wakefield.

I refereed a total of thirty-four games during the following campaign, 2004–05. It was a consolidation season for me, I suppose, a period in which I began to find my feet and settle into the rigours of the Premier League. By now I'd come to know my officiating colleagues a little better, too, although the deep chasms remained between Graham Poll's Red Wine Club and the others. This was in spite of the fact that one of his chief adversaries, Jeff Winter, had hung up his whistle in May 2004. The FA Cup final between Manchester United and Millwall ended up being his swansong game.

'Wishing you all the best, mate,' I'd said to him a few days earlier. 'What a way to go, eh …'

I was sad to see Jeff retire. He'd given me lots of help and guidance over the years, and I knew I'd miss him being around.

The new season brought with it some testing times. This included an on-pitch brawl during Manchester City v Chelsea in October 2004, which had been triggered by my awarding a match-winning penalty to the home side. Three weeks later, I'd reffed a feisty Newcastle v Fulham head-to-head which, despite the presence of big-name United players like Alan Shearer, Patrick Kluivert and Nicky Butt, the visitors had won 4-1.

In the first half, with the score at 0-1, I'd incensed the New-castle faithful by rejecting a penalty shout from Shearer. The England striker had gone to ground following a clash with Pape Bouba Diop, but I'd adjudged that he'd got his shot away before the defender had made contact. In my mind, this hadn't merited a penalty. As I waved away the appeals and gave a goal kick, Magpies boss Graeme Souness went completely apeshit, jumping and gesticulating on the sidelines, way outside of his technical area. I walked over to try and calm him down, only to be met with a barrage of abuse.

'Sorry, Graeme, but I'm not having that,' I said, shaking my head and pointing to the stands.

The Glaswegian became one of only three managers that I'd end up banishing to the backwaters during my career (Stoke City's Thordarson had preceded him, and Barcelona's Pep Guardiola would follow).

'Howard Webb had a rather tough afternoon,' said the following morning's *Daily Mirror* with some understatement, 'but the referee handled the game well. He allowed it to flow and got the big decisions right.'

Some Premier League grounds, I'd discover, were more hostile than others. One such cauldron was Goodison Park which, along-side Stoke's Britannia Stadium, tended to be the most challenging arena for me.

A particularly troublesome game – one of the toughest I ever reffed, in hindsight – took place at Everton in early December, ending in a 3-2 home victory over Bolton Wanderers. Both sides were teeming with tough, tenacious characters that day – Alan Stubbs and Duncan Ferguson for Everton, and Ivan Campo and Kevin Davies for Bolton – and I knew I'd have my work cut out trying to corral these extra-strong personalities.

In the first period, despite giving decisions as I saw fit, I was conscious that the majority were going in Bolton's favour. I soon became aware of the resentment slowly building among the Toffees supporters, and I felt the bad vibes transmitting on to the pitch. Every time I reprimanded an Everton player the crowd bayed for my blood, and their team got on my back.

Around the 30-minute mark, self-doubt began to creep in. This is, by some distance, the most damaging mid-match emotion for a referee to experience. *Was I being too harsh? Was I calling things badly? Was I letting the fans affect me?* From that point on I began to limit the stoppages, curb the whistle, and let more things go. As a direct result the tempo rose and the aggro escalated.

I'd started to hide, in effect, which is a cardinal sin for my profession. Rather than being intimidated by my surroundings, I should have maintained the courage of my convictions, followed my gut instinct, and thought *bollocks to you all*. But I failed to do so that afternoon.

Just prior to half-time, Bolton captain Gary Speed ambled over for a word.

'You're starting to let us down, ref,' he said, looking me straight in the eye.

'Don't be stupid,' I replied, feeling slightly affronted, although deep down I knew *exactly* what he meant. I *was* letting them down. I wasn't doing my job properly. I'd mishandled too many incidents. I'd allowed myself to be swayed by the febrile atmosphere, and as a result his team wasn't being protected. I was, to coin a phrase, bottling it. The game went from bad to worse and I just wanted to go home.

My Nightmare on Gwladys Street taught me a brutal lesson in game management. A dreadful day was compounded with an appalling assessment from the independent match delegate, former Football League secretary David Dent. My average score usually fluctuated between 23.8 and 24.0 out of 30, but that day he meted out a derisory 14.0, the lowest mark I'd ever receive in almost 300 top-flight matches.

George Courtney, by then a PGMOL referee assessor, also put the boot in by awarding me a similarly pitiful grade. *Twats, the both of you,* I remember thinking at the time but, once I'd had time to take stock, I knew these poor ratings were entirely justified. That evening, much to Mum's dismay, I returned Dad home with a melancholy *ding-dong* of the doorbell and a sorrowful shake of the head.

A few days later I hooked up with my refereeing coach, Keren Barratt, at the Hilton Hotel near East Midlands Airport. It took us five long hours to analyse the Everton v Bolton match DVD, going through it incident by incident and isolating all my frailties and failures. It became patently clear that, had I stuck to my guns and continued in the same vein as the first half-hour, I wouldn't have come a cropper.

This trial by video was a painful and embarrassing experience, but I needed to learn from this below-par performance.

'The moral of the story, Howard, is that you can't go hiding during a game,' explained Keren. 'Fans and players may disagree with your decisions, but you've got to trust your instincts, believe in yourself and persevere to the end.'

He also suggested I use this match as a yardstick for my future development, mentally referencing it whenever times got tough.

Never in a million years would I have guessed that Everton versus Bolton, December 2004, would cross my mind during the biggest match of my life, six years down the line.

In March 2005 I refereed Newcastle v Liverpool, the Magpies winning 1-0 much to the delight of Mr Souness who, on this occasion, was charm personified. After the game I met up with

Mark Clattenburg, the Select Group newcomer with whom I'd become quite friendly over the years. We'd first met in the late 1990s at a fitness test at Lilleshall, and had attended a few meetings together. He'd since earned a reputation as a naturally gifted young official, and I knew the PGMOL had high hopes for him.

Clatts had taken charge of his first ever Premier League game that day, at Crystal Palace, and had flown back up to his native Newcastle to join me for a night on the lash.

'Well done for getting through unscathed, mate,' I said as we toasted his refereeing milestone. 'The first of many, eh?'

The next morning, nursing a spectacular hangover, I had to report back to St James' Park, sporting my full referee's kit. Filming was taking place for the *Goal!* movie, featuring the story of aspiring footballer Santiago Muñez, and starring Kuno Becker and Anna Friel among others. The production team had used real-time action footage from the previous day's game, but still needed to capture some additional shots, and had asked me to pop over to the ground before I journeyed back to South Yorkshire.

For the next three hours – and while the icy north-east wind froze my knackers off – I had to re-enact a series of hand signals, whistle blows and card shows. Actors and extras scuttled around the Newcastle pitch, repeating the same moves and free kicks again, and again, and again.

'Thanks, ref,' said the director once we'd wrapped everything up. 'We'll make sure we get your name in the end credits.'

They did, as it happened. My kids were seriously impressed.

The remainder of my season went relatively smoothly. I showed only two red cards during the entire campaign, both of them dished out during a tense Crystal Palace v Southampton six-pointer. Iain Dowie and Harry Redknapp's charges had become embroiled in a four-way relegation fight, alongside Norwich City and West Bromwich Albion, and fraying tempers that day had led to dismissals for Peter Crouch and Gonzalo Sorondo. Both sides – together with the Canaries – would ultimately suffer the dreaded drop into the Championship.

The night before that game, Dad and I had booked into the Croydon Hilton. Unbeknown to us, the Saints entourage were staying there too and, when we arrived at nine o'clock, Harry Redknapp was already installed in the lounge bar.

In need of an early night – and not wanting to be seen fraternising with a boss on the eve of a big game – I left Dad and Harry to it. They ended up getting on like a house on fire, chatting about bygone players and classic matches until the early hours.

'They say Harry's going to retire from the game if Southampton get relegated,' said Dad over breakfast the next morning.

'Nah, I reckon he's got a few more years in him yet,' I replied.

From then on, whenever our paths crossed, the first thing that Harry would ask was 'How's Billy doing? Great fella, your old man …'

My 2005–06 season opened with the Chelsea v Arsenal Community Shield at Cardiff's Millennium Stadium. The game passed uneventfully – thank Christ – with three yellow cards (Claude Makélélé, Frank Lampard and Cesc Fàbregas) followed by a fair-and-square end result (Chelsea won 2-1).

Meanwhile, back on Planet PGMOL, things had kicked off yet again. In late July, Mark Clattenburg and I had missed the annual pre-season get-together, which had been held at the Aldershot army barracks. Instead, we'd been despatched to officiate the Premier League Asia Trophy in Bangkok, a biannual tournament featuring three English sides (Bolton, Everton and Manchester City that particular year) as well as the Thai national team. Clatts and I really enjoyed this diversion; it was a welcome change of scenery in a stunning part of the world.

When we returned to the UK, however, we realised that all was not well among our colleagues. It transpired that a booze-fuelled evening at Aldershot (with some army staff in tow) had spiralled out of control, culminating in Graham Poll clambering on to a car roof and causing some damage.

Shortly afterwards, Keith Hackett received an anonymous email detailing these indiscretions, which in turn prompted Poll's suspension. By the time Clatts and I had returned, two PGMOL investigations were under way: firstly, to establish the extent of Poll's wrongdoings and secondly, to expose the mole in the camp who'd sent the shit-stirring email, since it was widely assumed to be a fellow referee.

The next Staverton get-together was like an episode of *Poirot*. We were all called into a meeting room, where the PGMOL chairman, a well-spoken gent called Peter Herd, solemnly detailed the pending investigations, confirming that Graham Poll had received a two-match ban. Then Poll himself stood up. There was no apology as such, just a statement of betrayal aimed firmly at his colleagues, which surprised me.

'I'm so disappointed that one of you has done this,' he said, granite-faced. 'Whoever it is, shame on you.'

He then explained how medical reasons had provoked his mis-behaviour, before accusing the Select Group's resident secret agent of destroying what was left of our team spirit.

Then came a bizarre elimination from enquiries rigmarole. It was like being back at West Bar police station.

'Webb, Clattenburg, you were in Thailand, obviously, so you can leave now,' said Herd with a wave of his hand, before sum-marily dismissing more referees from the room.

Eventually the prime suspects were narrowed down to four

referees, but with each man pleading his innocence, and without any incriminating computer evidence, no action could be taken. There was to be no *Scooby-Doo*-style reveal, so the rogue was never unmasked.

'What a waste of bloody time and effort,' I remarked to my colleagues afterwards.

Poll's comments about dented morale were spot-on, though. Following Email-gate, the rift in the group grew so wide that the PGMOL's sports psychologist, Craig Mahoney, was parachuted in to try to sort things out, once and for all.

He sat us all down one morning, informing us that we had two options. We could either go the hard, painful route, which would entail airing our issues, reopening old wounds and addressing a few home truths. By doing this, though, we'd be able to draw a line under everything and move forward.

'Or,' he continued, 'you could go for the easier alternative. You could just walk out of this room right now, avoid the soul-searching, and carry on as you're doing, with no resolution to all this resentment. The choice is yours, gents.'

Unsurprisingly, we opted for the latter. I think we all had enough confrontation to deal with on the pitch, and just couldn't stomach a gut-wrenching, mud-slinging war of words at Staverton. As a result, the cliques and acrimony within the Select Group would prevail for many years.

The biggest game of my career at that stage – an FA Cup fifth round tie between Liverpool and Manchester United – took place on Saturday 18 February 2006. I hadn't been able to approach the match in the ideal frame of mind, however. The previous week I'd had a shocker at Arsenal v Bolton in the Premier League, missing a hideous two-footed tackle by Abdoulaye Faye on José Reyes – who was stretchered off – as well as failing to caution Mathieu Flamini for a reckless challenge on Ricardo Gardner.

Despite his team salvaging a point with a last-minute equaliser, Arsène Wenger was incensed afterwards, laying into Bolton for 'showing all the tricks that are creeping into the game' and accusing me of not displaying enough authority. Getting battered by the *Match of the Day* pundits that evening – as well as receiving timely 'You all right, mate?' texts from the Red Wine Club – added the finishing touches to a ruined weekend. And, as was the case following every dismal performance, my poor family would suffer 48 hours of down-in-the-dumps Dad sulking round the house.

'Can we go and play football in the park?' the kids would invariably ask on a Sunday afternoon. I'd always oblige, but would often disguise myself in a big woolly hat to avoid getting hassled by some smart-arse football fan.

It was at times like this that I'd draw on the moral support of Mike Riley. I had a high-profile cup tie looming on the horizon, yet I felt lower than a snake's belly.

The print and broadcast media had given the match a huge build-up, much of it focusing on the hostility between Gary Neville and the Liverpool faithful. Things had come to a head in the 90th minute of the Premier League clash at Old Trafford the previous January, a fiery game refereed by Mike Riley himself. Following Rio Ferdinand's winner, Neville had raced over to the away fans to engage in some serious fist-pumping and badge-kissing which, unsurprisingly, hadn't gone down too well among the Scousers.

Alex Ferguson had felt obliged to give me a name-check during his Friday afternoon press conference.

'Howard Webb is a young referee and there are big hopes for the lad, but this is a big test,' he was reported as saying. 'Handling the Neville situation is one thing but he has to be 100 per cent fair, otherwise all the talk about him may not be as hopeful as it should be.'

It was another textbook attempt at mind games, for sure, but the United boss's words genuinely had no bearing on my match preparation. They merely went in one ear and out the other. I was solely focused on the game itself – not the media circus surrounding it – and just wanted to marshal it to the best of my ability.

The tie itself, which Liverpool won 1–0, went like a dream from my perspective. I controlled the game well, the football flowed nicely and I was satisfied with most of my key decisions.

Souring the whole match, however, was a horrific injury to United's Alan Smith, who'd come on as a sub for Darren Fletcher. He'd blocked a free kick, had fallen awkwardly, and was left writhing on the pitch, emitting blood-curdling screams.

'Look at my leg, look at my leg,' he'd yelled, grabbing my left arm as I'd beckoned to the medical team with my right.

*I'd rather not if you don't mind, Alan,* I recall thinking, since out of the corner of my eye I could see a bone protruding from his sock. It was one of the worst injuries I've ever witnessed on the field of play.

My refereeing rollercoaster continued apace, and in March 2006 I was embroiled in yet more controversy after sending off Manchester City's Sun Jihai during an FA Cup quarter-final at Eastlands. I'd red-carded the Chinese full-back after he'd seemingly thrown a punch at West Ham United's Matthew Etherington while wrestling for possession. However, replays suggested it was more akin to a flailing arm and probably merited only a yellow. In hindsight, it was a harsh decision.

The City fans panned me for the rest of the match, no doubt blaming me for their cup exit following West Ham's shock 2–1 victory. Blues boss Stuart Pearce, with typical fair-mindedness, chose not to haul me over the coals, though.

'There'll be no criticism for the ref from me,' he stated in his post-match briefing. 'He has his job to do and he made the decisions as he saw fit.'

West Ham progressed to the FA Cup final, as it happened, and on Wednesday 26 April 2006 I was appointed to their Premier League match against Liverpool, their soon-to-be opponents at the Millennium Stadium.

If there was a game that didn't need any red cards, it was this one. The cup final was only a fortnight away, and the last thing any player needed was a three-match ban.

Lo and behold, with just eight minutes remaining, the Hammers' Hayden Mullins and Liverpool's Luis García decided to start scrapping. It was one of those 'this'll hurt me more than it hurts you' moments, but both players gave me no option but to dismiss them.

Alan Pardew and Rafael Benítez visited my dressing room after the final whistle. While they weren't disputing my decision – it had been pretty clear-cut – they wondered whether, in the circumstances, there was anything that could be done to reduce the ban to two matches in order to allow Mullins and García to feature in Cardiff.

It wasn't to be, however: the FA upheld the punishment and the players missed out. I was gutted, to be fair. Even though they'd been silly enough to have a spat in the first place – and were undoubtedly the architects of their own downfall – my decision had ultimately denied two footballers the chance to play in a cup final.

I couldn't beat myself up about it, though. Over the years I'd learned that there was no room for sentiment in elite sport. High-level refereeing was all about applying the laws, drawing upon my knowledge and experience and not succumbing to emotion. Moreover, at that point in my career I was being scrutinised more than ever before, not only by domestic assessors, but by overseas assessors, too.

FIFA and UEFA were on my case.

# CHAPTER 5

# We Will Not Let Them Kill You Here

I was working an evening shift at West Bar station when I received a four-word text from a fellow referee.

'There is a God,' it stated.

I messaged my colleague for an explanation and, a few seconds later, my phone buzzed with the reply.

'Poll has fucked up his career forever.'

Graham Poll, it transpired, had been refereeing Australia v Croatia in Stuttgart that night – a Group F game in the 2006 World Cup finals – and had monumentally cocked things up by booking Croatia's Josip Šimunić three times, only dismissing him from the field of play after the third yellow, and even then after the final whistle had been blown. Apparently the confusion had arisen because he'd marked one of the players' cautions against the wrong team, perhaps thrown by the fact that Canberra-born Šimunić spoke with a broad Aussie accent.

The sports media rounded on him the next day – *POLL LOSES THE PLOT* was the headline in the *Guardian* – and his fine reputation lay in tatters. While Graham and I weren't hugely close, I felt incredible sympathy for him (I doubt this view was shared by some of my other colleagues, though, who probably cracked open the champagne that night). We'd all made daft mistakes in our careers, but to have done so on the biggest football stage in the world, in front of an audience of millions, was every referee's worst nightmare. I took no personal satisfaction whatsoever from his misfortune.

Within days, Poll had acknowledged his error and had announced his retirement from international football, drawing to a close an excellent career that had spanned three major championships.

'It's time for somebody else in England to have a go and I'll do everything I can to prepare them,' he told the press, 'but for me, tournament football is over.'

Two years later, at the 2008 European Championships, that someone else would be me.

The English FA had nominated me on to the FIFA List of International Referees in January 2005, and a couple of months later I'd been dispatched to a UEFA Under-19s tournament near Madrid. The previous weekend I'd reffed Portsmouth v Liverpool – my twenty-eighth match in the Premier League – and I was feeling pretty buoyant about my officiating.

The opening fixture of the tournament pitched Portugal against Spain. I managed it in my usual fashion, trying to maintain good lines of communication with the players and aiming to keep the game moving with minimal whistle-blowing or card-showing. After the game I breathed a sigh of relief. *Job well done*, I thought to myself.

UEFA's referee observer that night – Aron Schmidhuber, a German who'd officiated at Italia 90 – clearly thought otherwise.

He put me firmly in my place when we met for our post-match debrief.

'You are a typical British referee, Howard. Too much blah, blah, blah,' he declared, doing that 'talky talky' gesture with his hands to illustrate the point. 'We don't need blah, blah, blah in European refereeing. Yellow is yellow, red is red. That is enough.'

A mark of 7.8 out of 10 for my general performance – pretty sub-standard, considering that 8.4 was an average FIFA grading – suggested that I had much to learn on the Continent.

It wasn't until the following November that I'd have my first taste of senior level international football. Belfast's Windsor Park was the venue for my inaugural game, as I'd been appointed to oversee a friendly between Northern Ireland and Portugal.

Managing two different football mindsets on one pitch was never going to be easy. As suspected, it was a battle between the high tempo, physical approach of the northern European side, and the slower, more technical style of their southern counterparts.

As an international rookie I wasn't best equipped to deal with this gulf in attitude, and a turbulent, distinctly unfriendly first 45 minutes saw me struggling to strike the right balance. The home crowd were particularly vociferous that night, too, barracking me for decisions that went Portugal's way, and heckling the 20-year-old Cristiano Ronaldo every time he touched the ball.

As I blew the half-time whistle and paced past the dugout, I was immediately accosted by Northern Ireland manager Lawrie Sanchez.

'Are you going to let this game flow or what, ref? Whistle, whistle, whistle all the bloody time. C'mon, let us play for God's sake …'

Portugal boss Phil Scolari also sounded me out, waylaying me as I headed down the tunnel.

'Referee! This is not rugby! You must give my players some protection!'

Short of asking Phil and Lawrie to get in a huddle and hatch a compromise plan, there wasn't much chance of keeping both camps happy that evening.

In September 2006 I took charge of my first ever Champions League game, Steaua Bucharest v Lyon. Not only was this a major step forward for me, it was also a tremendous honour. I'd be treading in the footsteps of some superb officials – Markus Merk, Anders Frisk and Urs Meier, for example – and would be refereeing elite European club football, which I'd worshipped since I was a kid. Growing up in the 1980s had given me the privilege of watching the likes of Liverpool, Nottingham Forest and Aston Villa playing on the Continent, and those vivid memories still resonated with me.

I was beset with nerves at the Stadionul Steaua as the Champions League anthem blared out. To all intents and purposes I was on trial for UEFA, well aware that there'd been instances of refs hashing up their first Champions League game and never being reappointed. Luckily for me it was a relatively straightforward tie without any powder keg moments. Lyon, who at that time were doing fantastically well under manager Gérard Houllier, secured a great 3-0 away win.

My team and I spent the rest of the evening in the Bucharest Intercontinental's basement casino, winding down with a few beers and shoving a few Romanian leus on the roulette wheel.

'So bloody glad that's over and done with,' I said to Phil Sharp, relieved to have overcome my first Champions League hurdle.

A year intervened before my next appointment, by which time I'd been promoted to UEFA's elite list of referees. It took me to my favourite venue of all time – the Santiago Bernabéu. A couple of hours before Real Madrid and Werder Bremen were due to kick off, I allowed myself a few minutes to take in the splendour of this magnificent stadium. I wandered down to the mouth of the tunnel and looked across the pitch, gazing up at the huge royal blue stands and the gleaming white REAL MADRID CF motif.

As I stood there, a UEFA delegate crept up behind me and tapped me on the shoulder.

'Take your chance,' he smiled, before turning on his heels and heading back down the tunnel. I think the implication was, *we've given you this opportunity, ref; don't mess it up.*

I didn't, thank goodness. The game passed by with just three yellow cards, ending in a clear-cut 2-1 home victory capped off with Ruud van Nistelrooy's side-footed winner, his fiftieth goal in the Champions League. I left the ground with an added spring in my step, hopeful that my assured performance would merit a decent UEFA assessment.

My satisfaction would be short-lived, however. The following month's match – a goalless affair between PSV Eindhoven and Fenerbahçe – proved to be a nightmare. A hot-blooded game littered with fouls and flashpoints, it would become one of the most gruelling Champions League ties I ever officiated. I dished out six yellow cards and one red, to Fenerbahçe striker Deivid de Souza after his late tackle on Mike Zonneveld. I also missed a spitting incident midway through the first half, and failed to spot an alleged stamp within minutes of the interval.

I was despondent after the match, furious at my erratic performance and fearful that I'd rankled UEFA's big shots. I felt anything but 'elite' that evening.

A poor grading of 7.8 confirmed that I hadn't exactly covered myself in glory.

'This referee has not really succeeded to control the players of this team,' stated the assessor's report. 'He has difficulties in disciplinary control. The mistakes were the results of not enough experience in officiating this type of match ...'

The following day I sat on a flight from Schiphol to Manchester, glumly contemplating the previous night's events. If I was to maintain my UEFA status, I needed to iron out my flaws and address my weaknesses. I decided to seek counsel from someone who had most certainly been there and done that.

Graham Poll, whose European experience was unrivalled among English referees, was more than happy to offer me advice.

'Howard, the reason you're struggling to keep control is because you're almost communicating *too* much,' he said when I called him up that weekend. 'On the Continent, they just want you to be the boss. They expect you to call the shots, to look strong in your body language, to show them that your decision's final.'

According to Poll, I'd mistakenly tried to rationalise and explain my decisions to offenders. By virtually pleading with players to believe me, I was appearing weak-willed and, as a result, was losing respect and authority on the pitch.

He went to explain that successful European refereeing wasn't a case of being a robot, or being aloof – naturally, there was a time and a place for taking a player aside for a quiet word – but it was about maintaining an air of control and confidence.

'Actions speak louder than words in Europe. Don't open up the dialogue, Howard, and don't invite a response. Impose your decision, keep interaction to a minimum, and make it clear that nothing is open for debate.'

Poll's wise words hit the nail on the head, and I couldn't thank him enough. As he suggested, if I was to keep UEFA happy I needed to adjust my refereeing style and adapt my mode of communication. No more 'blah blah blah', essentially.

I gleaned advice from other quarters, too. I studied video footage of the great Italian referee, Pierluigi Collina. He was a maestro of body language and facial expression, with the ability to switch from *ho-ho-ho* to *don't-fuck-with-me* within a matter of seconds. Players would be left in no doubt whatsoever about who was in charge, and what message he was sending.

A former colleague of Collina's also came to my rescue. Hugh Dallas, a hugely experienced and respected international referee from Scotland, had acted as the Italian's fourth official during the 2002 World Cup final in Japan. Following his retirement from reffing he'd taken up a new role within UEFA's referees' committee and, in addition to this, had been appointed as my mentor. As a consequence, I was partnered up with him at various training camps and seminars and he would become a hugely influential figure during the rest of my international career.

Having offloaded my European woes on to him, he volunteered his own unique analogy. You can safely assume that it hadn't been quoted in any UEFA handbooks.

'Refereeing is like riding a horse you've never met before,' he told me. 'When you first mount it, you're not sure what type of personality it has. You don't know if it's going to be a docile little gem that'll trot along obediently, or a misbehaving little shit that'll run out of control.

'If it's a shit, and you keep your reins too loose for the first few steps, you're going to have to pull it right back. But if it's a gem, and you keep the reins too tight, you might aggravate it.'

Hugh then explained that, if it was cantering along nicely, I could perhaps loosen the reins a little bit, allow the horse to relax and start to enjoy the experience myself. But, he warned, if the nag saw something that caused it to rear up, I'd have to take swift action.

'Then you'd have to tightly yank on the reins, just for a few minutes, to settle it back down again.'

Hugh's equine interpretation may have been unconventional,

but I digested every single word of it. If I was looking to progress on the Continent, I needed to be able to gauge and govern each game in the appropriate way.

One aspect of European football that didn't trouble me was the language, of course. English was the chosen tongue across the world of refereeing, and all the officials – even the native speakers – were regularly tested on their conversation and comprehension skills.

I found that most European footballers had a solid grasp of English, even those who hadn't played in the Premier League. Kakà from AC Milan was a case in point – he was virtually fluent – and even players like Roma's Daniele De Rossi, who swerved speaking English on the pitch, would have no problems chatting off it.

'Hey Howard, can I speak to you about this plaster cast on my arm?' he once asked me before an international match, conversing in perfect English. 'Just need to check I'm OK to play in it.'

I wasn't lazy when it came to European languages, though. Not at all. I memorised a long list of foreign swearwords so I could decipher whether I was being called a twat, prick or sonofabitch and – thanks to my refereeing friends – taught myself how to say 'wanker' in thirteen languages.

I had a few lost-in-translation moments, though; during a game between Porto and Seville I once told a player who'd committed two fouls in quick succession that his actions were incredibly stupid. He went absolutely crazy, running to the bench, gesturing at me, looking really aggrieved that I'd insulted him in this manner. I could only assume that 'stupid' had deeper connotations in Portugal, perhaps casting aspersions on his mental aptitude or something. Whatever the case, I apologised profusely.

I also remember encountering some communication problems during a friendly game between Middlesbrough and Chievo

Verona in August 2006. I never liked cautioning players in pre-season matches, but one of the Italians was being persistently aggressive and was throwing his weight around. Midway through the second half I'd had quite enough of this lad's antics, so I called him over and warned him that he'd be getting booked if he didn't calm down.

'No Inglese, no Inglese,' he protested, so I asked one of Boro's multi-lingual players – I think it might have been the Brazilian, Fábio Rochemback – to act as my translator.

'Can you tell this fella that if I see any more fouls, he'll be getting yellow carded?'

'No problem, ref,' he said, purposefully striding over to his opponent and prodding his finger.

'EH YOU, ANY MORA FOULSA, YOU GETA YELLOW CARDA,' he yelled at him, in Italian-accented English. He may as well have added a Joe Dolce-style SHADDAP YOU FACE for good measure. I almost cried laughing, and was still chuckling when I blew the full-time whistle.

I spent the most enjoyable four weeks of my professional refereeing career in North America. In April 2007 I'd attended a preparatory FIFA conference designed for listed referees who had yet to attend a tournament and, a couple of months later, was duly assigned to the Under-20s World Cup in Canada.

The significance of this was twofold. Not only did it represent my first major FIFA international competition, it also brought me together with Darren Cann and Mike Mullarkey, two supremely talented assistant referees who'd go on to play a huge part in my life and my career. I'd met them both before – in 2005 Darren had run the line at a UEFA Cup game in Zürich, and Mike had assisted me at Wolves in 2003 – but we'd never worked as a trio.

We were put together by pure chance, really. Linesman

Peter Kirkup was initially assigned to join Darren and me, but his employers, Barclaycard, weren't prepared to give him time off work. The FA hastily rang round some other Premier League assistants, and Mike was duly recruited as Pete's late replacement.

The three of us met up at Heathrow Airport in time for the Air Canada flight to Toronto, and had a quick pit-stop at the bar. In spite of our differing personalities, we instantly hit it off. Darren, from Norfolk, was adventurous, single-minded and had a huge knowledge of the game. Mike, a Devonian, was sensitive, conscientious and incredibly quick-witted. I slotted in somewhere in between, I think, but somehow the dynamic worked, and we all gelled.

We had a good feeling about the tournament as soon as we landed at Pearson International Airport. Toronto looked stunning in the June sunshine and, as we were chauffeured to our luxury city centre hotel in a FIFA car, we reckoned we were going to be well looked-after for the ensuing few weeks.

The next morning's introductory seminar, hosted by a referee instructor, was illuminating to say the least.

'Gentlemen,' he smiled, surveying the fifteen teams of officials sitting before him in the function suite. 'Welcome to the first step on the road to the 2010 World Cup.'

*Jesus H. Christ*, I thought, as the three of us from Team England exchanged astonished glances. While we were conscious that South Africa 2010 was just three years away, there'd been no indication from our FIFA superiors that this tournament was to form part of the selection process.

'Right, lads,' I said to Darren and Mike. 'It's time for us to make a good impression.'

We were appointed to the opening game, Brazil v Poland, under the closed roof of Montreal's Olympic Stadium.

'Have a great match, son,' said my dad when I phoned him that morning. 'It's on Eurosport over here, so your mum and I will be watching all the way from Brinsworth.'

The Poles won 1-0, in spite of playing with ten men after I'd dismissed one of their team for a second offence. I later learned from Dad that the TV co-commentator – ex-Arsenal midfielder Stewart Robson – had given me a mauling, accusing me of being overly harsh and not fully understanding and appreciating this level of football. Perhaps I was particularly firm that day, but Stewart wouldn't have known that I'd already had my fingers burnt overseas by being too lenient and that I wasn't prepared to take any more risks. FIFA had notoriously high standards and I wanted to show that I had the steel and mettle to succeed at this level.

Our team oversaw a total of five games that month, jetting between Toronto, Montreal and Edmonton in order to fulfil our fixtures. We had a brilliant time, enjoying all the trappings of a major competition but without the media scrutiny of a senior tournament. Being invited into the FIFA 'family' felt great, too: we loved the opportunity to rub shoulders with referees from all over the world, to take part in highly professional training sessions and to work with the world's most talented young footballers. Having plenty of downtime meant that we managed to fit in some sightseeing trips to Niagara Falls and the CN Tower, too, as well as a few nights out on the town.

Darren, Mike and I were thrilled to be appointed to the Nigeria v Chile quarter-final in Montreal. The game had also been designated as one of FIFA's 'Say No To Racism' awareness-raisers, with plenty of films, placards and banners – in English and French – to promote this worthy cause.

The match remained goalless after 90 minutes, but by the end of an extremely one-sided period of extra time the South

Americans had powered themselves to an emphatic 4-0 victory. It proved to be a very demanding half-hour for us. The Nigerians argued that the Chileans' first goal was offside – we begged to differ, allowing the goal and yellow-carding the complainant – and the second came from a penalty, their striker having been impeded by a Nigerian defender who I dismissed for denying an obvious goal-scoring opportunity.

The Africans were none too happy with our performance, however, especially their manager, Ladan Bosso. When asked in the post-match press conference to comment about the anti-racism campaign, Bosso went on the offensive in more ways than one.

'After what happened on the pitch – the officiating – I think FIFA has a long way to beat racism,' he sneered, 'because that official showed racism.'

I was furious. Our decisions had been correct, we'd handled the game capably – Darren was on fire that day, giving a string of outstanding offside calls – and to accuse us of racial discrimination was both unwarranted and unforgivable. Thankfully, FIFA came down strongly on Bosso, referring the case to their disciplinary committee and demanding he send me a written apology.

'After analysing my reaction I realised it was inappropriate,' he admitted. 'My comments were based on what I saw in the match and it was done in the heat of the moment.'

The semi-final between Czech Republic and Austria, in Edmonton's Commonwealth Stadium, proved to be the last game of our Canadian experience. There'd been much talk of Darren, Mike and me taking charge of the final, apparently, but we had an inkling that the Bosso furore may have intervened, despite our integrity never having been questioned by FIFA.

The lads and I managed to cast aside our disappointment and, the night before our departure, celebrated with drinks and pizza. Not only had we enjoyed a fantastic tournament, we'd clicked well as a trio, and had the distinct feeling that we'd be hooking up regularly in the future.

'It's been such a pleasure, guys,' I said, raising my bottle of Molson. 'Let's hope this is a springboard for us all.'

The 2007 FIFA Under-20 World Cup, incidentally, was lifted by an imperious Argentina team. Star of the show was the tournament's Golden Boot winner, a young lad by the name of Sergio Agüero.

With Graham Poll out of the mix, it became a straight race between me and Mike Riley for the honour of representing England in the 2008 European Championships. We'd both been officiating well in the Premier League, we'd been given our fair share of high-profile games and, apart from Mike's vastly superior experience, there wasn't much to separate us. We'd known each other a long time, too – we were fellow Rotherhamites who'd reffed the same local teams in our youth – and our rivalry had always been friendly rather than fierce.

One particular night, however – Wednesday 12 September 2007 – became pivotal for us both. I'd been posted to Kiev, refereeing the qualifier between Ukraine and Italy, whereas Mike had flown to Tirana to oversee Albania v Netherlands. Despite being racked with nerves beforehand – I'd been told that the chairman of UEFA's referee committee, Volker Roth, was that night's observer – my game went brilliantly. Thanks to a brace from Antonio Di Natale, Italy rode out 2-1 victors and there were no major calamities on my part.

Mike's match, on the other hand, had seemingly not gone to plan. A stormy, chaotic tie had seen him flashing six yellow cards and one red, as well as disallowing a good goal for Albania. Just to compound things, he'd been forced to suspend the match near the end after fireworks had been thrown from the crowd.

A couple of hours after full-time my phone rang. It was Mike, calling from his Tirana hotel room.

'Congratulations, Howard. Tonight's the night you've been selected for the Euros,' he said, sounding more resigned than resentful. He was a pretty rational, philosophical guy.

While I didn't want to assume anything, as far as Mike was concerned my progression to the finals was a foregone conclusion. His hunch proved to be spot-on, though, because in December 2007 I did indeed get the nod from UEFA, receiving a phone call inviting me to the joint Austria–Switzerland tournament, along with my linesmen pals Darren Cann and Mike Mullarkey.

In the wake of Steve 'wally with the brolly' McClaren's side failing to qualify, some newspapers dubbed us the 'only English team going to the Euros'.

Of all the referees picked for the finals in June 2008, I was the youngest and least experienced. Also making the elite list were such luminaries as Italy's Roberto Rosetti, Belgium's Frank De Bleeckere, Slovakia's Luboš Michel and Switzerland's Massimo Busacca, all of whom I greatly revered and respected.

Considering this array of refereeing talent, I knew that my chances of reaching the tournament's knockout phase were pretty slim. That being the case, I was still keen to officiate a couple of group stage games and, not only that, I wanted to referee them well. Not long before, the *Observer* had labelled a performance of mine as 'anonymously competent', implying that I'd managed the game smoothly and had only stepped into the breach when needed. A similar scenario, played out on this big stage, would have suited me just fine.

'The last thing I want is to be the centre of attention,' I

explained to Dad before I flew out to Switzerland. 'I just want to get the job done without any fuss.'

There were other omens to suggest that our stay on the Continent might be curtailed. As Darren, Mike and I arrived at the base hotel in Regensdorf, a town on the outskirts of Zürich, we found ourselves checking in at the same time as Roberto Rosetti and his Italian posse. Eavesdropping on their conversation with the reception staff, it became evident that their check-out date was five days after ours.

'Aye, aye, seems like they're already planning to send us home early,' I said to the lads, half-laughing.

UEFA denied this was the case when we challenged an official, claiming that some accommodation had been block-booked for longer spells than others, and that referees would be asked to swap and change hotel rooms if need be. We weren't convinced, though.

Our team's first appointment, we discovered, would take place on Thursday 12 June. We'd been allocated to Match 12, one of the second games in the group stage, Poland versus Austria, in Vienna's Ernst-Happel-Stadion. While the guys and I would have preferred an earlier-scheduled game (most officials liked to get involved sooner rather than later, thus limiting any long, edgy waits) we used the time to soak up the Euro 2008 atmosphere.

We watched all of the first round of group matches – some in the stadiums, some on the hotel's huge flat-screen TV – and nat- urally took a keen interest in our colleagues' handling of games. Everything seemed to be going pretty smoothly, we surmised, with few controversial decisions or incidents for fans and the media to seize upon.

Something else came along to keep us occupied, too. Together with five or six other refereeing teams, we'd agreed to participate in a fly-on-the-wall documentary. UEFA chief Michel Platini had personally sanctioned the film, which aimed to portray a warts-and-all, behind-the-scenes view of the tournament from the officials' perspective. There'd been absolutely no pressure to take part – some of our colleagues had politely declined – but the three of us decided to go ahead with it, believing it would be a nice way of capturing and chronicling our Euro 2008 experience.

'Something to show the grandkids, lads,' I said to Darren and Mike.

The camera crew followed us everywhere, from aeroplanes to people carriers, from meeting rooms to dressing rooms, from training exercises to physio sessions. They even latched on to our families, paying close attention to the views and opinions of my dad – who'd flown over for the tournament – and capturing the reactions of Mum and Joanne back home in Rotherham.

'Treat this like any other game, Howard,' said director Yves Hinant as his crew got set up, prior to our inaugural match in Vienna. 'Act as naturally as you can, and to try and ignore the cameras,' he added. 'We need this to be as authentic as possible.'

The crew trailed us as we performed our pre-match rituals, our warm-ups and our rally cries. They also filmed a nervy Billy Webb, perched on the edge of his seat as I blew the whistle to commence the action and kick off my first European Championships.

There were 30 minutes on the clock when Poland went ahead, Roger Guerreiro converting a whipped-in cross from close range. It was touch and go for offside but, reassured by Mike's decision to keep his flag down, I allowed the goal to stand. I stole a quick glance at the big screen replay – all refs do it – and the judgement looked sound enough to me. However, for the remainder of the half I was aware of Mike's anxious ruminations through my earpiece.

'I'm not sure that was correct, Howard, I'm not sure ...' he repeated over the radio, his voice quavering. 'Maybe he was off-side ... I'm really not sure.'

At half-time I headed off to the dressing room, where a stressed-out Mike was already searching for an answer from the fourth official, Hungary's Viktor Kassai.

'Be honest with me; was it offside?' Mike asked, although, without any TV replays available to us, no one could really say for sure.

The second half mirrored the momentum of the first, with both sides zipping the ball around the pitch and creating a host of decent chances. It was turning into a really scintillating game, and my team was handling it well.

And then, in the 91st minute, I awarded a free-kick to Austria, near the halfway line. The ball was clearly going to get bombed into the penalty area, and everybody went forward. I remember Darren saying 'Get right in there, Howard, it's going to come in!' and Mike, spotting a melee of holding and pushing, yelling 'Stop it, stop it, stop it!'

Bearing in mind that UEFA had issued strict directives to control such argy-bargy, I hit the whistle and stopped play before the free kick had been taken, warning the players to rein it in. I allowed it to be retaken and, as the players swarmed together and charged into the box, I immediately clocked Sebastian Prödl's shirt being pulled by Mariusz Lewandowski, prompting the Austrian to fall to the floor. It was a clear holding offence; I could even see his white undershirt being exposed.

*Shit. I'm going to have to penalise here*, I thought. I'd already fore-warned their teammates, I'd spotted an obvious yanking of the shirt, and I felt compelled to act upon what I'd seen. Having to make such a swift assessment can be very challenging when you're confronted with a crowded penalty area, and when you have so many other potential violations going on the background. This was more than just jostling, though; this was significant holding. In my opinion it couldn't be ignored, and I felt I had no option but to award a penalty to Austria.

The co-host's Ivica Vastić duly scored it – naturally, the stadium erupted – and a minute later I blew for full-time. While the Polish players were understandably devastated their reactions were largely contained, a few of them offering me limp handshakes as they trudged off the pitch.

In contrast, their coach Leo Beenhakker was apoplectic. He stomped over, screaming in my face and wagging his finger.

'English referee, English referee,' he yelled as I walked down the tunnel. 'Trying to prove you are a big man. Nobody saw it, nobody saw it. Fucking disgrace.'

I stopped in my tracks and fixed the silver-haired Dutchman with an icy stare.

'When you watch it back later, you'll see what I saw.'

Unsurprisingly, the atmosphere in the officials' dressing room was highly charged. We were utterly shell-shocked by the unexpected chain of events that had marred the final stages of our first game. Mike sat nervously on the bench, fretting that he'd cocked up that offside, while I paced round the room, anxious to find out if UEFA were going to support my penalty decision. Darren attempted to reassure us both.

'Lads, there's no point worrying until we see what the observer has to say,' he said, sensing our heightened anxiety. 'He'll be here soon. We'll know more then.'

Following a game, UEFA's observers would routinely pop into the dressing rooms to make initial contact before they set about compiling their detailed assessment. While they were always cautious and non-committal – particularly if there'd been any controversy – you could often gauge their likely angle by their choice of phrase.

If you'd done extremely well, they'd say 'Excellent!' If you'd coped reasonably, they'd say 'Good!' However, if you'd had a 'mare they'd say a very vague 'Thank you.'

'Thank you for your efforts,' said UEFA's Jaap Uilenberg when he made his appearance that evening, and my heart sank.

Soon, the texts from friends and colleagues began to flood in, the general consensus being that I'd been correct to give the penalty. Mike received a few messages, too, but his pained expression told me that his weren't so positive.

As these sentiments filtered over from the UK, Dad was still in the stands, being interviewed by the film crew.

'That's *good* news!' he boomed, his voice a mix of relief and gusto, upon being told that the TV pundits had largely agreed with my ruling.

Uilenberg paid us another visit while we were receiving our post-match massages.

'I've received confirmation that the penalty decision was correct,' he informed us, 'but I'm afraid there still remains an issue with the offside for the first goal.'

It was the last thing that Mike wanted to hear. The replays, it seemed, had shown that Poland's goal should have been disallowed. Guerreiro had, in fact, been offside, and Mike just hadn't adjusted his position well enough. It was an uncharacteristic mistake from a very talented linesman, and my heart went out to him.

Mike's eyes glistened with tears as we sat in the bus ready to go back to the hotel. He was an emotional guy at the best of times, but I'd never seen him looking so crushed.

We flew back to our Zürich HQ the next day, and as I was lingering at the baggage carousel I turned on my phone to catch up with a few voicemails. One had been left by a senior police officer at South Yorkshire Police HQ, Superintendent Simon Torr, asking me to contact him as a matter of urgency. Concerned that something had happened to my family, I searched for a quiet spot in the airport to return the call. The subsequent conversation came like a bolt from the blue.

'The force has become aware of some death threats made against you following last night's match, Howard,' warned the Superintendent. 'We've already been in touch with UEFA about putting in extra security patrols for you, but we need to talk about how we can keep your family safe over here.'

It had transpired that, in the aftermath of the game, the Polish media had worked itself up into a frenzy about my penalty decision. I hadn't seen any newspapers or TV reports that morning, but it appeared I was now persona non grata from Kraków to Warsaw. Apparently the internet was awash with images of me sporting a Hitler moustache, wearing a Dick Turpin-style robber's mask or with my head in a noose. Alongside this were mocked-up RIP tombstones and *Wanted: Dead or Alive* posters putting a £25,000 bounty on my head. ('If they increase it a bit more I'll hand myself in,' I said to Darren later that day.)

Even the country's Prime Minister, Donald Tusk, had stuck his oar in. He'd said something along the lines of, 'If I met Howard Webb, I'd want to kill him too,' prompting Rotherham MP Denis MacShane to table a motion in Parliament demanding an apology from the Polish government.

Being 800 miles from home amid all this tumult was really hard for me, and – first and foremost – I wanted to ensure my family's safety. I kept in constant touch with the police, who'd deemed some of the threats to be serious enough to act upon. They put a quick response marker on the police computer to flag up any emergency calls from Kay or my mum, and the local policing team visited my kids' school to make them aware of the situation.

Mum was particularly jittery about it all. She'd had strangers knocking on her door, loitering on the pavement and driving slowly past the house, although the police reckoned they were more likely to have been Polish journalists angling for a story than anyone with more sinister intentions.

I spoke regularly with Kay who, in fairness, was being pretty resilient about it all.

'We're fine, Howard, honest, and we're being looked after,' she said. 'Just you keep yourself safe over there, please.'

I was surrounded by tight security for the next few days: guards patrolled the hotel and training sessions were closed to the public to prevent any face-to-face hostility. As it happened, my biggest confrontation was with the media. Shortly after arriving back in Zürich, I'd been asked whether I wished to continue with the mid-tournament press conference, which had been scheduled weeks in advance.

'D'you still want to go through with it, Howard?' asked UEFA's director of communications. 'We'll totally understand if you want to give it a miss.'

I opted to front up and face the music; I didn't want to bury my head in the sand and, in any case, I felt I had nothing to hide. It turned out to be a very surreal experience, though. Referees rarely attended press conferences back in the UK, yet I suddenly found myself faced with dozens of journalists, with microphones lining the desk and cameras flashing every second. For a fleeting moment I did wonder whether I'd be making things worse rather than better, but it was too late to back out.

Interestingly, the English reporters defended me to the hilt, both in the press room and on the back pages. Without sounding too mawkish, it felt like they were almost looking after one of their own, and I genuinely appreciated their support.

One particular Polish journalist gave it to me with both barrels, though, asking me how it felt to be Public Enemy No. 1, his provocative line of questioning incurring the wrath of UEFA's media team.

'But if the penalty was clear we wouldn't be talking about it, would we?' he replied, unrepentant.

Following the events in Vienna, I didn't expect to be assigned to another Euro 2008 match and patiently awaited the instructions to return home. My pessimism was misplaced, however, because within 48 hours a very supportive UEFA had insisted that we fly to Salzburg to officiate one of the last group stage games, between Greece and Spain. On paper it seemed like a sexy match – the cup holders against the emerging favourites – but in reality it was a dead rubber. Spain had already qualified for the knockout stages and Greece, having lost both games, had booked their flights back to Athens.

Darren, Mike and I decided to try and put the Poland situation behind us – they'd since been eliminated, with Beenhakker still blaming 'the English referee' – and, as we flew over to Salzburg, we made a pact to enjoy what we fully expected to be our final game of Euro 2008. It was time to move on from all the menace and intimidation. It was time to end our tournament on a high.

Meeting us straight off the plane at the airport was the city's police chief, flanked by burly security staff.

'Velcome to Salzburg, Mr Vebb,' he announced, before looking left and right and lowering his voice. 'Ve vill not let zem kill you here.'

Well, thank goodness for that.

Things didn't end there. The next day, when we arrived at the stadium we were informed that they'd received a telephone warning of a bomb in the referee's dressing room, and that there had also been rumours of an impending anthrax attack.

'If this wasn't so tragic it'd be funny,' I said to Darren, as we headed off to inspect the pitch while a pack of sprightly sniffer dogs set to task.

Our swansong game went swimmingly. A Spanish side featuring Andrés Iniesta, Xabi Alonso and Cesc Fàbregas overcame the Greeks – they won 2-1– and there were no controversies or disputes to blemish the occasion. The post-match hugs between my assistants and I were more heartfelt than usual that evening.

The death threats, press attacks and bomb scares were manna from heaven for the UEFA film crew, of course, providing them with a hugely dramatic thread for their movie. I can't say I was enamoured to see them waiting for me at Manchester Airport, though, following my flight from Zürich. I was mentally and physically drained and just wanted to get straight back home to my family in Rotherham.

'Would we be able to film you watching the final?' a cameraman asked me as I loaded my luggage into the taxi.

'I'll think about it,' came my jaded reply.

I relented in the end – I've always found it hard to say no – so, on the evening of Sunday 29 June my house became jam-packed with assorted members of the Webb family and a team of European film-makers. I watched the Spain v Germany final from the comfort of my settee, with a steady supply of beer to hand. I enthusiastically applauded Iker Casillas when he hoisted aloft the trophy, and did the same for ref Roberto Rosetti when he mounted the steps to receive his medal.

Shortly after I'd returned home I'd become aware of the plight of a 62-year-old street lighting engineer who worked for Rotherham Borough Council. Not only did he have the misfortune of being called Howard Webb, he also had a work email address that incorporated both his name and his home town.

The day after the Poland v Austria game he'd logged onto his computer at council HQ and, instead of the usual handful of emails complaining about flickering light bulbs and faulty street lamps, he'd been faced with four thousand death threats from fuming Poles.

*HOWARD WEBB WE ARE COMING TO KILL YOU* and *YOU ARE BEING WATCHED, ENGLISH BASTARD WEBB* weren't exactly what he'd bargained for on a humdrum Friday morning and, such was the onslaught, the council had to suspend the poor fella's email account.

Kay showed me the article in the *Rotherham Advertiser* that had outlined this gentleman's ordeal.

'I have never been a referee and am not likely to become one,' he'd said, 'especially if this is the sort of abuse they receive.'

Welcome to my world, Mr Webb, welcome to my world.

# CHAPTER 6

# Don't Let It Ruin Your Christmas

Four o'clock on a Monday afternoon was always a crucial time for Premier League referees. That's when you'd find us glued to our laptops or staring at our smartphones, awaiting the all-important PGMOL email informing us which match we'd been assigned to that week. Competition was keen – there were eighteen of us, but only ten top-flight matches – and, while there was an element of squad rotation, it was the in-form refs who'd get the plum appointments.

I'd be restless and agitated for most of the day as I tried to second-guess my fate; within each round of games there'd invariably be one fixture that I fancied and one that I dreaded.

*Please don't give me that one, for God's sake*, I'd pray, remembering how I'd struggled like hell with the previous season's match-up.

Once I heard the message ping, I'd anxiously scroll down the attachment, my subsequent yell of 'Yes!', 'No!' or 'Shit!' being an indication of how happy, cross or uneasy I felt about my allocated game.

Following on from the appointment would be a PGMOL data pack comprising stats and spreadsheets relating to both teams:

previous formations, player disciplinary records, number of penalties awarded, that sort of thing. We'd also receive our meticulous weekly training programme from the PGMOL sports scientists, which we'd be expected to carry out at home.

Referees would be encouraged to do as much online research as possible, too – accessing match footage, media reports and clubs' official websites – and, if we happened to be at a PGMOL get-together that week, we'd sit down to analyse our respective fixtures. We'd often compare notes about particular sides and players; there were no agendas or vendettas to pursue, it was more a case of forewarning and forearming each other.

'So what was "you-know-who" like at the Emirates last week, then?' one ref would ask a fellow colleague.

'An absolute nightmare,' would come the reply. 'Diving like a dolphin. You'll need to keep an eye on him.'

My match-day preparations would generally follow the same set routine. Convening at the pre-match hotel, four hours prior to kick-off, would be my assistants (Darren and Mike, more often than not) as well as that day's fourth official. I'd initiate the usual discussion about tactics, teamwork and communication which, like an on-flight safety drill, was well-worn but necessary. As team leader, I felt strongly that certain key messages had to be entrenched, whether it was the first game of the season or the thirty-first.

'Right, lads,' I'd say to my officials. 'I'll need your viewing angles today. I'll need your experience and expertise. And, as always, I'll need you all to be confident enough to offer your opinions.'

We'd then be driven to the stadium in the usual Mercedes V-class people carrier. In the late 1990s, the Premier League had banned independent travel between homes and venues, partly to avoid any lateness but to also ensure our safety. A refereeing colleague had been attacked in his car following a West Ham game, having stopped at traffic lights near a pub full of aggrieved supporters.

Upon arrival at the ground we'd drop off our bags, sort out our guest tickets and head off for the pitch inspection. After checking its general condition we'd do a spot of 'visualisation', which may sound a bit mumbo-jumbo but merely involved gauging our vantage points on the pitch and assessing the zones in which we were likely to operate.

We'd also check the Hawk-Eye goal-line system, collecting the equipment from the technical team and taking a football to both sets of goals. There we'd enact a series of tests, positioning ourselves in different areas around the goalmouth and mimicking a series of likely scenarios. So, we'd roll the ball across the line, then we'd carry it over holding it close to our bodies, then we'd whack it into the top-right corner and then trickle it into the bottom-left corner, all the while monitoring the kit's audio-visual alerts (our Hawk-Eye watches would flash and vibrate when activated, and would also send a cue of 'GOAL GOAL GOAL' to our ear-pieces). We'd even aim the ball into the side netting from outside, to double-check that the system wouldn't react if it went wide but still bulged into the net.

At 1.45 p.m. the lads and I would attend a briefing from the club's head of security. This official – usually an ex-copper – would draw our attention to any potential risks in the stadium, ranging from delayed kick-offs to extreme weather, or from terrorist threats to parachuting campaigners. Preferred lines of communication and evacuation procedures would be outlined, too.

'It's your responsibility to get the players off the pitch and to a place of safety,' we'd be told, 'and, as per usual, the away team bus is on standby as a getaway vehicle.'

We'd come to know all the security supremos quite well, notably Arthur Roberts at Manchester United. A dapper, distinguished-looking guy, Arthur was superb at his job but had a habit of using exactly the same words and phrases during each pre-match spiel, to the point that Darren, Mike and I would often dissolve into giggles.

All it took was one mention of 'high-conspicuity jackets' or the confirmation that 'all arterial routes are flowing' to trigger us off and we'd be standing there, pinching each other like a trio of naughty schoolboys.

The two o'clock team-sheet exchange was a snigger-free zone, however. Taking place in our dressing room, it would often be a tense, solemn affair as both sides revealed their respective line-ups for the first time, and as both managers came face-to-face with the referee and his officials.

When I first joined the Premier League, this handover was pretty informal and could be carried out by any club representative: the commercial manager, the kit man or the physio, for example. But then the regulations changed, decreeing that team managers or senior coaches – plus their captains – had to perform the honours in a much more formal manner.

And not only that, following complaints from refs that some bosses were scanning the opposition team sheets instead of listening to officials' instructions – as if they gave a toss about us when they had a starting eleven to absorb – a new procedure forbade them from reading the line-ups until we'd finished our spiel. The fourth official would keep the papers out of reach, therefore, until he was given the nod to finally hand them over.

Not every Premier League club would send in their manager, however. Hands-on, in-yer-face bosses like Sam Allardyce, Mick McCarthy, Neil Warnock and Harry Redknapp would routinely turn up, probably seeing it as a good moment to try to psychologically impose themselves on the officials. Sir Alex Ferguson, José Mourinho and David Moyes rarely visited the dressing rooms prior to kick-off, and it was very uncommon for Roberto

Mancini or Arsène Wenger to pop in. They would instead send in their assistants, such as Brian Kidd at Manchester City or Steve Bould at Arsenal. One manager became notorious for knocking on the door and scornfully throwing the team sheets at the feet of refs he disliked.

All things considered, the team-sheet exchange could be an unsettling encounter for a referee, especially one learning the ropes in the Premier League. You'd find yourself at close quarters with some of the biggest names in football, whose attention you'd have to hold for two or three minutes. I've seen fresh-faced young refs trembling with nerves as they've shaken hands with players and managers, and going all jittery when they've attempted to speak. Although I never got overly edgy, I'd always have butterflies in my stomach beforehand.

This tiny window of opportunity with coaches and captains, I quickly learned, had to be used wisely and economically. You didn't want to bore them, or repeat yourself, or state the bleedin' obvious; ideally, you'd aim to be succinct and relevant, while all the time conveying an air of control and confidence. Refs' pre-match patter could range from the terse ('All right lads, you know me, I've reffed you before, have a good one …') to the tedious ('Can I draw your attention to this very interesting law change …?). Some could be plain bizarre. 'If you happen to lose your temper on the pitch,' I once heard a referee asking a hard-case captain, 'which of your teammates shall I find to calm you down?'

As well as the usual common-sense safety matters – don't jump into the crowd, don't celebrate at the wrong end – I'd try to broach issues that could benefit my own 90 minutes as well as theirs.

'You guys know your teammates better than I do,' I'd say, 'so, as captains, can I trust you to recognise any flashpoints and keep things under control?'

I'd go on to explain that a timely intervention between a

wound-up player and a card-carrying ref could mean the differ-ence between having eleven men on the pitch rather than ten. With this in mind, I'd implore these skippers to step in whenever necessary, whether it was having a quiet word with their col-leagues or giving them a damned good shake.

'Sometimes I'll need you fellas to get hold of these lads and put their heads back on, even if you don't agree with whatever deci-sion I've made,' I'd add.

The smart, seasoned captains – like Chelsea's John Terry and Everton's Phil Jagielka – would gladly take on this responsibility for the greater good of their team. Others, however, didn't seem to possess the same degree of emotional intelligence. Stoke City's Ryan Shawcross, for example, didn't seem to want to assist. From my perspective, he couldn't see the bigger picture and appeared more likely to give me stick than support.

My on-pitch, pre-match warm-up was a 13-minute sequence of runs and stretches performed with military precision, invariably alongside Darren and Mike. More often than not, this would be complemented with our regulation eye exercises. The PGMOL were particularly keen to promote good eye health – for obvious reasons – and recruited world-class vision specialists who encour-aged us to incorporate 'extraocular muscle workouts' into our match-day routines. I took it pretty seriously, and would stand on the halfway line, focusing on the dugout, then the corner flag, then the goalmouth and then the centre spot. My head would remain completely still while my pupils flitted from side to side, like one of those 1970s-style 'Eagle-eyes' Action Man figures.

I'd then return to the dressing room to get rigged up with all my officiating equipment. Fastened around my chest was the Polar heart-rate band, which linked up to the heart-rate watch on my left wrist (this also doubled up as my timepiece). The Polar device was programmed to give out a reading every five seconds and, after every game, its data would be uploaded to the Premier League sports scientists, Matt and Simon, who'd use it to analyse my aerobic fitness.

Secured on to my opposite wrist (from August 2013 onwards, when it was first adopted by the Premier League) was the Hawk-Eye goal-line technology watch. The electronic flag receiver – which buzzed to alert me to my linesmen's actions – was strapped to my left arm and held in place with Tubigrip. On my other arm, a holster housed the radio which connected to an earpiece in my left ear.

This new communications system had arrived on the scene in 2006, and had totally revolutionised the world of refereeing. Before then, the pitch had often seemed a very lonely place for the man in the middle, even with twenty-two players roaming around and thousands of fans looking on. With the advent of the radio, however, the ref suddenly had three good mates speaking in his ear, confirming his decisions, forewarning him of hazards, and offering him support and motivation.

A very basic radio system had been piloted in the 1990s, but it had felt like dragging around a breezeblock, with an earpiece so bulky that it weighted down the left side of my head. The inter-ference was ridiculous, too. I remember running the line at Watford FC for Steve Lodge, raising my flag and shouting 'OFFSIDE!' down this new-fangled piece of kit. There was no response, since all Steve could hear was the crackle of white noise. I yelled down the radio again; not a dicky bird. In the end I was screaming 'OFFSIIIIIIIIDE' so loudly that he heard me from the other side of the pitch, as did Elton John and David Furnish up in the directors' box, no doubt.

I was particularly paranoid about my yellow and red cards. This stemmed from the infamous incident at Goodison Park when my esteemed colleague, Peter Walton, had forgotten to take his set on to the pitch. TV cameras captured him booking Birmingham City's Jordan Mutch, before feverishly rummaging in his pocket for a card that didn't exist.

Peter, by then dying with embarrassment, decided to wield an imaginary one instead, flashing his thumb and forefinger in the air as the players looked on, utterly bewildered. The best part – and something that still makes me howl when I think of it – was the way he continued the charade by putting the 'card' back into his pocket. It took Peter a while to live that one down, poor sod.

So, to avoid any similar mishaps, I'd always carry two sets on a match day, yellow card in the front left pocket of my shorts, red card front right, and an extra pair in my left breast pocket for those occasions when there was a second yellow card offence. I never used a notebook, preferring instead to write directly on to the yellow card (home cautions on the left, away cautions on the right). Also in my pocket was the official FIFA coin (blue on one side, yellow on the other).

The final piece of equipment to be adorned, securely attached to an Adidas lanyard on my left wrist, was my Black Fox 40 pea-less whistle.

Seven minutes before kick-off, I'd ring the bell or buzzer to signal the players' exit from their respective dressing rooms. This wasn't as straightforward as it sounds. I often found myself having to chivvy them up, thumping on a locked door with a distinct lack of movement behind it, like a dad trying to get his kids up for school. Often this delay was brought about by playground-style antics, with one team petulantly refusing to budge until their opponents lined up in the tunnel.

This pettiness was such a pisser for a referee, firstly because you knew you'd already got a battle on your hands before you'd even begun and, secondly, because prompt kick-off times in the Premier League were so crucial, particularly if it was a televised game. Indeed, so keen were the head honchos to start on time that the Select Group were offered financial incentives to meet punctuality targets. So, just as the TV execs was going apeshit at the sight of an empty tunnel, I'd be thinking *get your arses in gear, lads, I've got a bonus riding on this …*

If all went to plan, the teams and officials would assemble with six minutes to go, and would make their way to the pitch with five left on the clock. I'd have to remember to pick the ball up – there were times when I totally forgot and walked past it – before lining up for the Fair Play handshakes. In the Premier League, home team players always walked first, crossing the away team for the handshakes. This was completely opposite to UEFA and FIFA football, which saw the away side moving while the home side stood fast.

Then, following the official photographs with captains, mascots and forty-three sponsors, I'd head to the centre circle to perform the coin toss. The laws state that the winner chooses the direction of play, while the loser gets to kick off. Even so, the number of skippers who'd call 'Heads' correctly and persist in saying 'Can we kick off instead?' was incredible.

'No you bloody can't,' I'd scold, before handing the ball to their opponent.

Some players failed to understand the implications of the choice of ends, too. Put it this way, if I'd been a visiting captain who'd won the toss at Anfield, I'd have forced Liverpool to kick towards the away end in the second half rather than have the Kop sucking in a last-minute goal. A fair few captains didn't appear to grasp this, though, or didn't seem to give it much thought.

At three o'clock, with the match ball placed on the centre spot, I'd have one final scan of the pitch. Then, following a shrill *peeeeeeep* of the whistle, we'd be off.

\*

If I was involved in a live televised game there'd always be a sure-fire way to decipher the story of the first 45 minutes. As I walked off the pitch I'd train my eyes on the TV steadycam man who, heeding instructions from his director, would hoist his camera on to his shoulder, run on to the pitch and zoom in on the half's most influential figure as they approached the tunnel.

If he scuttled up to Rickie Lambert, who'd thundered in an 18-yard volley, or hot-footed it over to Kasper Schmeichel, who'd pulled off a blinding save, I knew they'd be the main focus of conversation in the TV studio. However, if he sidestepped them both and rammed his camera in *my* face, I'd realise that I'd fucked up that fifth-minute penalty decision, and that my name was about to be flung like mud among the pundits. There had been a few occasions when the camera had trailed me all the way off the pitch, and I'd thought *BOLLOCKS*.

When I returned to the dressing room I'd glug down some water and munch on a Jaffa Cake before having the routine consultations and clarifications with my team. I'd cross-reference any cautions and dismissals with the fourth official, before discussing with my assistants the merits (or otherwise) of that sending off or that penalty decision.

'It'll be interesting to see a replay of that tackle later, fellas,' I'd say. 'Not convinced it was enough for a red ...'

For those 15 minutes we'd exist in a media vacuum, without any TVs, radios or mobiles in our midst. I know for a fact that the phone ban was often flouted by certain refs and assistants, though. Some would sneak off to the toilet and have a furtive peek at texts, particularly if they wanted to verify a borderline decision.

This wasn't because these refs were in any way bent or corrupt; it was simply because they couldn't bear the uncertainty. It could be a risky tactic, though. If their first-half call had been spot-on, they'd return to the field of play feeling like the cock of the walk.

If they'd got it wrong, however, they'd often trudge back on to the pitch with their confidence dented.

While players and managers were barred from our dressing room during the interval – the exception being to alert us to second-half substitutions – you'd experience plenty of mind games and barbed comments in the tunnel as you were lining up for the restart. Some individuals would try to influence and unnerve you, doing their utmost to gain that psychological advantage for the next 45 minutes.

I remember Gary Neville once having a serious go at me in the Britannia Stadium tunnel, complaining about a messy tackle by Stoke's Robert Huth on Michael Carrick. It was a borderline red/yellow – an 'orange' as we often termed it – but I'd erred towards caution and plumped for the lesser sanction. This decision was playing on my mind as we waited to go back on to the pitch, however, and it was obviously at the forefront of Neville's, too.

'Have you seen that tackle back?' he yelled down the tunnel, knowing full well that I wouldn't have done. 'It's a fucking shocker, ref. Leg breaker. Horrendous. You'll be embarrassed when you see it on *Match of the Day*.'

*Oh shit*, I thought. *Maybe I've dropped a bollock there.*

Later that night I tuned into BBC1 at 10.35 p.m. – virtually watching the footage through my fingers – only to discover that my decision had been correct, and that it had been a clear-cut yellow. Nothing like a bloody red. It had taught me a valuable lesson, though.

'Never believe anything you hear from players or managers at half-time until you've seen it with your own eyes,' I'd warn any rookie refs who worked alongside me. 'They'll try every trick in the book to get into your head and alter your mindset. Be strong. Don't be swayed. Believe in yourself.'

\*

Following the final whistle, and once we'd got showered and suited-and-booted, I'd fulfil my duties with the Press Association – they always liked to double-check their tally of cautions – and would meet up for a quick debrief with the referee assessor.

Occasionally we'd receive a post-match visit from a manager on the warpath. All bosses had to abide by the Premier League's 'cool-off period' rule, which meant that, after full-time, they couldn't barge straight into our room and had to wait at least 30 minutes before discussing any burning issues. Our side of the bargain was never to close a door on a manager; we were obliged to speak to any bosses with grievances, regardless how livid they were.

One particular Boxing Day at the Stadium of Light had seen Sunderland boss Martin O'Neill demanding to see me after a game against Everton. In the 51st minute I'd ruled that Lee Cattermole had committed a foul on Leon Osman, so had awarded a penalty against the Black Cats. I hadn't really seen the contact, I admit, but everything about it had suggested a spot-kick. Over the years I'd learned to trust my gut instinct; very rarely did it let me down.

Leighton Baines converted to make it 1-1, and O'Neill, it's fair to say, was fuming. Precisely half-an-hour after the final whistle, he came hammering on my door.

'Come in, Martin,' I said, and steeled myself for a dressing down.

'It wasn't a fuckin' penalty, it wasn't a fuckin' penalty,' he raged, peering at me above his glasses. 'I can't believe you fuckin' gave that. I just can't. It's a fuckin' disgrace.'

I decided that a conciliatory approach might mollify him. While we weren't supposed to analyse video replays after the game, I made an exception on this occasion, asking Sunderland's Prozone guy to have a look at the incident and give me a steer.

'Come back in five minutes, Martin, OK?' I said, and he shuffled out of the room, muttering to himself and shaking his head.

I was pretty confident that my judgement had been correct, but I just required corroboration. However, as the Prozone chap replayed the footage, it became crystal clear that the Irishman did indeed have grounds for complaint. I'd got it wrong, and I shouldn't have given the penalty. On this occasion, my gut feeling had fallen short.

'Martin, I've got an apology to make,' I said once I'd called him back into my room. 'I just didn't read it right. Everything told me it was a penalty,' I sighed, hanging my head dejectedly. 'The bottom line is I messed up, and I'm so, so sorry ...'

Seeing me so dismayed, Martin's mood changed completely. Within minutes he'd gone from calling me a disgrace to killing me with kindness. 'Ah, don't you worry yourself, Howard, these things happen,' he said gently, sitting beside me and placing his arm around my shoulder.

'Don't let it ruin your Christmas ...'

Depending how my match had gone, when I returned home at night I'd either launch my kit bag into the corner of the kitchen, vowing never to referee again, or I'd fix myself a drink, collapse on the sofa, and breathe a sigh of relief.

I'd watch *Match of the Day* regardless. Sometimes I couldn't stomach it until the Sunday morning repeat – usually if I'd ballsed up, and wasn't in the mood for a roasting from Hansen and Lawro – but typically I'd watch it in real time. My phone would start vibrating with texts as soon as the opening titles rolled. Like me, my refereeing colleagues would be perched on the edge of their seats, hoping they'd get through their highlights unscathed.

'How did it go at Spurs, mate?' my pal Martin Atkinson would text.

'Think I missed a bad tackle in min 37,' I'd reply. 'Bit worried about it TBH ...'

I'd be on tenterhooks as I watched my match footage, my eyes darting to the time at the top of the screen, praying that it would fast-forward past the 37th minute. Then the 'Second Half' caption would flash up and my Kettle Chips would go flying as I punched the air. *YES!!!* They'd leapfrogged it. And if my error wasn't on *Match of the Day*, it wouldn't exist to a vast swathe of the British public and my trial by television would be averted.

'Lucky bastard,' Martin would text.

You couldn't rest on your laurels, though. Later in the show the panel would sometimes revisit your game, perhaps to compare one incident with another.

'Now let's return to the Spurs game to have a look at this tackle we noticed,' Gary Lineker would say. 'It's a real shocker that really should've got red carded by Howard Webb ...'

'SHIT!' I would shout.

'LOL,' Martin would text.

I'd spent just over three years as a Premier League referee when the 2006–07 season kicked off. Having effectively served my apprenticeship, and having garnered some decent assessments, I started to be appointed to some high-profile games. Manchester United v Chelsea on Sunday 26 November was a case in point. The media had focused in on this Alex Ferguson v José Mourinho 'match of the season', not just because it was a top-of-the-table clash between the two title contenders, but also because it had raised some pertinent refereeing issues.

A few weeks previously, Mourinho had publicly questioned the integrity of Graham Poll following the dismissal of John Terry during a hostile game at White Hart Lane, which had prompted Chelsea's players to mob the referee in a pretty unseemly manner.

A budding ten-year-old footballer for Whiston Junior and Infants School first XI in 1981-82.

(Clockwise from top left) Dad, Mum, me, Joanne and Claire. I was aged 12 when this photo was taken.

A grainy picture of my dad refereeing a local game in about 1985. It was he who pointed me away from playing and into officiating.

Modelling the worst referees' kit, with its random white splats it was instantly christened the 'birdshit kit'.

January 2001, Brentford v Northampton. Early in my journey through the professional ranks of referees – you can see why I decided it would be best to shave my head. (Getty Images)

Joleon Lescott of Wolves and Andy Hughes of Reading battle it out in the Championship play-off semi-final – the match that helped ensure I would be working in the Premier League the following campaign. (Getty Images)

I developed a warm-up routine that helped ensure things ran as smoothly as possible. Here I'm with my assistants Andy Martin and Graeme Atkins. (PA/Empics)

Following Jeff Winter, during a Select Group training session in 2004. There was plenty of lively, and not always friendly, competition between the referees. (PA)

Graeme Souness protests, while Alan Shearer looks on, after I'd turned down his penalty claim in November 2004. In the end, I had to send the Newcastle manager to the stands. (PA)

Another tough game, this time between Bolton and Everton in December 2004. During the match, Gary Speed had told me: 'You're starting to let us down, ref.' He was right – and I received the worst mark of my career that day. (Getty Images)

Sir Alex Ferguson billed the FA Cup tie between Manchester United and Liverpool in February 2006 as a 'big test' for me. In these encounters, the pressure was always high – from the players, the dugout and the stands. (Getty Images)

In the thick of it. The brawl at the end of the 2007 Carling Cup final resulted in three red cards. At the time, I felt I had lost control, but I received praise for my handling of the situation. (Getty Images)

Before I took charge of this game between Brazil and Poland in the Under-20 World Cup in June 2007, I was told it was my first step on the road to the 2010 World Cup. It was also the first time I teamed up with my assistants, Darren Cann and Mike Mullarkey. (Getty Images)

Pointing to the spot, as Poland are penalised in the 91st minute in their European Championship game against Austria in Vienna. Because of this decision, I received death threats. (PA)

Leading the teams out at an emotional Old Trafford in February 2008, on the 50th anniversary of the Munich air disaster. (PA)

Waving away the Spurs protests, I award a penalty to Manchester United that sparked a stunning comeback in April 2009. It was a mistake, and from then on I was plagued with allegations that I was a closet United fan. (Getty Images)

You only ever referee the FA Cup final once, and happily the match between Chelsea and Everton in 2009 went smoothly. (Getty Images)

Poll took a few days off shortly afterwards, thus opening the door for me to officiate the Old Trafford showdown.

The day before the match, FA Director of Football Development, Trevor Brooking, had come out in strong support of Select Group referees, accusing certain managers and players of showing disrespect and setting a bad example to young footballers and budding officials.

'We don't want to drive referees out of the game,' he'd said. 'We need an environment to allow young refs to come through, not to get pressured from the sidelines.'

PFA chairman Chris Powell waded in, too.

'No one wants to see players hounding the referee,' he commented, 'but, equally, refs can help themselves by showing a bit of common sense instead of sticking to the letter of the law every time.'

So with all this unrest as a backdrop, and tasked with refereeing such a key game at the league's summit, my nerves were a-jangling that afternoon. I couldn't have wished for a better performance, though. Seventy minutes into the action I remember thinking *I've got this game in the bag*. Some days you see the ball like a beach ball – you don't miss a trick – whereas other times it's more like a golf ball, and you feel yourself searching for every decision.

I received a full complement of twenty-two handshakes after the game (which finished 1-1), a host of positive comments in the media, and a congratulatory message from Premier League chief Richard Scudamore.

Three days later I put in another assured performance, marshalling a hot-tempered London derby between Fulham and Arsenal. Craven Cottage was like a cauldron – I gave out one red card and nine yellows, my highest ever tally in the top flight – and it tested my mental and physical resilience to the limit.

*I think I might have finally cracked this refereeing lark ...* I remember thinking to myself as I drove back up the M1 to Rotherham, listening to a phone-in caller bigging-up my performance on BBC Radio 5 Live.

The Carling Cup final took place at Cardiff's Millennium Stadium on Saturday 25 February 2007, an all-London affair between Chelsea and Arsenal. With one minute left on the clock, Chelsea were hanging on to a 2-1 lead, with their opponents pushing for an equaliser. For the final half-hour the Blues had been without their captain, John Terry, who'd been knocked out cold in the penalty area and had been replaced by Jon Obi Mikel.

I felt relatively happy with proceedings; while I'd had to show five yellow cards, I thought my team and I were controlling the game pretty well. As full-time approached – and as I started to think *job's a good 'un* – Kolo Touré latched on to the ball, advanced upfield and was impeded by a shirt-pulling Mikel. I blew the whistle, only to see Touré reacting aggressively by throwing an arm towards Mikel, who duly retaliated. Then Frank Lampard and Cesc Fàbregas entered the fray, their teammates steamed in, and a huge brawl ensued. Even Arsène Wenger and José Mourinho marched on to the pitch, followed by their respective coaches, subs and physios.

*Shit, shit, SHIT*, I thought. *It's a cup final and it's all kicking off around me.*

Also going through my mind was the fact that I'd not long been on a UEFA course that had tackled mass confrontation, the strong message being that, if there was an affray on the pitch, yellow cards rarely sufficed. The last thing I wanted to do was dismiss a player in a cup final, but in this case there was an air of inevitability.

Large-scale skirmishes can be horrendous for referees, since it's so easy to lose the identity of the wrongdoers or to forget who's guilty of which offence. Your eyes can't physically see every punch and shove that's going in, especially if you're trying to pull various players apart, as I was doing. However, as the scuffling continued there came a point where I felt there was nothing much I could do, so I took a step back to observe, gather evidence and plan my course of action. It was like being a copper again.

I was determined not to lose the first two offenders – I was chanting *Touré-Mikel-Touré-Mikel-Touré-Mikel* under my breath – and I actually grabbed hold of the latter so he couldn't elude me. Everything else around me seemed like a blur, though, and I began to panic, petrified that I'd be forever remembered for losing complete control in a showcase cup final.

*What a fucking disaster,* I thought. *I can't believe this is happening.*

Once the ruckus had calmed I sent off Touré and Mikel. Then my assistant Darren Cann approached me near the centre circle.

'Red card for Emmanuel Adebayor, Howard; he's thrown a punch,' he asserted, so Arsenal's target man received his marching orders too, protesting his innocence as the physio dragged him down the tunnel. Dave Babski, my other linesman, instructed me to caution Fàbregas and Lampard, whose names were consequently added to the book.

By the time I'd blown the final whistle my head had gone. I could hardly speak when I went to collect my medal from my refereeing idol, Jack Taylor. I was in shock. I was dumbstruck.

'Well done, son, well done,' he said, smiling and shaking my hand.

*Well done?* I thought to myself. *I was rubbish.*

I didn't hang around for the trophy presentation, instead storming off to the dressing room where I flung my Carling Cup medal against the wall, screaming a few choice words as I did so.

A stupid, infantile thing to do but that's how pissed off I felt. In my mind, I'd cocked up a prestigious cup final.

Once the dust had settled, though, and much to my surprise, some positive text messages from friends and colleagues started to trickle through. Keith Hackett was extremely complimentary when he visited me after the game, maintaining that I'd handled a tough situation incredibly well. My team and I had managed to pinpoint five of the six chief troublemakers (Emmanuel Eboué's whack on Wayne Bridge had gone unnoticed) which, in the scheme of things, wasn't so bad at all.

The football media were pretty gracious, too. I was 'a beacon of maturity in a sea of tantrums,' according to one journalist, and most back pages suggested that it was the belligerent players who were to blame for marring a match dubbed the 'Snarling Cup Final'.

Later that year I had yet another on-pitch encounter with José Mourinho. I'd reffed Chelsea v Blackburn at Stamford Bridge on Saturday 15 September, a game that had finished 0-0. It hadn't been without controversy, however; Salomon Kalou had assumed he'd bagged the opener, celebrating wildly behind the goal, only for linesman Peter Kirkup to rule his attempt offside.

A few minutes later I became aware of a commotion on the touchline and saw a fractious Chelsea boss pointing at his tablet and dishing out some serious verbals to the fourth official. In a fit of pique he then threw the device to the ground, which promptly shattered into tiny pieces. I should've probably sent him to the stands – his behaviour was bang out of order – but for whatever reason I decided against it and had a word with him instead. All the while I was thinking *shite, maybe that goal wasn't offside.*

After the game, I was told that Mourinho wanted to see me. As he knocked on my dressing room door I braced myself for the mother of all rants, especially as the replays had suggested that Kalou's goal may well have been legit. Instead, in wandered a very subdued, forlorn-looking manager – his hair ruffled, his tie loosened – who then sat himself down on the opposite bench.

I apologised immediately for the offside decision and, to my surprise, he just shrugged and smiled weakly.

'This was an important goal, yes, but mistakes can happen,' he said sadly, looking like the weight of the world was upon his shoulders. 'But you do know the man will now fire me.'

He didn't call him Roman, or Mr Abramovich; just The Man.

'Don't be daft, José,' I replied. 'You won the Premier League title last year. Your lads were unbelievable. I don't think you're going anywhere.'

He was adamant, though.

'I say it again, ref. This match will cost me my job. The man will fire me.'

I drove home that night with our conversation playing on my mind, hoping that one of football's most charismatic leaders wouldn't be out on his arse.

Chelsea drew 1-1 with Rosenborg in the Champions League a few days later, and the following morning news filtered through that Mourinho had been shown the door. His dressing room prophecy about The Man had been spot-on, and I felt sad about it. Very sad, in fact.

A month later, on Sunday 28 October, I approached the huge Liverpool v Arsenal game with my confidence utterly sapped, since I'd just infamously botched up the PSV v Fenerbahçe Champions League game. I was determined to get myself back on track, though, and knew I needed to show some fight and resilience. In the first minute I bit the bullet and yellow-carded Ukrainian striker Andriy Voronin for scraping his studs down Cesc Fàbregas's Achilles tendon. That early, decisive caution served to calm my nerves and to nail my control and, for the rest of the 90 minutes, everything went to plan.

'You did brilliantly, Howard,' said Keith Hackett when he rang me later. He then revealed that he was planning to allocate me to another big match the following week, namely Arsenal v Manchester United at the Emirates Stadium. I was in two minds about this, to be honest. While flattered to have been handed two prominent games in succession – it was a coveted tie, and being given back-to-back games with the same team was almost unheard of – I knew it would be a huge mental challenge for me. The chance of delivering these high-octane matches without some kind of to-do was always very slim.

Ordinarily I'd have preferred at least a fortnight's breathing space between them, if only to physically and mentally recharge and to give myself a break from the intense media scrutiny. As it transpired, though, these sandwiched-together games would actually work in my favour, marking the start of a successful purple patch for me.

The match at Arsenal witnessed the best lining decision I have ever seen in my life. It was 2-1 to Manchester United and, in the very last minute, the ball was pinging around the visitors' penalty box. William Gallas volleyed it goalwards, only for Edwin van der Sar to leap up and make a fabulous mid-air save to thwart the Frenchman. Play continued, and the ball was subsequently cleared by a United player.

Meanwhile, Darren Cann was flagging furiously and yelling 'GOAL GOAL GOAL!' down my earpiece. *What bloody goal?* I was thinking – there'd been no appeals from the players, and no telling roar from the crowd – but, such was my faith in Darren's judgement, I blew the whistle, gave the goal and, moments later, signalled for full-time.

An incensed Ryan Giggs immediately accosted Darren,

demanding to know what the fuck he was playing at, and why the hell this phantom goal had been awarded.

'Trust me, Howard,' said Darren as we walked off the pitch together, past a fuming United bench. 'It was a goal. One hundred per cent.'

TV replays completely vindicated Darren's bold decision; the ball had been a full metre behind the goal-line as Van der Sar had clawed it back. It was a truly outstanding piece of linesmanship. Giggs himself acknowledged the fact, too, profusely apologising to Darren the next time he saw him.

Sir Alex Ferguson was seething, though – no shit Sherlock – and gave me no end of stick in his post-match comments, claiming that I'd missed an Arsenal foul in the build-up to the goal. The offence he was alluding to had taken place a couple of minutes before Gallas's strike, between which time there'd been a goal kick, a throw-in and probably about four changes of possession.

I watched his reaction on *Match of the Day 2* with my wife and found myself laughing at the ridiculousness of it all.

'How far back is the fella gonna go, Kay? Unbelievable ...'

I was deeply honoured to be asked to officiate Manchester United v Manchester City at Old Trafford on Sunday 10 February 2008. This derby match would also mark the fiftieth anniversary of the Munich air disaster in which twenty-three people, including eight Manchester United players, had perished.

Both clubs were desperately keen to ensure that this poignant occasion would be respected by the visiting City fans, and had worked tirelessly in the run-up to try and avert any offensive chants or gestures.

As the match referee, it was my job to manage the minute's silence. With this in mind, early that morning I met with a Greater

Manchester Police Chief Superintendent to run through the procedure.

'The minute's silence will define how today goes, Howard,' she said. 'And I don't mean just inside and outside the stadium, but in Manchester city centre too.'

It was my responsibility, she explained, to gauge the atmosphere and, should there be any disturbances, to assess the situation as best I saw fit.

'So if the City fans start up any offensive chants, what should I do?' I asked her. 'Do I abandon the silence, or do I just bear with it?'

She paused, and thought for a second.

'It's your call,' she said.

I'd never been so nervous in my refereeing career as I was that day. At 1.20 p.m., a lone piper led the United and City teams out of Old Trafford's corner tunnel, both sets of players wearing specially manufactured kits without sponsors or logos. Once Sir Alex Ferguson and Sven-Göran Eriksson had placed their wreaths on the centre spot, I set my watch, I blew my whistle and I bowed my head. *Please, please let this go smoothly*, I said to myself.

The silence was deafening. Other than a couple of firecrackers outside the stadium, there was no sound whatsoever for the full 60 seconds as thousands of supporters stood in tribute, holding aloft their retro scarves. The behaviour of the 3,000-plus Manchester City fans was exemplary, and seeing the red and blue halves of Manchester joined together in tribute was simply amazing. It was one of the most emotional moments I've ever experienced in football.

April and May could be challenging months for match officials. League campaigns were reaching their endpoint, with tussles at both ends of the table. Faced with crunch games being played for crucial points, every referee needed to be at his best and on his toes.

In April 2009 the battle for the Premier League title had come down to a two-horse race between Liverpool and Manchester United. On the last Saturday of the month, I'd been assigned to United v Tottenham at Old Trafford, a game that the home side needed to win to keep up the pressure on their Merseyside rivals. By half-time – and much to the delight of the Liverpool fans everywhere – Spurs were 2-0 up thanks to goals from Darren Bent and Luka Modrić, and were quite possibly heading towards a shock away victory. I'd had a decent 45 minutes in the middle and, as the game restarted, I felt well on top of everything.

Then, on 58 minutes, United's Wayne Rooney skilfully latched on to the ball. I was in line with him, occupying a great position with everything in view. Suddenly, though, he played a slide-rule pass to Michael Carrick which instantly cut out about four defenders and put 25 metres between me and the action. I tried to adjust my view and was able to see Carrick and Spurs' goalie, Heurelho Gomes, both racing for the ball in the 18-yard box. From my vantage point I saw the United player flick it away from Gomes, who proceeded to clatter into him.

As far I was concerned it was a nailed-on penalty – and no one in my earpiece told me otherwise – so I duly pointed to the spot. Gomes then clambered to his feet and careered around like a madman, throwing his arms up into the air in protest. *Shit*, I said to myself. *This isn't as straightforward as I thought. I think I might have missed something.*

I remember standing in the middle of the pitch feeling sick to the stomach, my gut instinct telling me that I'd just made an appalling error.

I'll be honest; as Cristiano Ronaldo stepped up to take the penalty, I was thinking *miss, you bastard*. But he didn't, of course, and his goal became the catalyst for a United fightback. They went on to run riot, turning the match on its head and scoring four more to secure a 5-2 victory. Their title charge had been well and truly reignited.

That final half-hour was among the most torturous of my career. My emotions were all over the place. Not only had my apparent blunder been a game changer, it had also potentially impacted the final outcome of the Premier League title race. Three guesses as to who was ambushed by Sky's steadycam fella at full-time.

The post-match replays confirmed my worst fears. Gomes had made clear contact with the ball, and had in fact pushed it out for a throw-in. Never in a million years should it have been a penalty.

I felt so distraught – and so remorseful – that I asked for permission to give a post-match interview so I could front up to the media and acknowledge my error. This was kyboshed by the PGMOL but, a couple of days later, I seized upon another chance to say my piece. I was reffing an English Schools match in Peterborough and, during an interview with BBC Radio Cambridgeshire, shoehorned in my apology-cum-explanation, hoping that it would get syndicated across the national network.

The next day I awoke to hear the 7.30 a.m. sports bulletin on BBC Radio 5 Live.

'Now here's something you don't hear often,' announced the presenter. 'We've got a referee admitting he's made a mistake.'

Three weeks later, Manchester United won the Premier League championship by four points, prompting accusations from some quarters that I was a closet Red who'd gladly given them a helping hand.

It was a myth that would plague the rest of my career.

# CHAPTER 7

# Champions League, We're Having A Laugh

I'd always been quite an intense kid; something of a worrier. My family remember me as a curious and inquisitive youngster, my over-active imagination often running away with me.

During the time of the Cold War, in the early-to-mid-1980s, I developed a real fear of nuclear attacks. I'd seen articles in my dad's *Daily Mirror* about the United States and the Soviet Union being at loggerheads, and would lie in bed at night fretting about President Brezhnev pressing the red button, launching missiles and wiping out Western civilisation.

Compounding these anxieties was the 1984 airing of *Threads*, a BBC TV drama set in Sheffield that fictionalised the effects of a nuclear holocaust. I was too scared to watch the programme myself – it was quite literally too close to home – but my class-mates gleefully regaled the film's sequence of a four-minute warning, an earth-shattering explosion and a mushroom cloud suffocating some poor buggers on Sheffield Moor.

I remember sitting in my lounge with the TV tuned to the

*Nine O'Clock News*, scaring myself shitless whenever a grim-faced Angela Rippon outlined the perilous state of East-West relations. My dad would always try to allay my fears, though.

'The Russians won't be bombing Brinsworth any time soon, Howard, I promise,' he'd say. 'Now go and get your pyjamas on, it's way past your bedtime.'

It wasn't the only time I needed Dad's reassurance. Once, when I was about ten, I fell over while playing football in a nearby field and, as I did so, my hand brushed against a toadstool. I'd read in my *Encyclopaedia Britannica* that they were deadly to the touch, and I fled home in tears.

'I'm going to die, I've been poisoned, I'm going to die,' I shrieked as I burst through the back door. I got so worked up that Dad had go to extreme lengths in order to calm me down. He dragged me back to that same field, whereupon he lay on the grass and licked the offending fungi to prove that I wasn't going to croak.

'Behave, lad, there's nowt wrong with you,' he barked and, duly placated, I picked up my football and carried on from where I'd left off.

However, as I entered my teenage years, more profound psychological behaviours began to materialise, possibly born out of these childhood neuroses.

Whenever my mum left for work in the morning, for example – she was employed by Garnett Dickinson, a local printing firm – I'd always give her a goodbye kiss. As I did so, though, a worrying thought would occasionally cross my mind, like her having a car crash or a workplace accident. To eradicate this doom-laden image, I'd have to run down the drive and either give her another peck on the cheek or touch her car while I thought about something nice, in order to almost cancel it out.

Also, while at Brinsworth Comprehensive, I recall sitting an exam as part of my short-lived A level studies. As I wrote down an answer, I remember having a sudden, random thought that I was going to flunk the test badly and get kicked out of school. To remove this scenario from my head I'd have to scrub out the entire sentence, before rewriting it with a positive mindset. Consequently, many of my answer sheets and exercise books would become defaced with crossings-out and deletions.

Things became worse as I grew older. Sometimes, as I prepared to go to sleep, I'd find myself having to repeatedly get in and out of bed until any lingering anxieties were erased, and until my mind was effectively reset (this could take up to twenty attempts). Outdoors, I'd often have to ritualistically tap the driveway with my foot before my head was clear enough to get into my parents' car. It could get really bloody frustrating for everyone involved.

'Hurry up, Howard, we're going to be late,' Mum would say as I dithered next to their Chrysler Alpine.

Mum and Dad euphemistically referred to my idiosyncrasies as 'Howard's habits'. A friend of mine, Curtis Frost, nicknamed me 'Habit National' (a pun on the Abbey National Building Society) having noticed my tendency to touch doors and floors after I'd played a snooker shot that, unbeknown to him, would have coincided with one of my quirky little thoughts.

My unusual behaviours were never brought up in conversation, though, and were never directly addressed. As far as friends and family were concerned, these whims were merely a facet of my character, a part of my personality. Back in the 1980s they wouldn't have been expected to recognise the symptoms of what is now commonly known as obsessive compulsive disorder, the condition that I was so clearly exhibiting.

There are many strands of OCD, of course, and countless people who live with it on a daily basis. Some sufferers are preoccupied with neatness, order and symmetry (David Beckham will remove a drinks can from the fridge if there's an odd number of them, apparently) and others will have hygiene-related issues, stemming from a phobia about germs and bacteria.

My form of the condition isn't linked with issues of orderliness or cleanliness, however, and is instead associated with intrusive thoughts. This occurs when a person becomes fearful that a negative feeling can directly influence an outcome, and believes that this consequence can only be prevented by carrying out some kind of neutralising action.

The 'obsessive' element of my OCD, therefore, was the invasive thought, which was often attached to something bad happening to myself or a loved one. The 'compulsive' element was the undoing response, usually involving touching, tapping or making some other connection in order to clear my head and dispel my anxiety.

As the years went by, trying to stave off these thoughts and limit these actions became both tiring and infuriating. Take my issues with Mum leaving for work, for example. I'd spend the five minutes prior to her departure almost forcing myself to think positively, but it rarely worked. The more pressure I heaped upon on myself, the more I over-thought, and the more my mind would play tricks on me. The only solution would be to counterbalance this negativity in my own eccentric little way.

These silly compulsions would make me feel so bloody stupid. *Look at the state of you, tapping your mum's car while the neighbours aren't looking*, I'd say under my breath. *You're pathetic …*

I was forever at odds with myself. On the one hand here was a normal, rational and intelligent lad who knew damned well that touching a car or tapping a floor would have no impact whatsoever upon a person or a circumstance. On the other hand, however, here was a nervy nutjob who felt compelled to perform absurd rituals to stop bad stuff from happening. And, while I wasn't at all religious or superstitious – and had never believed in psychics and spiritualists – I sometimes found myself being controlled by these mind-over-matter urges.

It wasn't an incessant struggle – days could pass with hardly any OCD-type episodes – but some days proved to be more wearisome than others. New Year's Eve was always an ordeal. When the clock struck midnight – the most significant minute of the entire year – I dreaded being invaded by negative thoughts that, in my mind, could affect the whole course of the ensuing year. I was a nervous wreck on the evening of 31 December 1999, when the world and his wife awaited the dawning of the new Millennium.

*I hope my head's not full of crap when that clock strikes twelve ...* I remember thinking as this historic, pivotal moment approached.

Fortunately, my mind stayed clear that night, but had I experienced a passing thought about Rotherham United getting relegated at the end of the season, for example, I'd have felt duty-bound to counteract this nightmarish scenario by making a tangible connection. I might have brushed past the clock while no one was looking, or covertly touched a Rotherham scarf hanging in the cloakroom. My daft little actions weren't going to make a jot of difference to the Millers' end-of-season fate, of course, but those were the lengths to which I felt obliged to go. It became absolutely exhausting.

The issue I need to address, I guess, is whether or not my OCD affected my refereeing performance on a football pitch. I can say, with 100 per cent nailed-on certainty, that it didn't. On the contrary, in fact. Officiating, I discovered, was probably one of the few refuges that I had from the condition. The frenetic on-field activity never allowed time for any intrusive thoughts to linger and, during those 90-plus minutes, my mind was far too focused and occupied for there to be any impact whatsoever. Once I crossed that white line, with the ball under my arm and my linesmen by my side, I felt almost shielded from my OCD, like I'd somehow entered a protective force-field.

I freely admit, though, that 'Howard's habits' could impinge upon my pre-match preparation. Sometimes it would take a few attempts to pull on my shirts or shorts, as it was imperative that the act of donning my kit coincided with some upbeat thoughts about the match ahead. Occasionally I'd have to walk in and out of the dressing room until I was in the right frame of mind – touching the door as I did so – or else I'd be compelled to ring the pre-match alarm bell twice if the first *brrrrrring* gave me the wrong vibes.

As the seasons went by, I honed and developed my own coping strategies, whereby any anxieties were addressed and combated well before kick-off. I'd often go through my kit-changing rigmarole in the toilet, for example, which allowed me some privacy and solitude and afforded me enough time to get my head in gear.

Concealing my condition from my colleagues wasn't always easy, though, and one particular incident brought my OCD into sharp focus. In October 2006, along with assistant referees Glenn Turner and David Bryan, I'd been appointed to referee France Under-21s v Israel Under-21s (it was the first leg of the play-off for the following year's European Under-21 Championship). The match was due to take place in the Normandy town of Caen, so we'd taken the Eurostar to Paris and were catching a connecting train out of the capital's St Lazare station.

As we awaited departure, I remember idly contemplating that night's game, and catching sight of the Eiffel Tower through the carriage window. As I did so, however, a poor assessment grade – 7.9 – suddenly flashed into my mind. It's a very specific mark, usually signifying what UEFA terms a 'key match error'. This can be a missed penalty, or an overlooked red card, either of which can severely damage a referee's reputation.

Feeling anxious, I fixated on Paris's most iconic landmark, willing myself to replace the crap mark in my head with a higher grade 8.4. I couldn't, however, and 7.9 became lodged in my head. But then the train started to pull away and I felt the panic setting in. Tall buildings were now blocking the Tower that I'd felt compelled to focus upon, and I was gradually losing sight of it.

By now sweating, and still visualising 7.9 in my head, I strained to catch a final glimpse, lifting myself out of my chair and craning my neck. I contemplated running further down the train carriage and sticking my head out of the window, not unlike that famously gory scene in *The Young Ones* where Vyvyan literally loses his head.

'You OK, Howard?' asked Glenn, no doubt perplexed by my erratic behaviour.

'Yeah. Fine,' I replied, unconvincingly. 'My seat's not very comfy, that's all.' I was anything but fine, though.

Most of the two-hour journey was horrendous. I was fractious and agitated, convinced that this failure to feed my compulsion had condemned my refereeing performance and, worse still, had potentially ruined my UEFA career. Fortunately, I managed to pull myself together as we approached Caen, doing my utmost to adopt the air of a professional referee who was in full control.

Two days later, I was back on the same train for the return journey to Paris. The previous night's game between France and Israel had gone brilliantly, earning me an assessment grade of 8.5. My ridiculous Eiffel Tower-related theories had therefore been blown out of the water, and I was left feeling totally and utterly foolish.

I wasn't allowed to log this incident for future reference,

though. The OCD mindset never let you do that. Any semblance of logic or reason would be completely erased in time for the next thought invasion.

I never felt the urge to 'come out' to the PGMOL or the Select Group about this. First and foremost, I saw my OCD as a personal rather than a professional matter. It had never affected my competence on the pitch and, for that reason alone, I simply didn't think there was a need to reveal all to my colleagues and superiors. Secondly, no matter how much I'd have emphasised this personal-professional distinction, I have a feeling that – in certain quarters – my OCD would have been wrongly perceived as a weakness and a limitation. I think it would have been held against me, whether consciously or subconsciously, and might have even curbed my career progression.

*All this OCD stuff sounds a bit bloody bonkers to me …* I could have imagined some less-than-sympathetic person remarking. *Can we trust Webb on a football field? Or shall we hand that semi-final to a ref who's, erm, not so flaky …?*

I'm expecting that these disclosures may come as a surprise – a shock, even – to my refereeing counterparts. The only two officials who won't be remotely taken aback, though, will be my trusty wingmen.

Over the years, Darren and Mike witnessed enough of my strange dressing-room behaviours to suss that I had some deep-seated issues. Like my family, however, they avoided broaching the subject and never asked any searching questions; they just let me crack on with my odd little fixations. It was the great unsaid; the elephant in the dressing room. I vaguely recall Darren once taking me aside to ask if I was OK – I can only assume my compulsions had gone into overdrive one afternoon – but I think I just brushed him off.

But my assistants weren't daft. They'd see me furtively knocking on the dressing-room wall. They'd see me repeatedly walking in and out of the door. They'd see me anxiously pulling on my shirt for the umpteenth time.

Darren and Mike knew the score.

Mike Mullarkey was one of the linesmen at my side when I walked out to referee the 128th FA Cup final on Saturday 30 May 2009. Gracing the Wembley pitch that afternoon were David Moyes' Everton and Guus Hiddink's Chelsea, both aiming to get their team's ribbons on that famous silver trophy.

Ask any trainee ref to reveal their burning ambition, and I reckon the majority would cite the FA Cup final. It's the ultimate domestic honour; the pinnacle of English refereeing.

'Who knows, one of you could be taking charge at Wembley in fifteen years' time,' I remember Alan Young saying to us in that Rotherham training room, back in 1989. 'That's your benchmark, lads. That's the game to aim for. Somebody's got to do it – why can't it be you?'

The fact that FA protocol allowed refs to oversee only one FA Cup final during their career made this appointment feel extra-special. Not all elite referees were lucky enough to live out their FA Cup dream – Mark Halsey and Uriah Rennie were two top-notch officials who never got the chance – so I was going to cherish this once-in-a-lifetime opportunity.

The National Referees' Association's annual Eve of Final Rally – held that year at the Russell Hotel in Bloomsbury – was a long-established event. Tradition dictated that the match official had to deliver a speech to all attendees and, aware of its huge significance, I spent a couple of days painstakingly piecing it together.

I talked about my childhood FA Cup memories, outlining the

iconic players and teams that I'd watched over the years, from Mick Mills' Ipswich to Pat Rice's Arsenal. I also spoke about some more recent encounters, notably an eventful cup tie that I'd overseen between Birmingham City and Wolverhampton Wanderers earlier that season. In the 50th minute the ball had comically bounced straight off my arse, landing right at the feet of Wolves' Sam Vokes. He then ran the full length of the pitch to score the winner. I felt dreadful afterwards, and had issued a formal apology in the media.

'So you're looking at the only man in history to have set up a winning goal in a third round match before going on to referee the final,' I told the assembled officials.

I also used my speech to acknowledge my many mentors, whose words of wisdom and constant encouragement had shaped my refereeing career. People like David Marshall from the Rotherham and District FA, Ron Skidmore from the Northern Counties East League and Trevor Simpson from the Football League. Finally, I thanked my family, not least my parents and my long-suffering, ever-supportive wife.

'And to Kay, I love you dearly,' I said. 'I hope I've made you proud.'

The final took place on one of the hottest days of the year. The pitchside thermometer soared to 32°C, and myself and my team – Dave Richardson was partnering Mike, with Martin Atkinson as fourth official – were already sweating buckets as we lined up prior to kick-off.

*Wow, I'm reffing an FA Cup final,* I told myself as the band struck up the familiar chords of the national anthem. All those years I'd spent watching this footballing showpiece from my lounge in Brinsworth, glued to the telly and slurping my Tizer, and here I was, standing proudly in this historic stadium, about to oversee this most illustrious of cup finals.

*Savour this moment, Howard* ... said a voice in my head. *It's as important as anything you'll ever do.*

Chelsea went on to beat Everton 2-1 in the searing heat. This was despite the Toffees' Louis Saha opening the scoring with the fastest-ever goal in FA Cup history, having unleashed a spectacular volley after just 25 seconds. Didier Drogba equalised 20 minutes later, and Frank Lampard's scorching 72nd-minute winner finally earned the Blues their victory.

All things considered, the game went well, although post-match replays brought into question a Florent Malouda effort that we'd judged not to have crossed the line (it was a close call, and this was a few years before the introduction of goal-line technology). When I blew the final whistle I was engulfed by a huge sense of relief, and within minutes I was climbing the steps to the Royal Box to receive my cup final medal (handed over by former United Nations Secretary General Kofi Annan, no less).

After the match Kay and I, together with the other officials and their partners, were invited to join David Elleray for some celebratory drinks at Harrow school in north-west London. He'd been a housemaster there for nearly 30 years, successfully combining his teaching with his top-flight refereeing career.

I can still picture us all standing on the balcony that balmy late-spring evening, sipping champagne and chatting happily. Stretched out before us was a magnificent view of our capital city with Wembley stadium in the foreground, its towering arch lit up in Chelsea blue.

A month later, it was Mum and Dad's turn to enjoy a slice of VIP treatment. The time had arrived for the official premiere of the UEFA-commissioned Euro 2008 movie, and we'd been invited by the production team to attend the prestigious Locarno Film Festival.

My parents and I – along with Darren, Mike and my sister Joanne – were flown to Switzerland in business class, and were put up in a swish hotel in the town of Lugano. My globetrotting lifestyle had made me quite blasé about travelling, I suppose, but it was lovely to see the delight on Mum's face when she first caught sight of Lake Lugano and the surrounding snow-capped mountains.

'Isn't it just beautiful, Billy?' she beamed, bowled over by this stunning Alpine panorama.

On the morning of the big premiere we were invited to a private screening in the hotel. The fact that Darren, Mike and I had absolutely no idea what to expect, or how we'd be portrayed in the film, made it all quite nerve-racking.

'This'll be interesting,' I smiled, plonking myself down in the seat between them.

The director, Yves Hinant, explained that the movie's working title had originally been *Kill The Referee* – alluding to the vengeful Poland supporters – but had since been sanitised to *The Referees* in the UK, and to *Les Arbitres* on the Continent.

'Hope you all like it,' he smiled, as the opening titles rolled.

Compared with the other featured officials, our team had the lion's share of screen time. In addition to the behind-the-scenes footage in the dressing room, the cameras focused on our handling of the Austria v Poland game although, unbeknown to us – and much to our horror – they'd recorded our mid-match conversations over the communications system. Had we been aware of this at the time, we might have been more guarded and less sweary.

'Thank goodness we didn't insult anyone,' I whispered to Mike.

As suspected, the fallout from that particular match featured heavily. While it was a grim time for my family and me, it was an absolute gift for the film-makers since all the death threats and witch-hunts provided the movie with an incredibly dramatic hook.

The star of the show, however, was none other than Billy Webb. Dad came over really well in the film – he wasn't shy and retiring on camera, put it that way – and his love of refereeing and his pride for his 'lad' shone through.

'I love him to death,' he said at one point, wiping away a tear.

The movie's closing scene took place at the Referees' Association Centenary Dinner in Solihull, which I'd attended in the wake of the tournament. At the end of the night – by which time I was suitably well oiled – I'd been dragged up on the stage by the organisers. Within moments the band had struck up the opening bars of *You'll Never Walk Alone*, and someone had thrust a baton in my hand. So there I was, pissed as a fart, conducting a hearty singalong to Liverpool FC's famous anthem, thinking *I bet this comes back to bite me on the arse one day.*

In the summer of 2008, I'd decided to take a five-year sabbatical from South Yorkshire Police. Although I'd gone part-time a few years earlier, I found I was still struggling to manage my sergeant role and felt unable to give it the attention it deserved.

I effected a clause in my contract that permitted staff to take a career break to 'pursue sporting ambition', thus allowing me to concentrate solely on refereeing and to avoid any more troublesome job-juggling.

As the 2008–09 season approached I was really keen to take my FIFA and UEFA refereeing up a gear. I was already being monitored at home and abroad as a potential candidate for the 2010 World Cup finals and, in order to maintain my profile, wanted to get as many Champions League matches under my belt as possible.

I presided over five such games that campaign including, in

April 2009, the first leg of the quarter-final between Barcelona and Bayern Munich. Barça, boasting a star-studded cast list that included Lionel Messi, Dani Alves, Xavi Hernández and Thierry Henry, raced to a 4-0 lead at the interval, a scoreline that remained intact until I blew the final whistle.

In the first half, however, I committed the sin of booking Messi for a dive. Believe me, I'm shaking my head just writing this. At the time it had seemed a tad theatrical from The Best Player In The World Who Never Knowingly Dives™, but post-match replays showed that it had been a brain-freeze of a decision on my part. He'd clearly been fouled – although I still maintain it was an exaggerated fall – and I should have awarded a penalty instead.

Moments after the booking, however, and with 90,000 home fans spitting venom, I heard my fourth official, Martin Atkinson, yelling down my earpiece.

'Pep Guardiola's going insane on the touchline, Howard. Absolutely crazy. Think you might need to sort it out …'

A quick glance to my right confirmed that the Barça boss had gone completely loco and, following futile attempts to placate him, I had no option but to banish him to the stands. Suffice to say that I didn't make many amigos in Barcelona that night; in fact, I was never asked to officiate at the Nou Camp again.

That season's other ties had passed by without too much drama, though – I came through fixtures at Shakhtar Donetsk, Lyon, Inter Milan and Atlético Madrid relatively unscathed – and, the more experience I accrued, the more I grew to love refereeing in the Champions League. Indeed, working on the Continent often came as a welcome antidote to the pressure-cooker environment of the domestic league and the petty politics of the Select Group.

UEFA, it has to be said, were ultra-professional and ran the Champions League like clockwork. On the morning of the game, at ten o'clock sharp, organisational meetings for club representatives, team coaches and match officials would be convened. These gatherings were always held in English, regardless of the nationality of the respective teams (this would mightily piss off any French contingents, funnily enough) and would usually kick off with a quick overview of the projected media attendance.

'OK, guys, so we have seven hundred and fifty journalists, thirty-six TV crews and sixty-two radio broadcasters,' the UEFA co-ordinator would announce, and I'd sit there thinking *shit, no pressure there, then*. Such a huge media presence for just 90 minutes of football.

Match officials were then given the floor to outline the key messages that needed to be conveyed to both sides, most of which related to stringent UEFA directives.

'You guys need to tell your players that, if they mob or surround me after a decision, I'll take action,' I'd state firmly. 'Any holding in the penalty area won't be tolerated by my team, and if I see any showing of imaginary cards – from players or managers – there'll be consequences.'

The hope was that the team coaches would relay this guidance to their players, but this was rarely the case. With that in mind I'd hand out hard copies of my speech, too, simple stating-the-bleedin'-obvious crib sheets that featured the officials' names and mugshots and which reiterated my main points. I suppose it was a case of trying to be proactive during the game, too; contrary to public opinion, referees didn't like showing cards, and much preferred the prevention rather than the cure.

'What d'you mean you didn't realise?' I'd be able to level at an enraged player who'd just been cautioned for wielding a pretend card. 'Did your coach not pass on my message?'

If we had any time to spare after the meeting, the lads and I would take the opportunity to do some sightseeing in our host European city. Over the years we visited the Colosseum, the

Acropolis, the Vatican, Prague Castle and – a particular favourite of mine – the wine region of Porto. Spending time in Paris was always fabulous, whether it was embarking upon a scenic, two-hour climb up the Eiffel Tower (the lift had bust) or having an – ahem – entertaining meal at the Moulin Rouge, renowned for its flamboyant cancan shows.

How those memories endured depended on how the game went, though. You could see all the nicest views and enjoy all the best excursions, but if that evening's game turned to shit, those recollections would often be shelved in the back of your mind.

On the eve of a Champions League match, the officials and I would usually have a bite to eat with UEFA's referee observer and the referee liaison officer, the latter of whom was attached to that country's football federation. In previous years, the match officials had been entertained by the host club, but UEFA had decided to change this arrangement, deeming it too cosy for comfort.

There was no pre-match drink ban as such – I'd usually limit myself to a small beer – but we had to be sensible with our meal choices. The last thing a ref needed before a game was indigestion, or worse still, food poisoning. Pierluigi Collina, UEFA's chief refereeing officer, rightly believed that officials were ambassadors for the profession as well as their country, and as such were obliged to take good care of their health, fitness and nutrition. He'd become incredibly irate if he ever got wind of any over-indulgence.

'I receive some very interesting feedback from observers,' he once revealed, stony-faced, during a speech at a UEFA conference. 'Honestly, I once got told about a ref having oysters before a match! Can you believe that? Oysters! *Oysters!*'

Post-match refreshments weren't so restrictive, though. I'd always have a few lagers afterwards, whether it was to celebrate my success or to drown my sorrows.

If we'd had a 'mare of a game, the officials and I would often end up having what became known as a 'tumbleweed' meal, where we'd just sit round the table looking blankly at each other, the sound of cutlery on plates punctuating the silence. Our mood would deteriorate further if the UEFA assessor's debrief was delayed, which was often the case. Sometimes, following an interminable wait, we'd find ourselves having to analyse our match performance at two o'clock in the morning.

I remember one assessor, after a particularly difficult evening game, asking us if we could reschedule the debrief for the following day since he was feeling really tired. Yeah, no problem, we said, before heading to the residents' bar for a nightcap. As I sipped my drink I happened to gaze out of the window, only to spot the man himself athletically clambering from one hotel room balcony to another, naked as the day he was born.

'Didn't I see you in a bit of bother last night?' I asked him the next morning (I knew he was about to give me a below-average grading so felt obliged to wind him up). He reddened slightly, before offering up some half-baked story about how his door had slammed shut behind him, and how he'd had to ask an obliging neighbour for help.

'But anyway, enough about me,' he said, hurriedly changing the subject, '… on to last night's game—'

On the occasions that a European match went well – and if my team and I were rewarded with a decent, timely assessment – we'd always go out for a slap-up meal in a local restaurant before piling back to the hotel, armed with some beers. We'd chat, drink and listen to music until the early hours, rounding things off with a spirited game of iPod *Guess The Intro*. I count those chilled-out post-match nights, spent with such warm, funny and like-minded people, as among the best times of my life.

\*

My first two Champions League games of the following season – Bayern Munich v Juventus and Milan v Marseille – both went well, prompting two more beery nights in Germany and Italy. The third – Dynamo Kiev against Barcelona, in December 2009 – was the coldest match that I'd ever refereed in my life.

On the eve of the game I did my best to prepare for the wintry, sub-zero temperatures. Kiev's stadium was attached to a small health spa complex, and I thought it would be sensible to have a therapeutic sports massage to get my blood pumping and my circulation flowing.

I entered a spartan treatment room with a towel around my waist, and was welcomed by a female therapist who proceeded to put a large, woollen, cone-shaped hat on my head (to this day I don't know why). Then she led me to the wood-panelled sauna and asked me to lie down on the bench, before speaking to me in broken English.

'You relax, and we give you special Ukrainian massage,' she said. This got me mildly excited, I admit; I thought I was only going to get a bog-standard rub-down.

And then in lumbered Igor, all 6-foot-8 of him, holding what looked like half a Christmas tree.

'I your masseur,' he said, before thwacking me with this big branch for the next 20 minutes. A popular therapy in Eastern Europe, I later learned.

*Oh well*, I thought to myself as the pine needles pierced my skin. *You can't say my job's not varied* ...

I guess minus 15°C was relatively mild for a Ukrainian winter, but the following night I ran on to the pitch with maximum insulation. I'd swaddled myself in thermal underwear and, for the first time in my career, sported leggings and long sleeves (partly for warmth, partly to hide Igor's branch-welts).

The freezing conditions, however, meant that the game was played at an incredibly slow pace, which made it so much easier for me to referee. Lionel Messi scored the winner – his side won 2-1 – and, considering the previous season's Pep palaver, I was glad to not only have the chance to ref Barça again, but to ref them competently.

The assessors seemed happy enough with all three performances, and UEFA duly handed us a fixture in the round of 16. The February 2010 match between Olympiakos and Bordeaux passed smoothly, other than a histrionic penalty appeal from the home side which I'd dismissed without hesitation. The protestations continued after the final whistle, though, exacerbated by the fact that the Greeks had lost 1-0. The following day's back page headlines screamed *ROBBED BY THE REF*.

By the time I'd been awarded a quarter-final first leg – Inter v CSKA Moscow – I was starting to keep a close eye on the progress of Arsenal and Manchester United. The previous success of English teams – they'd reached the final five years on the trot, between 2005 and 2009 – meant that many compatriot referees had been prevented from officiating in the latter stages. Philip Don had been the last Englishman to referee a Champions League final, getting selected for Inter Milan v Barcelona in 1994. The original choice, Holland's John Blankenstein, had been forced to step down because there were so many Dutchmen in the Barça set-up, including their coach, Johan Cruyff.

So, as I journeyed back to our Milan hotel, having successfully reffed a pretty undemanding tie, I couldn't help but wonder whether I'd be in with a shout for a semi-final. There was even more food for thought, when, on Tuesday 6 April, the cup holders Barcelona knocked out Arsenal, Messi having illuminated the Nou Camp with a glorious first-half hat-trick. And there was more English woe when, the following night, Manchester United let slip a 3-0 lead against Bayern Munich, the Germans going through 4-4 on aggregate via the away goals rule.

'Bloody hell, Howard, you might have a chance here,' texted a refereeing mate. I crossed my fingers and hoped he was right. I didn't for once think I'd be a realistic candidate for the final – this was only my fourth year as a Champions League official, and there were more experienced refs above me in the pecking order – but the prospect of a semi-final was mouth-watering.

As it happened, I wasn't allocated to either tie. Italy's Roberto Rosetti and Switzerland's Massimo Busacca took charge of the Bayern v Lyon games, with the Inter v Barcelona legs being overseen by Olegário Benquerença from Portugal and my Belgian friend, Frank De Bleeckere. I watched the match action from home, sitting on the sofa with my three footy-mad children. Rosetti had a great sending-off of Franck Ribéry, if such a thing exists. It was an example of what we call a 'television red', whereby in real time a tackle can look pretty innocuous, but slo-mo replays show it to be utterly reckless, with excessive force.

'Now that's what you call a brilliant decision, kids,' I said, delving into my bag of Doritos. 'Top-class refereeing, that.'

The following week, I was driving to Doncaster to ref Balby Carr School's Under-15s final when my mobile rang.

'Hello, Howard,' said UEFA's Head of Refereeing, Yvan Cornu. 'Congratulations are in order, I think. I'm delighted to inform you that you've been appointed to the Champions League final in Madrid.'

Anyone travelling up the M18 that morning might well have seen a bald bloke with a broad grin struggling to control his steering wheel.

I spent the next hour running round a school field, trying to corral twenty-two kids and thinking *WHAT THE FUCK*. I remember one pupil having a go at me for a decision I'd made, and I was so close to saying 'Oi, you gobby little git, you're talking to a Champions League final ref here ...'

The reaction from the other Select Group referees was over-whelmingly positive. To be fair, there was never much envy among colleagues when it came to prime European appointments, bearing in mind that only one or two of us were in contention in the first place. In fact, you'd often find yourself flavour of the month because certain refs – usually Lee Probert, Andre Marriner or Lee Mason – would get the chance of a nice trip to Munich or Milan as my fourth official or, in the later stages of my career, a goal-line additional assistant referee.

The after-effects of Iceland's volcanic ash cloud meant that my team and I – Darren, Mike, fourth official Martin Atkinson and reserve assistant referee Peter Kirkup – had to fly to Madrid a day earlier than planned. I vividly remember driving along the M62 towards Manchester and, as I passed the Lancashire red rose mile-stone, having the misfortune of hearing talkSPORT's Alan Brazil mid-rant.

'I can't believe Howard Webb's been chosen to referee the Champions League final,' he moaned, or words to that effect.

'He's a shocking ref. There's no way he's up to standard.'

*Cheers Alan, you miserable twat*, I remember thinking to myself, before flicking over to 5 Live.

My mind went into overdrive as I neared the airport, though. I was so keen for everything to go well, yet I was acutely aware that just one fuck-up could both define my career and jeopardise my reputation. That self-same scenario had happened to the Swedish ref Martin Hansson, a part-time fireman from Gothenburg who was not only a brilliant official but who'd also become a good friend of mine. In November 2009, he'd been delighted with his assignation to the second leg of the 2010 World Cup play-off final between France and the Republic of

Ireland. Only the finest officials were entrusted with such do-or-die games, and he was determined to do a great job.

I'd watched the match from home and, midway through the second half, my phone had buzzed with a message from my PGMOL coach, Keren Barratt.

'Your mate Martin's having a fantastic game,' he'd texted. Indeed he was. Until he missed Thierry Henry's infamous hand-ball incident, that is.

Neither he nor his assistants had spotted the Frenchman's unlawful intervention, which had taken place during the build-up to William Gallas's extra-time goal. The 2-1 aggregate scoreline would scupper the Republic's chances of World Cup qualification, and that one error of judgement would tarnish the rest of Martin's refereeing career.

'Gutted for you mate, simply gutted,' I said when I rang him the next day.

There are rare occasions when, around the 60-minute mark, a referee will know instinctively that he's got a game in the bag. That may sound presumptuous – so much can happen in half-an-hour, after all – but sometimes you just feel it. You're in the groove. You're seeing things clearly. The players are reacting well to decisions. And, if something blows up in the 89th minute, you know for certain you'll be able to handle it. The Champions League final, on Saturday 22 May 2010 at Real Madrid's Santiago Bernabéu, was one such game.

With ten minutes to go before kick-off, the two teams had begun to assemble in the stadium's distinctive landing area, its chrome grille dividing the reds and whites of Bayern Munich and the blacks and blues of Inter Milan. Following in their wake were twenty-two little mascots, probably aged about eight or nine, all seemingly thrilled to be escorting their football heroes. But bringing up the rear, looking

If ever there is a good time to show a card, midway through the first half is it. Here Bayern Munich's centre-back Martin Demichelis goes into the book during the 2010 Champions League final. (PA)

Mike Mullarkey, me and Darren Cann making our World Cup debut in the Spain v Switzerland game on 16 June 2010. Happily, we received praise for our teamwork from the FIFA assessor. (Getty Images)

Thumbs up! After the Brazil v Chile game went well, I signalled to my dad in the stand how happy I was. Little did I know that my next game would be the final. (Getty Images)

Nigel de Jong's flying 'tackle' on Xabi Alonso in the World Cup final merited a red card, but I just didn't see it well enough to send him off, so I gave a yellow. (Getty Images)

Receiving my World Cup final medal from Sepp Blatter, with South Africa's President Jacob Zuma looking on. I was worried that the match might have ruined my career. (Getty Images)

Dimitar Berbatov goes to ground after minimal contact from Daniel Agger in the first minute of the FA Cup tie between Manchester United and Liverpool in 2011 – I'd been caught cold. (Getty Images)

Summoning urgent help after Fabrice Muamba collapsed on the pitch in March 2012. (PA)

Luis Suarez is right to protest. I'd missed a clear foul by Samuel Eto'o in the penalty area during the Chelsea v Liverpool game in December 2013. (Getty Images)

My final Premier League game: Hull City v Everton, 11 May 2014 – it was time to call it a day. (Getty Images)

Preparing to go out for my last game: Brazil v Chile in the 2014 World Cup finals. (Getty Images)

I made one of the biggest calls of my career in the match, correctly disallowing a goal that could have knocked out the hosts if they had lost. (Getty Images)

I've had the privilege of refereeing in many great venues, but none to match Buckingham Palace, as part of the FA's 150th celebrations.

Another Champions League final, but this time in a different role. I've really enjoyed working with BT Sport since I retired from officiating.

The Saudis love their football, so I was pleased to have the opportunity to help develop their officials – a role I can combine with my work for BT Sport.

Receiving an honorary degree from Robert Winston, the chancellor of Sheffield Hallam University.

Kay and our children look on as I am granted the Freedom of Rotherham.

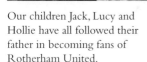

Our children Jack, Lucy and Hollie have all followed their father in becoming fans of Rotherham United.

Very proud to be asked to unveil the name of Rotherham United's new ground: the New York Stadium. (James Brailsford)

thoroughly pissed off, was a young girl dressed in a black referee's kit. She'd probably dreamed of being paired up with Diego Milito or Bastian Schweinsteiger, but in the end she'd got boring old me instead. I couldn't help but smile.

*She's definitely drawn the short straw, bless her*, I thought to myself. Then I caught sight of a mini-Darren and a mini-Mike trudging behind her, with even glummer expressions, and realised that their straws were even shorter.

I took hold of my mascot's hand and gave it a friendly squeeze. Together we walked down the twenty-three steps to the ground level and along the maroon and gold carpet, towards the pitch. As we entered the arena we were ambushed with the fabulous sight of the European Cup, in all its gleaming glory, slowly emerging from within the black trophy podium. As I strode past I caught a glimpse of my reflection, and I felt a sudden surge of adrenalin. I was within touching distance of a cup that had been lifted by some of the most iconic teams in history: Liverpool, Benfica, Celtic, Manchester United, Real Madrid, Ajax, Nottingham Forest, AC Milan. *Wow. Just wow.*

Remaining calm and composed when you walk out to the sights and sounds of a full-to-capacity Bernabéu – particularly on a beautiful springtime evening – isn't easy. I remember doing a quick 360-degree turn and taking a mental snapshot of this architectural wonder, with its five steep tiers of chanting, banner-waving supporters.

'Just look at that,' I said to Darren and Mike, who were similarly awestruck, doing their utmost to absorb this amazing atmosphere. We smiled at each other, no doubt sharing the same thought. *My God ... how did we get here?*

As the teams and officials assumed their positions for the line-up and prepared for the Champions League anthem, José Mourinho and Louis Van Gaal shook hands and took their seats in the dugout. The sense of anticipation was incredible. One managerial ego versus another managerial ego. One European giant versus another European giant. Eleven world-class players versus eleven more world-class players.

*This is the real deal, Howard,* I said to myself. *This is massive. This is not the time to mess up.*

Much to my relief, it turned out to be one of those painless games that presented me with few challenges. A total of three cautions across the whole match bore testimony to that, the earliest being a yellow for Martín Demichelis following his clunky 26th-minute challenge on Milito.

Bayern's centre-back did me a favour, in some ways, because the first half's mid-point is always a good time for a referee to show his opening yellow card. With high-profile matches like these, teams can often start cagily, and will sometimes take 20 minutes or so to find their feet, as was the case in the Bernabéu. Then a sudden flashpoint – like Demichelis' robust tackle – will not only shake the game into action, but will also provide an opportune moment for the ref to make his presence felt and tighten the reins (Hugh Dallas's horsey analogy comes in handy yet again).

So, with 20 minutes left on the clock – and with Inter heading for a 2-0 victory courtesy of a Milito brace – I felt in total control. Everything was going like a dream. It was possibly the best I'd ever felt on a football field.

'You're doing great, Howard,' piped up Darren in my earpiece. 'Not long to go now. Just stay in the zone.'

It was at that moment, safe in the knowledge that I'd got the game in my pocket, that Alan Brazil's remarks sprang to mind. *Cheers, mate,* I thought, making a mental note to thank him for the extra motivation.

I can't say I shed a tear after I blew the final whistle, but I did feel incredibly emotional. The 90 minutes had gone completely to plan – the football, as opposed to the officials, had been the primary focus – and the sense of relief among our team was immense. The usual post-match heaviness in my legs seemed to disappear as I bounded up the steps to collect my medal from UEFA president Michel Platini.

'Well done, Howard,' he said. 'Your team did a great job.'

It took me a while to leave the pitch afterwards; I admit, I wanted to milk the moment and to savour the scene of my one and only Champions League final. When fourth official Martin Atkinson finally managed to drag me off to the dressing room, the first thing I did was flake out on the bench. It had been a physically demanding night – every muscle in my body ached – but mentally I was floating on air. And while I hadn't done anything particularly special in the game – I'd just done my job to the best of my ability – it was gratifying to see all the congratulatory texts flooding in from my pals back home.

A beaming José Mourinho came into the dressing room shortly afterwards, his winners' medal swinging from his neck, and hugged each official. I hadn't seen him properly since his Stamford Bridge heart-to-heart, and it was nice to witness him smiling again. Pierluigi Collina also popped in to say congratulations, but seemed distinctly unimpressed to see the four of us swigging from bottles of San Miguel. We reckoned we'd earned some post-match refreshments – and it was the end of the football season, when all was said and done – but he obviously thought otherwise.

There was no such disapproval when we partied with the English officials' contingent that night, which also included referee coach Keren Barratt, PGMOL chief Mike Riley and assorted family members. The Spanish football federation had thoughtfully hired us a private room in a city-centre restaurant where, after feasting on tapas and Cava, we staged a good old-fashioned singalong. Following raucous renditions of 'Molly Malone', 'Ilkley Moor Baht 'At' and 'Champions League We're Having A Laugh', the oldest swingers in Madrid dived into a nearby nightclub, before staggering back to our hotel as dawn broke.

I was a complete waste of space the next morning, so much so that I slept through my alarm and missed my plane home. I eventually managed to drag myself to the airport in time for the next flight, slumped in the departures lounge, bog-eyed, as hundreds of unassuming Italian and German football fans walked by. I took time out to call Dad, who'd watched the final back home in Rotherham.

'Well done, lad,' he said. 'You did yourself proud. Now for the next challenge, eh?'

Indeed. Within a couple of weeks, I'd be waiting for another flight. A flight bound for Johannesburg, South Africa.

# CHAPTER 8

# Today's Your Day

By the summer of 2008, FIFA had shortlisted sixty referees' teams for the 2010 World Cup and, for the next couple of years, they watched us like hawks. The governing body needed to reduce this elite group by half in time for the finals and, in order to whittle it down, instigated a rigorous programme of continuous assessment and aptitude testing. Darren, Mike and I were flown to FIFA seminars all over the world – Zürich, Pretoria, the Canary Islands – and were assigned to a number of international tournaments that included the Under-17s World Cup in Nigeria as well as the 2009 Confederations Cup in South Africa. The latter was, to all intents and purposes, a dress rehearsal for the following year's football fest.

We attended a variety of intensive training camps, too, where we tackled the four principal areas of FIFA's referee coaching remit: the technical, the physical, the psychological and an experimental directive dubbed 'energy'. The latter purported to help us utilise our senses on the field of play and to find our inner positivity; it was all very new-agey and I can't say everyone bought into it.

We were handed a blindfold, for example, before being planted in the centre circle and told to locate a corner flag so as to 'absorb our environment'. Cue groups of disorientated refs staggering around like zombies, curses of *merde* and *scheisse* echoing round the stadium as they stumbled into goalposts and advertising hoardings. Another time we were asked to 'hone our sensory processing skills' by running around the pitch while reading a newspaper, like some bizarre *Monty Python* sketch.

'Are they taking the mickey or what?' I moaned, trotting past the penalty spot while holding aloft that day's *Pretoria News*.

Some monitoring and evaluation was carried out remotely, too. Every week, over a period of 18 months, each World Cup candidate had to log on to an online platform and answer questions about certain scenarios. A photo of a referee dealing with a player would flash up on my computer screen, for example, and I'd be asked to interpret his emotions and body language. Then I'd have to click on to a video link and, after scrutinising footage of a contentious decision, would have to describe in detail how I'd have managed it.

Furthermore, we were set long dissertations to complete, we had to sit Laws of the Game examinations, and we had to undergo language and communication tests. The process was both intense and uncompromising. At every stage, underperforming refs and assistants would be scratched off the list, raising the hopes of those remaining.

In May 2008, FIFA requested that all the candidates sit down to watch the Champions League final between Chelsea and Manchester United. We were all connected to a special online forum and were encouraged to share our real-time views regarding the performance of the Slovakian referee, Luboš Michel. It was a severe test for him – the match was ill-tempered, the rain torrential – but he did a good job overall.

*One hundred per cent correct to send off Drogba*, posted an Asian referee, who'd had to stay awake until the early hours to log on.

*A clear slap on Vidić. Nailed-on case of violent conduct*, I typed, as the second period of extra time came to a close.

While we'd never assumed anything, Darren, Mike and I were quietly optimistic about our World Cup chances. We'd sailed through the initial selection process, including a high-pressure, high-stakes fitness test in Zürich that we'd had to pass collectively as a team (had any of us failed it, we'd have all been eliminated).

Our South African dream finally became a reality in January 2010, when we received the official nod via a message on FIFA's e-platform. I remember sitting in the conservatory, my laptop on my knee, and whooping like a kid when I spotted our names among the officials' roster.

'We're on the list!' I hollered down the phone to various relatives as I spread the word. My dad, of course, was beside himself.

'I'm off to Thomas Cook to sort out my flights, son,' he said excitedly. 'Wouldn't miss this for the world ...'

In the wake of our good news, and not long before I departed to South Africa, close friends, family and colleagues were invited to a huge party that I threw at a local hotel. Alongside the bucking bronco and the bouncy castle was the legendary Maltby Miners' Welfare brass band, whose tuneful renditions of 'Abide With Me' and the *Match of the Day* theme tune went down a treat.

Only a few days earlier I'd been awarded the Champions League final, yet UEFA had sworn me to secrecy until the official announcement. The more beer I knocked back, however, the more I found myself blabbing about my prestigious double-whammy.

'Reffing the Champions League and World Cup in the same year?' gasped my friend Mark Carratt, who'd known me since my

Rotherham and District Sunday League days. 'Bloody hell, Howard, it's a far cry from running the line at Sunnyside Working Men's Club,' he laughed, as the brass band struck up 'The Great Escape'.

Darren, Mike and I arrived at our World Cup base on Tuesday 1 June, following an 11-hour flight from Heathrow to Johannesburg. I'd bumped into England players Steven Gerrard, Jamie Carragher and Stephen Warnock on the Manchester-to-London connecting flight, and had wished them all the best for the forthcoming tournament.

'Cheers Howard,' said Jamie, 'and good luck to you guys, too.'

Our home for the next six weeks would be Kievits Kroon, an exclusive country retreat located on the outskirts of Pretoria.

'This'll do nicely,' said Mike as we relaxed with a coffee on the veranda of our whitewashed lodge, watching the sun set over the distant hills.

The following morning, we made our way to the nearby training ground, where we hooked up with a group of local footballers who'd been drafted in to mock up some on-pitch scenarios for us. Continually blaring out of the stadium's public address system, however, was the ear-splitting din of a thousand vuvuzelas. It wasn't just the high altitude we'd have to acclimatise ourselves to, it seemed.

'That loud enough for you?' smiled one of FIFA's technical instructors, who'd been asked to organise the sound effects so we could accustom ourselves to the deafening honks.

The first round of referee appointments was announced at a swanky welcome dinner at Kievits Kroon. The showpiece opener – South Africa v Mexico at Johannesburg's Soccer City – was handed to Ravshan Irmatov, a classy ref from Uzbekistan. Our match was the last of the sixteen to be called out, and we were thrilled to be assigned to Switzerland v Spain on Wednesday 16 June, at Durban's Moses Mabhiba Stadium.

Technically you weren't deemed a 2010 World Cup official until you'd crossed the white line and blown the whistle, and I couldn't get to Durban fast enough.

'Darren, Mike, we've been working towards these finals for three years,' was my dressing room rally-cry on the afternoon of the game. 'Let's go out there and do ourselves proud.'

The reigning European champions kicked off as clear favourites and predictably dominated the first half. Not long after the interval, however, Swiss midfielder Gélson Fernandes scored a really sloppy, messy goal. Spain somehow couldn't force an equaliser and, against all expectations, it remained 1-0 until the final whistle.

From our standpoint, we couldn't have wished for a better start. We'd handled the game adeptly, the flashpoints had been minimal, and there were high-fives all round when the lads and I reconvened afterwards.

'Congratulations, guys. Great teamwork,' commented the FIFA assessor in his post-match debrief. 'Job well done.'

Later that night, Darren, Mike and I met up with our respective fathers for a bite to eat. Dick Cann and Mike Mullarkey Senior had also made the trip over to South Africa, and all three dads were staying at the gated Johannesburg home of Ari Soldatis, an ex-World Cup linesman and a good friend of David Elleray's who'd kindly offered to put them up. Whether Ari regretted that decision was debatable. Within ten minutes of arrival, Dick had gone the full Frank Spencer by falling through a jacuzzi cover and, later that night, Ari had noticed Dad munching on what he'd thought were fig rolls, my old fella having clearly gone rooting through his kitchen cupboards.

'Billy, you do realise you're eating dog biscuits, don't you?' he'd asked as Dad was mid-gnaw. Poor Ari. It must have been like living on the set of *Last of the Summer Wine*.

Our next game, one of the third matches in the group stage, took us to Ellis Park in Johannesburg. We were faced with a win or bust, last-chance saloon match between the champions from Italy and the underdogs from Slovakia, both of whom needed a victory to progress to the knockout phase.

It turned out to be one of the most enthralling games of the finals. A humdinger of a match finished 3-2 to Slovakia and – shock of all shocks – Italy were bundled out of the tournament, star players like Andrea Pirlo, Giorgio Chiellini and Gianluca Zambrotta trudging dejectedly off the pitch with their World Cup dreams in tatters.

It was a hugely intense game for us to officiate – there were plenty of tight calls, and I had to show seven yellow cards – but we managed things well. Darren was absolutely outstanding through-out, correctly calling an off-the-line clearance from Martin Škrtel and disallowing an Italian goal that had been centimetres offside.

After the game I handed the match ball to Italy captain Fabio Cannavaro – it was his last ever international game, after all – but I managed to blag another one from FIFA for Darren to keep as a memento of a supreme performance.

Three days later, and my linesmen and I were lying in front of a TV in a Kievits Kroon bedroom, watching the crunch England v Germany tie in Bloemfontein's Free State Stadium. Our mood darkened as Joachim Löw's boys went 2-0 up, but lightened again when, just before half-time, Matthew Upson pulled one back with a header. Then, moments later, we almost hit the ceiling when Frank Lampard's superb volley smashed against the bar and bounced behind the line, past goalie Manuel Neuer.

'YESSSSSSSSS,' I yelled, while dad-dancing on the bed. 'GET INNNNNN!'

It was only when I finally calmed down, and noticed the TV camera panning in on a stony-faced Fabio Capello, that I realised the goal hadn't been given.

'What the hell's happened there, lads?'

Uruguayan referee Jorge Larrionda – one of the best officials in the business – had been let down by an assistant who'd judged that the ball hadn't crossed the line. The TV replays, however, confirmed that they'd made a colossal error, possibly one of the worst cock-ups in World Cup history. We all just sat there, agog, knowing that this game-changing gaffe (Germany went on to win 4-1) would have huge footballing and refereeing ramifications. And, just to compound matters, a few hours later – during the Mexico v Argentina match – Italian referee Roberto Rosetti and his team would allow a Carlos Tévez goal to stand that was clearly yards offside.

Sunday 27 June 2010 proved to be a dark day for international refereeing. Not only did it lead to calls for FIFA to seriously consider goal-line technology, it also placed match officials like myself under more scrutiny than ever.

The following day, therefore, my nerves were jumping when I returned to Ellis Park to oversee the round of 16 game between Brazil and Chile. I'd never reffed two South American teams before and this pair had history, with the Chileans a regular thorn in their rivals' side. I decided to seek the counsel of Horacio Elizondo, the Argentinian who'd officiated over the 2006 World Cup final and who, in the process, had dismissed Zinedine Zidane for his infamous headbutt. Horacio was more than happy to dispense some tips on how to approach the tie.

'With both sets of players, your body language will need to be so clear, so obvious,' he said. 'When you show the yellow, don't just show the card. Look the player straight in the eye. Send a message that a line has been drawn.'

I took his excellent advice on board, and I refereed out of my skin. Once we'd kicked off, my pre-match anxieties ebbed away, and for the entire game – which Brazil comfortably won 3-0 – I felt calm, strong and confident.

As I walked off the pitch at full time, I looked up towards the stand where Dad was sitting and held my thumbs aloft. While I couldn't pinpoint his face among the crowd, I just wanted him to know how happy I felt.

*Let me have another game, FIFA*, I thought as I surveyed the colourful throng of vuvuzela-tooting supporters. *I can't get enough of this. I'm in my element.*

What I didn't know then, of course, was that my next game would be the final itself.

An hour or so after the nail-biting Match 64 announcement, I'd found a quiet spot outside the Kievits Kroon conference room to calm down and have a breather. I think I was in a state of shock, the words 'Webb, England' still echoing round my head, the good wishes of my colleagues continuing to ring in my ears. Me, a World Cup final official, for God's sake. That same kid who'd once reffed the Under-11s at Orgreave in his dad's baggy kit. To say it was beyond my wildest dreams was an understatement.

I checked my phone, which had been vibrating in my pocket for the previous hour, and was amazed to have received nearly 500 messages from well-wishing friends, family and colleagues.

Naturally, the first person I rang was Kay, who'd been watching Sky Sports when news of our big appointment had filtered through. While I'd have much preferred to have broken the glad tidings to her myself, it was still fantastic to hear her voice down the line, sounding so overjoyed.

'We're all so pleased for you, love,' she said, in between happy sobs, as my three children whooped in the background. 'You deserve this so much.'

There then followed a call to my proud-as-punch parents. Dad had flown back home after the Brazil v Chile game, but it seemed he was already planning a prompt return visit.

'Wild horses wouldn't keep me away, son,' he said. 'See you in Johannesburg.'

That night, in our Kievits Kroon lodge, Darren, Mike and I celebrated our appointment with a glass of Coke. We also reminded ourselves of a pledge that we'd made on the first day of the tournament, as we'd sat admiring the panoramic view across the Pretoria hills. We'd promised each other that, in the unlikely event that we got the final, after the match we'd race through the complex and jump into the swimming pool wearing our FIFA suits.

'Looks like we're going to get a bit wet on Sunday night, lads,' I grinned.

Our conversation then turned to England's previous World Cup final referee, Jack Taylor. I happened to mention that he'd received an OBE for services to football back in 1975, and half-jokingly wondered whether we'd get the same. I was speculating more than presuming, imagining how wonderful it would be.

'I promise you this, though,' I said to Darren and Mike. 'We're a team, and we've been together a long time, so if I get an honour, we *all* get an honour.'

'We'll hold you to that,' replied Darren.

Friday 9 July was classed as a rest day, so all the remaining match officials took time out to visit Kwalata Game Ranch in Gauteng province. With my pre-announcement nerves now fully exorcised, I felt incredibly relaxed and really enjoyed riding in a rickety jeep, taking in the stunning terrain and spotting all sorts of wild animals (I got the chance to feed a hungry giraffe at one point).

The eve of the final, in contrast, was a mad-busy day. The three of us spent the whole morning training, concentrating mainly on speed and agility exercises. With hindsight, I was probably in the shape of my life: fit, lean and without an ounce of excess weight. I'd got myself a decent suntan, too, courtesy of six weeks'-worth of South African winter sunshine.

After our warm-down, the football media descended upon us for the obligatory pre-final press conference. Seats, benches and sponsors' hoardings were rigged up on the training pitch and, for the next hour, my team and FIFA's head of refereeing, José María García-Aranda, were quizzed by print and broadcast journalists from all over the world.

The majority of the questions were directed at José María and me. Rather than focusing on our plans and preparations for the final, however, they mostly centred upon the few contentious calls that had peppered the tournament, notably the Lampard oversight, the Tévez offside and a disallowed goal for the USA.

Towards the end of the press conference the questioning changed tack, though, with an English journalist asking for my opinion on my wife's comments in the media back home in the UK.

Kay, it transpired, had been interviewed live on *GMTV*, and had said something along the lines of me hardly being able to take charge of my three children at home, let alone twenty-two players in a World Cup final. It was a tongue-in-cheek remark reflecting our ordinary family life, she'd thought. The tabloids seized upon this, of course – they don't half love a good angle – and the *Daily Star* gleefully printed a *WEBB CAN'T CONTROL HIS OWN KIDS* banner headline, alongside a family photo.

I rang Kay after the press briefing to give her some gentle ribbing. She hadn't yet seen that morning's newspapers and was horrified – and quite upset – that they'd latched on to a seemingly throwaway remark.

'I only meant it as a daft joke, Howard,' she said, apologetically. 'I wouldn't have said it had I known they were going to splash it all over the headlines.'

But I was fine with it, and I told her so. In fact, it had added some much-needed light relief to a pretty heavy-going press conference.

At 8.30 p.m. on the Saturday night, precisely 24 hours before the big game, I found myself surveying the pitch at a virtually empty Soccer City. I'd already visited this magnificent arena once (I'd been to the opening ceremony prior to the South Africa v Mexico game, bouncing up and down like a kid when the air force did a loop-the-loop flyover), but FIFA had granted my special request to pay a return visit for preparation purposes.

'I just want everything to be right, y'see, and I don't want any hassle or stresses on the night,' I'd said while stating my case, explaining that a dummy run would really help Darren, Mike and me to fine tune the logistics and iron out any problems.

As far as I was concerned, all bases had to be covered. We travelled to the stadium, familiarising ourselves with the route and the journey times. We explored the dressing rooms and the tunnel area, monitoring how long it took to walk from one to the other. We assiduously checked all our radio and communication equipment, thus ensuring that all was in order. We walked on to the pitch at exactly 8.30 p.m., noting the temperature, the humidity, the air pressure. Finally, we spent time alone on the playing surface to assess dimensions, distances and positioning. Only when I was satisfied that I'd tried and tested everything did I summon the car to take us back to Pretoria.

As we sped down the motorway – FIFA dictated that we travelled everywhere with a police escort – the convoy suddenly veered off into a shopping centre on the fringes of Johannesburg.

'Erm, where are we going, exactly?' I asked the driver, worried that something was amiss and that we were going to end up bound and gagged in the boot.

He smiled enigmatically, before revealing that something special awaited us.

We followed the driver into a coffee shop, only to be noisily greeted by the three dads – Billy, Dick and Mike – as well as Mike Riley, David Elleray and none other than Jack Taylor. A FIFA camera crew were also in tow, to capture this *Surprise, Surprise*-style reunion for their official film, *Match 64*.

I'd known that Dad was coming over, but hadn't been told exactly when, so it was all pretty unexpected. I have a feeling David 'Cilla Black' Elleray had probably instigated it all; if so, he played a blinder.

Dad, bless him, enveloped me in a huge hug, told me how proud he was and promptly burst into tears (it was a genuine show of emotion from him, in spite of the cameras whirring over our shoulders). It was a special moment for me, too, but I managed to keep my composure, ever conscious that – with my big day ahead – I had to conserve my energy and control my feelings. Hard-headed though it may sound, I wanted to save any outpourings for after the match, not before.

I was absolutely thrilled to see Jack Taylor, too. This wonderful man had always given me great support, and I valued his mentorship so much. He and I had a 15-minute chat over a coffee and a cake, Jack advising me to maintain a positive and confident approach, and to focus upon my man-management skills.

'It's a huge honour, this, Howard,' he said, 'and it's such a great reflection of English refereeing. So go out there and do your colleagues back home proud.'

Then Jack regaled the story of how, in that classic 1974 World Cup final, he'd bravely awarded a penalty to Holland in the opening minute, against the West Germans, in Munich. Franz Beckenbauer's boys hadn't even had chance to touch the ball.

'It was such a clear penalty, Howard, I could have given it from the car park,' he laughed.

Afterwards, Beckenbauer had made a point of saying 'Jack, you are an English referee,' very much implying that the man in black had displayed the courage, honesty and integrity to make such a crucial decision.

'Leo Beenhakker said something similar to me at Euro 2008, Jack,' I smiled, 'although I think his sentiments were slightly different ...'

It was dark by the time Darren, Mike and I returned to Kievits Kroon, but we managed to catch a rerun of that day's third-place contest between Uruguay and Germany, a hugely entertaining match that saw the latter winning 3-2. The fifth minute had witnessed a pretty clear red-card tackle from Germany's Dennis Aogo, who'd gone studs up on Diego Pérez's shin; a proper leg breaker. Much to the consternation of the Uruguayan bench, referee Benito Archundia had only deemed it worth a yellow.

I looked my linesmen straight in the eye, and posed the million-rand question.

'So, guys, if that happens to *us* in the first five minutes, what do we do?'

'We send the player off, that's what we do,' responded Darren, quick as a flash. I shuddered at the thought.

'Shit,' I said. 'I hope nothing like that happens tomorrow night.'

It was while sitting in bed, nursing a cup of tea, reading Andre Agassi's autobiography and listening to Snow Patrol's *Eyes Open*, that the magnitude of the next day's match hit home.

*What I'm going to do tomorrow is just huge*, I mused. *Football's the biggest sport in the entire world. Millions of people will be watching this one game. And I'm the man in the middle. Bloody hell fire ...*

Maybe I should get some kip, I thought, conscious of the text that I'd received from Pierluigi Collina the night before, admonishing me for replying to his good-luck message at midnight.

'It's two days before the final! You should be asleep!' he'd quite rightly pointed out.

With that in mind I closed my book, unplugged my iPod and sank my head into the pillow.

The following morning, after our customary breakfast of Jungle porridge oats, Darren, Mike and I had a sit-down meeting with Leslie Irvine, our technical instructor. Leslie, an ex-FIFA international referee from Northern Ireland, discussed the format of the day, as well as the general protocols and procedures. He also emphasised the need to try to get into the heads of the players, suggesting we consider the huge pressure that they'd be under and prepare for any resulting flashpoints.

'I'll ask you to remember the old phrase,' he said, nodding sagely. 'Expect the unexpected.'

There then followed a session with the officials' designated psychologist, Mañuel Lopez, during which we addressed strategies to help us keep cool and composed, including some positive visualisation and some pre-match breathing techniques. With the hours ticking by, we returned to our rooms for some chill-out time; we listened for a while to *Catnapper*, a CD given to us by FIFA's 'energy' chaps which featured a husky American actor lulling us into relaxation mode.

Feeling calm and serene – and following a quick Skype chat

with Kay and the kids – I began to gather together my things for the game.

After a smooth, glitch-free journey, the lads and I reached Soccer City in good time, roughly two hours before kick-off. Approaching the Johannesburg city limits and seeing the beams of blue light emitting from the copper-coloured stadium was a moment I'll never forget.

The closing ceremony was in full swing as we arrived and, after dumping our kitbags in the dressing room, we headed down the tunnel to savour some of the on-pitch party. Shakira, the hip-swivelling Colombian (and wife of Spain's Gerard Piqué) was its centrepiece, performing the official World Cup anthem, 'This Time For Africa'.

'Today's your day,' she sang, as the crowd swayed, the flags fluttered and the vuvuzelas blared. 'I feel it, you paved the way, believe it …'

Watching this vibrant spectacle gave me such a buzz. *Look at the state of this*, I remember thinking to myself. *What a beautiful venue. What a fantastic atmosphere. What a momentous occasion. And what an absolute privilege to be able to play my part in it.*

I didn't want to become overwhelmed and overawed, though, so after five minutes I decided to make my way back up the tunnel to begin my pre-match preparations. As I did so, I spotted a large England banner draped over the wall, with HALIFAX emblazoned across its centre in big black lettering. The bloke holding it frantically waved at me and, amid the deafening stadium din, began shouting at the top of his voice.

'Do Yorkshire proud, Webby,' he yelled, pumping his fist. 'Do Yorkshire proud!'

Then I spied another, smaller, flag of St George among the sea of orange and red. The wording suggested that its owner was another England fan, still sore about his team's premature exit from the tournament: CAN'T PLAY, CAN REF, was written across its four corners.

The lads and I had an hour-and-a-half to get organised while the closing ceremony was concluding and the pitch was being cleared. After the customary massage, it was time to rig ourselves up with our usual officiating equipment: the Polar heart-rate monitor, the electronic buzzer flag device, the radio communication system.

Then, sporting our FIFA training kit, Darren, Mike and I jogged back out on to the pitch for our warm-up. We'd already become renowned in refereeing circles for our synchronised pre-match exercise routine, which lasted precisely 13 minutes and followed the same regimented sequence each time (UEFA once even filmed it to demonstrate best practice and good team-work for other refs).

So it was shuttle runs followed by ankle circles, hamstring stretches, sidesteps, jogs back, groins in to out, groins out to in, high knees, bum kicks and so on. The routine became as much of a superstition as a discipline and, to give us the right positive vibes, had to be executed perfectly.

Then it was back again to the dressing room, where we hooked up with the fourth official and reserve assistant referee, namely Yuichi Nishimura and Toru Sagara from Japan. They'd already conducted the full pitch inspection, as well as speaking with the respective team managers and checking players' kits, boots and jewellery.

So, with a matter of minutes to go until kick-off, and with all the talking done and the measures taken, it was time for a quiet moment to ourselves. The three of us had uniquely different ways of getting 'in the zone', to put it mildly.

A highly focused Darren stood in front of a mirror, holding his flag and going through a slo-mo semaphore-style routine. Mike, the big softy, kissed his treasured wedding ring before putting it in a special box, to be retrieved immediately after the game.

And, as for me, I endured my time-honoured, obsessive-compulsive battle to keep my sodding shirt on. It was a rigmarole that, on this momentous evening, took place in the dressing-room toilet so as not to distract the lads in any way.

I reached into my kitbag and grabbed my azure blue Adidas shirt. However, as I pulled it on, a negative thought invaded my head, my anxiety levels rose, and I took the top off again to erase that niggling feeling.

*Come on, Howard,* I said under my breath, willing myself to think positively. *Let's get this out of the way.*

I went through the exact same routine a fair few times. In the end it took me about six attempts to keep that bloody shirt on my back. But when I did, and when that upbeat thought finally crossed my mind, my anxiety completely evaporated and I was firmly in the zone.

So, with my pre-match OCD battle won, my body was relaxed, my mind was clear and, notwithstanding a few butterflies, I was ready for action. My thoughts drifted to my family – Dad sitting among the fans here in the stadium, Mum, Kay and the kids watching on telly back home – before a loud knock on the dressing room door signalled our exit.

There was just time for a quick hug with my assistants and the shortest of pep talks – 'Be the best, lads' – before they headed off to the teams' dressing rooms for the final checks, leaving me the sole official in the tunnel.

I peered out towards the pitch and caught sight of the white and gold Adidas 'Jo'bulani' World Cup ball perched on a plinth and, a few metres ahead of it, the FIFA World Cup trophy. The presence and proximity of this beautiful cup – and the way it seemed to radiate its own golden yellow glow – simply took my breath away.

I asked FIFA's head of media, who'd been buzzing around the tunnel area, whether he had an idea of the game's expected audience figures.

'We're looking at nearly a billion viewers worldwide,' he grinned, 'so no pressure, ref.'

But it wasn't pressure that I felt right then, I explained to him. It was pride. It was joy. It was honour.

Soon, the players began to filter into the tunnel, as did the mascots and officials. Iker Casillas headed up the Spanish side to my right, with Giovanni van Bronckhorst leading his Dutch teammates to my left. There were a few smiles and nods exchanged between both camps but any chat was minimal; it all felt very serious, solemn even.

The pre-match tension was momentarily broken, however, when a pitch invader sprinted towards the trophy (a Catalan separatist called Jimmy Jump, apparently, who'd vainly attempted to crown the cup with a traditional red hat). As I craned my neck I saw him being rugby tackled by a posse of security guards, before being hastily dragged through the tunnel.

We then received the signal from the FIFA media guy that the TV control room was good to go.

'Five … four … three … two … one: NOW!!!' he shouted, ushering us forward.

And, just before 8.30 p.m. on Sunday 11 July 2010, a miner's son from Rotherham strode on to the Soccer City pitch, lifted the World Cup final ball off its plinth, nestled it in the crook of his arm and walked out to referee the biggest sporting showpiece on earth.

\*

As we lined up with the teams and shook hands with South African president Jacob Zuma and FIFA president Sepp Blatter, the latter paused for a moment.

'Webb, we've chosen you because you're the best man for the job,' he smiled. 'Hope you have a great game.'

Blatter didn't stick around long enough to give me a chance to reply but, had he done, I'd have told him that it wasn't just about me. My assistants and I were the best *team* for the job.

While the anthems blared and the crowd roared I tried to remain focused, pondering Leslie Irvine's brief: *trust yourself, believe in yourself, keep doing what you've done so far …*

Then I headed over to the centre circle, whereupon I shook hands with both captains, performed the coin toss, placed the ball on the centre spot, and blew for kick-off.

The first notable incident – a really strong tackle by Robin van Persie on Sergio Busquets – occurred on two minutes. I hadn't deemed it worthy of a yellow card, but I called him over for a warning, and to bid for calm. I'd reffed Robin a few times in his Arsenal days and, being quite a straightforward, easy-to-read player, had never found him hard to handle. This particular day, though, I saw a marked difference in attitude. There was no apology or acknowledgement. He seemed preoccupied, disengaged almost. *Aye aye*, I thought. *Reckon I'm going to have my work cut out for me today.*

Then came another heavy challenge, this time by Mark van Bommel on Carles Puyol, which, once again, I felt merited a talking-to rather than a caution. By the 15-minute mark, however, I'd had to twice reach for my yellow card for crude tackles by van Persie and Puyol, the former clattering Joan Capdevila and the latter sliding into Arjen Robben.

With a third of the half gone, then, I thought I was doing OK. My game management had been decent enough, I reckoned; I hadn't over-reacted, I hadn't gone in with the cards too quickly, I'd kept my powder dry for as long as I could, but when I'd needed to step up to the plate I'd done so. I was building up my input gradually, as opposed to going all gung-ho.

*Those yellows will settle the game down nicely*, I told myself.

Like hell they did. Shortly after, I had to mete out two more cautions, the first to van Bommel for a really strong tackle from behind on Andrés Iniesta, the second to Sergio Ramos for clipping Dirk Kuyt.

*Shit*, I thought. *Four yellows in 22 minutes. This isn't calming down at all. This isn't going to plan.*

I remember conveying my fears to Darren and Mike on the radio.

'Believe in yourself,' they both replied, almost simultaneously. 'Keep doing your job.'

'Whatever you do, don't hide,' added Darren.

For a fleeting moment the Everton v Bolton match of December 2004 sprang to mind, when I'd gone missing after half-an-hour and had virtually thrown in the towel. Darren was right; in no way did I want a repeat of that, especially not on a world stage.

Then, on 27 minutes, Xabi Alonso headed the ball forward to David Villa but, as he did so, Nigel de Jong crashed into him. At that moment I'd been positioned just behind Alonso, about ten yards away, so I hadn't seen the actual point of impact or exactly how de Jong had connected. However, I knew that it was a late and forceful challenge, and that it warranted a caution. None of my team spoke up on the radio to suggest otherwise, so I showed a yellow card for what I'd seen unfold before me: an untidy, reckless challenge from the Dutch midfielder.

Hand on heart, it never, ever crossed my mind that this was a red card. In that instance, on that pitch, I was utterly convinced it was a yellow; not one per cent of me thought otherwise. I hadn't bottled out of the big decision, I hadn't felt intimidated by the occasion, and I'd certainly not felt under any pressure from FIFA to curb dismissals. I'd simply handed out the appropriate penalty for what I'd seen with my own eyes, from my vantage point. And that's the truth.

As I brandished the card, however, there was a furious reaction from the Spaniards, both on and off the field. I genuinely thought they were pissed off because of the general physicality of the Dutch team, not just this one particular offence. I also presumed they were riled because I'd chosen not to play advantage when the ball had dropped to David Villa from Alonso's header.

It wasn't until half-time that I realised de Jong's tackle might have been worthy of a red card. In the dressing room, Darren grabbed hold of his phone (unlike the Premier League, FIFA had no mobile restrictions) and, as he scrolled through his texts, his expression darkened.

'What's up, Canny?'

'De Jong's tackle, Howard. Some of the refs at Kievits Kroon HQ are saying it should've been a red.'

'Really? Shit …'

I felt gutted beyond belief. It looked like I'd missed a red-card offence in the World Cup final. What a fucking nightmare. I returned to the pitch with my head pounding and my heart thumping.

The second half carried on where the first had left off. Around the 60-minute stage, with the tackles still flying and the yellows being flourished, I remember thinking *just go with it, Howard. What will be will be. Deal with what you see. Trust yourself, trust your team …*

After 90 minutes – and a tally of nine cautions – it remained goalless, thus heralding extra time. There was a really strong penalty shout for Spain in the first period which I waved away, rightly, as it happened, since their player had kicked the floor and hadn't been tripped. I ended up sending off Johnny Heitinga in the second period, though; he'd already been cautioned for pulling a player back, and I finally gave him his marching orders for a foul on Iniesta on the edge of the box. By this point, I felt myself starting to waver, both emotionally and physically. I was exhausted. I was spent. I'd never known a match like it.

I was fully expecting the game to go to penalties but, with about three minutes left on the clock, Spain went on the break. Cesc Fàbregas played a clever ball into Iniesta, who drove a superb half-volley past goalie Maarten Stekelenburg to send the red half of the stadium wild.

My heart sank as I saw the Barça man sprinting away and ripping off his number 6 shirt, his vest bearing a tribute to Espanyol defender Dani Jarque who'd sadly died a year earlier. By that point I'd booked twelve players, and my head was so mashed that I simply couldn't remember if he was among them. If so, I needed to show him a second yellow for excessive celebration.

*Shit, shit, SHIT* said a panicky voice in my head. *Please don't tell me I've got to dismiss the match winner ...*

In the meantime, as I tried to work this out, I had to caution Joris Mathijsen for slamming the ball down in anger. It was while pencilling his number on to my yellow card that I noticed the absence of the number 6 in the Spain column.

*Thank fuck for that*, I thought, as I brandished the yellow, not the red, at Iniesta.

Four minutes later I blew for full-time. As the Spanish lads celebrated madly, I found myself being surrounded by a cluster of enraged Dutch players. They were joined by their coach, Bert van Marwijk, who'd angrily stomped over from the dugout.

'You performed like this because Spain complained about you in the first game!' he yelled, which puzzled me; that was the first I'd heard of it.

I spent a few moments trying to placate the Dutch team, but I swiftly realised it was futile. They'd been beaten in the final, and nothing I could say was going to quell that disappointment. I decided to remove myself from an increasingly febrile situation and, together with Darren and Mike, moved to another part of the pitch.

Waiting for the medal presentation was possibly the longest ten minutes of my life. My mood was grim, and my mind was racing. It had been so tough out there, and I'd really tried to do my best. But had my performance been good enough? Had it been at the level you'd expect for a World Cup final? Would another referee have handled things better?

*I hope this match hasn't ruined my career,* I remember thinking to myself. *I don't want this to define me forever.*

'Ladies and gentleman, from England, Howard Webb ...' announced the PA as I traipsed up the steps, while a loud boo rang out from the stands. Sepp Blatter looked really uneasy when he presented me with my medal; like me, he probably didn't know what to think of it all.

Before heading back on to the pitch, the media assistants asked my assistants and I to pause for a moment and have our picture taken. As the photographer merrily snapped away, the Dutch fans continued to hiss and catcall. I felt like I'd been put in the stocks. It was torturous.

'I'm off to the dressing room,' I muttered to Darren, and began walking towards the tunnel. This should have been the proudest moment in my life, but I felt so downbeat that I couldn't even stomach the trophy presentation.

'Whoa, stop right there!' barked my linesman. 'When are you ever going to get the chance again to see the World Cup being lifted, after the final that you've just refereed? You're not leaving this pitch, Howard.'

He was right, of course. Looking back, I was glad that I witnessed captain Casillas hoisting aloft the trophy, beaming with joy amid all the fireworks, streamers and chants of *campeones*.

A couple of hours later, back at Kievits Kroon, our ruse to jump fully clothed into the swimming pool was quietly shelved. All three of us were mentally drained, and weren't in the mood for high-jinks of any kind. Instead, we ambled over to the half-empty restaurant for a tumbleweed dinner.

Afterwards I rang my dad, who was back at Ari's place in Johannesburg.

'Bloody hell, son, that was a bugger of a game. I really felt for you,' he said. 'But I'm proud, all the same. So, so proud.'

I flew back to Manchester Airport the following evening, and shortly afterwards caught up with Mike Riley in the glamorous surroundings of Stockport Tesco Extra, just off the M60. It was good to see him, and he couldn't have been kinder.

While I was still really upset about the game, I'd become aware that a groundswell of support had been building for me, particularly in the UK. Over the space of 24 hours I'd received hundreds of sympathetic texts and emails ('What a bastard of a game that was, Howard …') and Mike had come armed with some benevolent newspaper articles. *SHAME ON THE DUTCH* said the *Daily Star*. *I DID MY BEST, SAYS WEBB* read the headline in the *Independent*.

During the taxi ride home to Rotherham, I rang Kay, who told me that the media were already camped outside the house, awaiting my return.

'They've been here ages, Howard,' she said, 'so I've just taken out some tea and biscuits.'

As the cab approached our house, I could see that the road was lined with satellite trucks and radio cars. *Bollocks*. I quickly phoned Phil Dorward, the Premier League's press officer, who advised me to go indoors and draft a quick statement. Talking to the media was the last thing on my mind – I just wanted to shut myself away with my family, basically – but I did as I was told.

I couldn't have been more succinct – I was pleased to be back home, I explained to the assembled reporters, and I would be speaking at greater length with the media later that week. Once I'd had my photo taken in front of the kids' 'Welcome Home Daddy' banner, I sloped off.

After a couple of days, I felt ready to pick myself up, dust myself off and analyse the final. I took my laptop to a local pub, met up with Premier League linesman Scott Ledger, and replayed the entire match.

I was pleasantly surprised to find that, other than the de Jong incident, I'd had a better game than I'd remembered. Van Bommel could have perhaps walked in the first half, and I'd lost my way somewhat for a short period in the second but, in my eyes, it wasn't the unmitigated disaster that I'd initially feared.

As regards the match's main flashpoint, there was no doubting that de Jong's now infamous kung-fu kick was a red-card offence, especially when viewed in slo-mo. Had my positioning been better, I'd have clearly witnessed the incident and would have sent him off, no question. But I hadn't seen it, pure and simple. To my dying day I'll wish I had.

Watching the match footage was painful, though. An analogy from a South Yorkshire-based journalist, Les Payne – who I admire greatly – perfectly summed up my emotions.

'You feel like a bride who, having enjoyed sunny days in the run up to her wedding, has torrential rain on her big day,' he said. 'She's still got the photos to prove that she got married, and she still sees it as a momentous, memorable occasion, but it'll be forever dampened by that downpour.'

In late July, the family and I jetted off for a holiday in Turkey. Within minutes of arriving in Dalaman, however, any hopes of a peaceful getaway were dashed. It was mayhem. Whenever I hit the beach or the bar I'd be waylaid for chats and photos, and I didn't get a minute's peace. I met some lovely people, don't get me wrong, but it wasn't the head-clearing, cobweb-sweeping break that I'd craved.

'Are you famous now, Daddy?' asked my younger daughter after I'd autographed a holidaymaker's beermat.

'I'm not sure about that, Lucy,' I replied, but, deep down, I knew my life had changed forever.

I started the 2010–11 season a little later than planned. Mike Riley had phoned me after I'd arrived home from Turkey, insisting that I took my time to return to the hurly-burly of the Premier League.

'You've got to be both mentally and physically ready, Howard,' he'd maintained. 'It's been a long, tiring summer. Don't make the mistake of rushing back too soon.'

So Saturday 11 September – West Brom v Tottenham Hotspur – became my first appointment of the campaign. I arrived nice and early at The Hawthorns and, following the usual pre-match preparations, ventured outside to warm up.

As I paced over to the far corner of the pitch, a ripple of applause arose from a section of the home fans. I think a few of them even stood up. *That's a nice touch*, I thought, as I smiled and raised my hand in acknowledgement.

Half-an-hour later, just a couple of minutes into the game, I awarded a free-kick against the Baggies, right in front of the same set of fans.

'*World Cup, and you fucked it up, World Cup, and you fucked it up …*' came the chant.

Home sweet home.

# CHAPTER 9

# They Tell Me You're A Football Referee

Let's get something straight, once and for all. Contrary to what you might have seen on the internet, I have never shared a bed with Sir Alex Ferguson. There is no statue of me outside Old Trafford. My kids are not called Rio, Wayne and Cristiano. There is no Red Devil tattoo inked on my left buttock. The only United I have ever supported – hand on heart – is of the Rotherham variety. And that's the whole truth and nothing but the truth.

That said, as my Premier League career progressed, I was becoming aware that I was gaining a reputation as a ref with Manchester United leanings. While it was complete and utter bollocks – I genuinely didn't give a toss who won the games I reffed – I realised that some of my decisions may have sown those seeds. That 5-2 victory at Old Trafford in April 2009 was the big catalyst, I suppose; aided and abetted by my dubious penalty decision, United staged one of the season's greatest football comebacks and paved their way to the league title. 'How-Red Webb' and

'Fergie's love child' were just a couple of the barbs levelled at me in the aftermath.

The fact of the matter is that, throughout my career, I hardly had any dealings with Sir Alex. He never turned up to the pre-match team sheet exchange, and rarely came into the referees' dressing room afterwards. He and I were not remotely friendly; I can't recall having a meaningful, convivial conversation with him and certainly wasn't one of those refs who claimed to have had his number on speed dial. When our paths did cross he was at best, civil and at worst, hostile.

I remember an encounter we had in December 2009, prior to a Fulham v Manchester United game. It was a Saturday lunchtime kick-off at Craven Cottage but, as there'd been a frost, I'd been asked to conduct an early-morning pitch inspection. I rocked up bright and breezy at nine o'clock, only to find Ferguson lurking in the tunnel, waiting for me.

That particular month, Manchester United's defence had been ravaged with injury, meaning that neither Nemanja Vidić or Rio Ferdinand, nor Jonny Evans or John O'Shea were available for selection. It was looking likely that the Reds' boss would have to field a weakened team against Fulham, and he was clearly angling for a postponement.

'I've already had a look at it,' he snapped, scanning the pitch. 'It's horrendous. It's a bloody death trap.'

'I'll check it out and let you know what I think,' I replied.

After some pacing and prodding I surmised that the pitch was absolutely fine; soft underfoot with no hazardous icy patches. *Right, here goes*, I thought, as I walked towards the tunnel to break the news.

'See what I mean?' Ferguson barked as I approached him. 'So the game's off, then, yes?'

'Nope,' I said. 'The pitch is fine.'

'You fuckin' what?' he yelled. 'You're trying to tell me the game's still on? I cannae believe that!'

'I am. The surface is clearly playable,' I countered, bracing myself for another tirade. Instead, he just paused and tutted.

'Yeah, I know it is,' he smiled, the wily old sod, and headed back up the tunnel. Five hours later his makeshift team got battered 3-0.

Another confrontation, a few months later, saw Ferguson's famous hairdryer being whacked up a notch or two. In March 2010 Manchester United were up against Liverpool at Old Trafford and at half-time, with the score one apiece, I blew the whistle and sauntered off the pitch, slightly concerned about a close-call penalty appeal by Manchester United involving the opposing goalie, Pepe Reina.

I noticed the United boss storming down the touchline and, as I entered the tunnel he was standing there, glowering at me, as his players filed past. *Here we go*, I thought. *That penalty shout's pissed him right off.*

'I saw you in that film,' he yelled as I neared my dressing room. 'I saw you singing "You'll Never Walk Alone". Fucking says it all, that …'

Ha. He'd obviously had the pleasure of watching my starring role in *The Referees* film from Euro 2008. I'd always known that my drunken rendition of Gerry and the Pacemakers' famous anthem would return to haunt me one day. That day had arrived.

However, the fact that he was creating such a stink in full view of his players, and was I felt virtually accusing me of cosying up to Liverpool, made me very, very angry indeed.

'I need a word, *now*,' I hissed. It was the one and only time I'd ever summoned a manager to my dressing room during the interval. I was seething.

'You know that's bullshit,' I yelled once he'd closed the door behind him. 'It was just a bloody singalong. It had nothing to do with Liverpool,' I added, explaining the circumstances behind my impromptu turn at the Referees' Association dinner in Solihull.

'All right, fair enough,' he said, his newly calm demeanour suggesting his tunnel histrionics had all been for effect.

'Anyway, I know you're a Rotherham fan,' he added with a wink, before striding back out to the tunnel.

There's no getting round the fact that, towards the end of my domestic career, I approached games involving Manchester United with great trepidation. Accusations of bias and favouritism continued to be bandied about, causing me much angst and frustration since they were so wide of the mark. I found it difficult to cast the allegations to the back of my mind, though; I used to go into these matches feeling edgy and apprehensive and, instead of keeping an open mind, would find myself over-analysing everything.

I'd cling on to the hope that nothing would happen to fan the flames and perpetrate these falsehoods, and would pray that any incidents involving the Reds would be clear-cut and controversy-free. Such pre-match emotions could be dangerous and destructive for a referee; if you succumbed to them you knew you were going to be less likely to believe in yourself and trust your own instincts.

And while my OCD behaviours never encroached on to the pitch, they'd often be heightened in the lead-up to United games. Niggling thoughts would swirl around my head as I got changed into my referee's gear and, in order to purge them, my shirt would be pulled on and off until my arms ached.

It was with all this as a backdrop that, on Sunday 9 January 2011, I had to prime myself for the FA Cup third-round match between Manchester United and Liverpool. Kenny Dalglish was making an emotional return to the hot seat for his second stint as Liverpool manager, a full-to-capacity Old Trafford was pulsating with excitement, and the stage was set for an exhilarating Manchester-versus-Merseyside cup tie.

*Come on, Howard,* I urged myself as I shook hands with captains Rio Ferdinand and Steven Gerrard. *Let's get this one right, for fuck's sake.*

It took me all of one minute to cock things up. Dimitar Berbatov had been challenged by Daniel Agger in the corner of the penalty area near the byline and, after halting briefly, had hit the deck. Had I been more vigilant, I'd have realised that there'd been minimal contact from the Liverpool centre back, I'd have surmised that it wasn't enough to justify a penalty, and I'd have waved away the appeal. But I did none of those things, and I signalled for a spot-kick.

I'll be honest. The situation had slapped me in the face and I hadn't been ready for it. I'd not switched myself on from the very first second – one of the cardinal sins of refereeing – and had been caught cold. Put it this way, had Agger's tackle happened in the tenth minute, I think I'd have been more alert and attentive, and would have probably told Berbatov to get up before awarding a goal kick.

The immediate reaction from the enraged Liverpool players spoke volumes, suggesting that my decision had been overly harsh. Moments later, Ryan Giggs placed the ball on the spot and slammed it into the corner of the net to make it 1-0.

I mentally berated myself as play resumed at the centre circle. *You stupid, stupid bastard. You've ruined the game in the first fucking minute with a soft-as-shit decision.*

Things didn't get any easier for me when, after 32 minutes, Gerrard recklessly tackled Michael Carrick near the half-way line.

I knew it was forceful, I knew that the studs had been shown, and I felt pretty sure that it was a red-card offence. However, having sensed that I'd erred with the penalty decision, this time I needed to be cast-iron certain. With impatient fans' howls ringing in my ears, I decided to consult with my fourth official Andre Marriner.

'It was two-footed, Howard,' he said. 'It's a dismissal.'

The ever-professional Gerrard left the pitch without fuss, but the Liverpool bench and the away end support were much less charitable. It ended up being a tough old game for me; the score-line stayed at 1-0, Dalglish's men were knocked out of the cup and, yet again, my name was mud on Merseyside.

The storm continued to rage after the match, too. Liverpool defender Ryan Babel, clearly upset with my performance, took to Twitter to post a mocked-up image that depicted me wearing a Manchester United shirt, with the message 'And they call him one of the best referees. That's a joke.' It went viral on social media, attracting thousands of retweets.

I know it was probably meant as a daft prank – and, to be fair, Babel did issue an apology later – but my heart sank when I saw it. Images like this served only to tarnish my integrity and impartiality, two things that I held most dearly as a referee. The FA recognised that Babel had overstepped the mark, though, and subsequently charged him with improper conduct, issuing him with a £10,000 fine. I gather this Twitter-related reprimand was the first case of its kind in English football.

It was around the same time that other photoshopped images began to circulate, all poking fun at my supposed penchant for Manchester United. Me sharing pillow talk with Alex Ferguson, me celebrating wildly with United players, me holding a Red Devils' scarf. Someone even took the trouble to doctor a family photograph, replacing my wife and kids' faces with four mini-Fergies. At the time I felt really uneasy at the message they were conveying, but nowadays I tend to take them with a pinch of salt. A few of them even make me laugh.

The 2010–11 campaign turned out to be my most problematic season as a referee, not just in the Premier League, but in the Champions League too. The Spain v Holland final in South Africa had undoubtedly had its ramifications, with my confidence, my self-belief and my reputation all taking a knock in the aftermath. My elevated professional status brought with it prestige, undeniably, but it also burdened me with a heavy weight of expectation.

'Ah, it's yer man Webb from the World Cup,' you'd hear – and sometimes worse – when you trotted out of the tunnel.

As usual I'd been appointed to three Champions League group stage matches that season – and I reckoned they'd gone OK, albeit nothing special. As such, I was somewhat surprised when, during a UEFA elite course in Cyprus in early 2011, chief refereeing officer Pierluigi Collina pulled me into a side office. David Elleray – himself a UEFA committee member – was sitting next to him.

'Howard. Let me give you some advice. You've got to get back to basics,' said the Italian, proceeding to tell me how, the previous month, he'd watched me officiate an Everton v Chelsea FA Cup tie. 'Your interaction with the players was all wrong,' he continued, as David sat there quietly. 'You were too tactile, too demonstrative. Some of your gestures were over-dramatic. It just didn't seem to be the old Howard Webb out there.'

Collina was clearly implying that I'd become a bit 'big time'. While I valued his opinion and respected his judgement – he was one of my refereeing idols, after all – on this occasion his criticism jarred with me, as I thought he was being unduly harsh. While I was the first to concede that the World Cup had undoubtedly changed the way I was perceived, and that I wasn't having the greatest of seasons, I hadn't noticed a huge change in my interaction and communication. I certainly didn't recognise myself as the referee he was describing. Perhaps, for my own good, he was trying to rein me in a little, clip my wings, bring me back down to earth after my eminent year at refereeing's summit.

I found myself at a really low ebb after the meeting, having been slated by one of the world's finest referees while David had remained tight-lipped. *I'll bloody show them*, I thought.

Then, as it happened, a Champions League opportunity arose, providing me with the perfect chance to prove my worth to any doubters. Martin Atkinson had been due to oversee the round of 16 game between Shakhtar Donetsk and Roma on Tuesday 8 March, but had fallen ill the day before. I'd been at Doncaster swimming baths with Jack when the FA had called, requesting that I fly over to Ukraine early the next morning.

But guess what; I botched up the match. It was a complete disaster. I managed the game badly throughout and, to compound matters, missed an off-the-ball elbowing incident by Daniele De Rossi on Darijo Srna. As I traipsed off the pitch, Shakhtar's referee liaison officer, my ex-colleague Luboš Michel, ambled over.

'It must be difficult for you, Howard, carrying the label of World Cup final referee,' he said.

Unsurprisingly, I wasn't appointed to another Champions League game that season. It was the bitterest pill for me to swallow. To have experienced the heady heights of 2010, but not to have progressed past the last sixteen the following year, said everything about my change in fortunes. At one point I questioned whether I should even carry on with refereeing – perhaps I should have just quit after 2010, I pondered – but, thanks to help and advice from friends and family (and some great sport psychology support from Professor Ian Maynard at Sheffield

Hallam University) I decided to get my act together and haul myself out of this rut.

Being surrounded by inspirational colleagues, some of whom had suffered adversity themselves, helped to spur me on. This included my colleague Sian Massey, a talented assistant referee who occasionally worked alongside me, often deputising for Darren or Mike. In January 2011, she'd unwittingly become embroiled in a sexism scandal involving Sky Sports' Richard Keys and Andy Gray. Sian had been appointed to a Wolves v Liverpool game at Molineux, and the presenters' ridiculous off-air barbs about female officials 'not knowing the offside rule' – as well as chauvinistic comments about West Ham chief executive Karren Brady – had led to their dismissal from the broadcaster.

She found herself thrust into the spotlight and, for her own safety and well-being – and to avoid a media circus on the touch-line – the PGMOL withdrew her from Premier League matches for a few weeks. Sian's comeback game turned out to be Blackpool v Aston Villa on Saturday 12 February, which I happened to be reffing.

'You OK?' I asked, as we walked past the photographers camped outside the players' entrance. She was a tough cookie – her steely nature had helped her rise through the ranks – but she'd definitely been taken aback by all the media attention.

'I'm fine, Howard,' she replied. 'I just want to get this game over and done with.'

Fair play to her; she did brilliantly that afternoon. It was quite interesting to see some players' reactions towards her during the match, though. One lad, having been penalised for offside, legged it over to berate the assistant, as they tended to do. Once he realised it was Sian, however, he stopped dead in his tracks. Then, following a quick about-turn, the cheeky bastard decided to give me a mouthful instead.

'That was never offside, ref! Unbelievable!'

My efforts to deflect attention away from Sian even stretched to having a totally shite performance in the middle. Well, that was my excuse when the assessor came knocking, anyway.

Aside from my trials and tribulations in the Premier League, it was nice to receive some recognition from other quarters. In February I was granted the Freedom of the Borough of Rotherham for my contribution to football and my work with local charities. Then, a couple of months later, Darren, Mike and I were delighted to be honoured with the Professional Footballers' Association's Merit Award.

Prior to our presentation at the PFA's annual awards ceremony – hosted at the Grosvenor House Hotel – a video montage was shown on the big screen, with the likes of Jack Taylor and José Mourinho paying tribute to us. David Elleray featured, too.

'Howard and his team of Darren Cann and *particularly* Mike Mullarkey excelled at the World Cup,' said David.

I found this over-emphasis a bit odd. Granted, Mike had enjoyed a great tournament – he hadn't put a foot wrong – but neither had Darren, who'd been simply outstanding throughout.

Despite that, it was a great night that lasted well into the early hours. At one point I found myself talking to a twenty-something lad about football, or as best as I could after eight pints of lager. In the course of our chat, he mentioned that I might have heard of his dad, since he worked in sport media.

'Yeah?' I replied. 'Who is he?'

'Alan Green. The football commentator.'

Oh, I'd heard of Alan all right. He'd always been a bit of an acquired taste for us referees, shall we say, and had been known to frequently scold me over BBC 5 Live's airwaves.

'Haaaaaaard Webb's having a shocker,' he'd declare in his broad Belfast tones.

By about 4 a.m., and after a couple more beers, me and Green junior were absolutely rat-arsed. For some reason he suggested that I give his father a call. *Don't bother, mate*, I thought. *He's not exactly going to be very happy about being woken up at dawn, is he?* Green Junior was insistent, though.

'Hey Dad, I've got someone who wants to speak to you,' he grinned, thrusting his mobile into my hand.

'Hello? Hello? Who's that?' croaked a groggy, grumpy voice.

'Top of the morning, Alan,' I slurred in a mangled Northern Irish accent.

'It's Haaaaaaard Webb here. I've had a shocker ...'

I proceeded to dissolve into gales of laughter before handing the phone back to his son.

Alan, I'd like to apologise now for the rude awakening. You have indeed slagged me off countless times – sometimes justified, sometimes not – but maybe you didn't deserve that.

Maybe.

A much more genteel visit to London took place a few weeks later. On Wednesday 11 May 2011, with Kay and my three children in tow, I travelled from Rotherham to Buckingham Palace to receive my MBE from HRH The Prince of Wales. My name had been among those announced in the Queen's New Year's honours list, and I was absolutely thrilled to be nominated, as were my family.

'My son, a Member of the British Empire,' said Mum. 'We're so pleased for you, Howard ...'

Putting a slight dampener on the proceedings, however, was the fact that my loyal assistants, Darren and Mike, had been overlooked on this occasion. My decision to gratefully accept my MBE had also meant that I'd reneged on my vow made in South

Africa to only take up an honour as part of 'the team'. While my two pals said they understood my reasons – once I'd opened the letter from Buckingham Palace I'd felt unable to refuse – deep down I knew they were disappointed in me. And, to be honest, I think they had every right to be.

On the day itself, I'd arrived at the Palace at 10 a.m. Once I'd been drilled in all the royal protocol, I sat in an ante room with a hundred other people, waiting to be called up.

The announcement of 'Howard Webb, for services to football …' was my cue to walk over for my audience with the Prince, who'd then present me with my medal.

'They tell me you're a football referee,' said Prince Charles as I stood nervously before him.

'So what's that like, then? Must be jolly tough for you gents.'

'Indeed it is, Sir,' I said. 'Very tough indeed. But it's a job I love and enjoy very much.'

'We should be extremely grateful for all the work that you do,' he continued. 'Let's hope many more people get involved. Very well done.'

Then he extended his hand for me to shake, which was the signal for me to make a sharp exit. I got the distinct impression that His Royal Highness – not known for his ardent football support – had believed I was a local referee, who'd perhaps been nominated for dedication and long service. But hey, that was completely fine with me.

Later that year, in October, I oversaw the Greece v Croatia European Championships qualifier at the Olympiakos Stadium near Athens. Travelling with me were Peter Kirkup and Jake Collin as my assistant referees.

Jake, a Scouser, was a lovely lad and a brilliant linesman. He was, however, a slightly gullible type who'd often be the butt of our jokes, particularly if chief prankster Mike Dean was on the scene. Once, when we were officiating in the French city of Lille, Mike had mischievously informed Jake that we'd all been handed a free €100 voucher for the club shop.

'Buy what you want,' he'd said, and Jake had duly filled up a basket with loads of Lille FC stuff that he'd have never normally bought in a million years: T-shirts, tea towels, aprons and the like. Mike had then kindly offered him his own (non-existent) voucher too, which prompted Jake to embark on an in-store trolley dash, grabbing all sorts of crap off the shelves, key rings, paperweights, fridge magnets, everything.

'That's €199,95, monsieur, 'ow would you like to pay?' asked the cashier when he reached the till, Jake's Lille FC clobber almost toppling over the side of his trolley. At that very moment he clocked us outside the shop, saw that we were crying with laughter, and sussed that he'd been hoodwinked.

'I'm ever so sorry, Madame, but I've forgotten my pin number,' he said to the cashier, before abandoning his trolley and storming over, red-faced, to give us a piece of his mind.

We'd also pull Jake's leg about his fellow linesman, Peter Kirkup. Pete had gained the nickname 'Rev' due to his vicar-like demeanour. I've no idea if Pete was religious or not, but he was a strait-laced, clean-living bloke who rarely swore and who swerved alcohol. Jake had convinced himself that Pete was a bona fide man of God, though, and would often grill him about his unconventional double life.

'So how d'you manage to fit in your Sunday reffing with your church services, Rev?' he'd ask, as me and the other officials stifled our giggles.

Pete happily joined in all the ribbing and would often wind up our colleague during our trips to Europe.

'Jake, my child,' he'd say, pressing his palms together in prayer, 'I'm just going to venture into this church to say a few holy words for tonight's match, and to ask the Lord to protect us from dodgy offsides.'

We'd then all wait outside as Pete – who worked for Barclaycard in Northampton – lounged in a pew and idly checked his emails for five minutes.

'My prayers are done,' he'd say as he walked back out, before looking skywards. 'God has blessed you, Jake, and will be looking down upon you as you run the line tonight.'

So, when Jake was in the Olympiakos stadium that October evening, just minutes after kick-off, shouting 'HOWARD, HOWARD, THERE'S A MAN ON FIRE,' down my earpiece, you could have perhaps forgiven me for being sceptical.

*Somebody's winding him up again*, I thought. *Either that or he's got the wrong end of the stick.*

But then I looked across to him and, sure enough, there was a man engulfed in flames in the stand behind him. The Greek and Croatian fans had evidently been attacking each other – Molotov cocktails and plastic seats had gone flying – and this bloke had copped the worst of it. Naturally, I stopped the game immediately. This was a grave situation and, as far as I was concerned, the match was heading for an abandonment.

The coaching staff were having none of that, though. Their reaction, including that of Croatia boss Slaven Bilić, was impassive. This kind of disruption was pretty commonplace in this part of the world, I was told, and there was absolutely no need to call the game off.

Worryingly, the players then began brawling – I think both teams were fearful they'd have to forfeit the game to their opponents – and it all got a bit too feverish for my liking. I herded my assistants into the tunnel while the police regained control in the stadium, and crossed my fingers that the poor fella in the stands was receiving the right treatment.

'OK, we begin again,' came the message from the stadium officials ten minutes later and, after everyone had piled back on to the pitch, we kicked off for a second time. For the remaining 90 minutes I was absolutely shitting myself, worried that one dodgy decision could spark off more aggro in the stands. Never before had I felt more nervous in an overseas game but, as it turned out, I officiated it well (as did Jake and Pete on the sidelines). I had to dole out nine yellows, and had to fight hard to maintain control, but I managed to get through it. Greece won 2-0, although the football seemed secondary that night.

As the 2011–12 season reached its midpoint, Manchester City had hit a great vein of form and were pushing for their first league title in over four decades.

On Sunday 22 January I'd refereed their home game against Spurs, a superb 90 minutes of football that had been decided by a last-gasp penalty. Ledley King had fouled Mario Balotelli, and the flamboyant Italian had blasted in the spot-kick to make it 3-2.

I'd already had a few run-ins with Spurs that season. White Hart Lane was one of my favourite venues – the stadium was fabulous, as were the staff – but it had been the location of some controversial decisions on my part. I don't think assistant manager Joe Jordan was a member of my fan club, something he made abundantly clear once I'd drawn proceedings to a close at the Etihad that afternoon.

'You better be fuckin' right with that penalty, Mr Webb,' growled the Scot menacingly as I passed the Spurs dugout. 'You've done enough fuckin' damage to this club already ...'

TV replays confirmed that I'd got the penalty right. However, they also showed that Balotelli shouldn't have been on the pitch to take it in the first place. Footage revealed that, in the 83rd minute, he'd clashed with Scott Parker and had back-heeled the Spurs captain's head while he was on the floor. I was close to the incident, admittedly – and subsequent photos suggested it had been in my eyeline – but I genuinely hadn't spotted it. Had I done so, the Italian would have unquestionably received his marching orders.

As I expected, the FA contacted me after I'd submitted my official match report, asking me to clarify whether my team had seen the incident and, if so, whether we'd made a judgement at the time. Having answered 'no' on both counts, I was then obliged to watch a video of the offence before outlining the action I would have taken.

I confirmed to the FA that I'd not seen the stamp on Parker but, having viewed the clip, I would have shown Balotelli a red card. This triggered a retrospective investigation, which saw City's striker being charged with violent conduct and being handed a four-match ban. (Incidentally, contrary to allegations made by ex-referee Mark Halsey regarding his own career, the PGMOL never once pressured me to lie in these circumstances.)

Balotelli's agent, Mino Raiola, went berserk when the FA finally meted out their punishment to the player, labelling me a coward and a cheat and blaming me for his client's predicament. He accused me of trying to cover my tracks, alleging that I'd clearly seen the incident and had failed to admit that I'd misread it. While he wasn't pleading Balotelli's innocence, he was in effect querying my competency and integrity, claiming that the player wouldn't have been punished had I admitted to an error.

'If he had not changed his mind, the television proof would not have been enough,' raged Raiola. 'I'm really mad, and I think the Football Association should send this referee to the optician.'

All this rumbled on in the media for a couple of days – I

received a proper mauling in some newspapers – yet I wasn't allowed to comment to the press, and no one from the FA or the PGMOL had come out to support me publicly. My wife rarely interfered in work-related matters, but she was so angered by this chain of events that she felt compelled to ring Mike Riley.

'Mike, can you please tell me why no one at the PGMOL is speaking up for my husband?' Kay demanded. 'This agent bloke is telling all and sundry that Howard should be banned from ref-ereeing for life, yet he can't defend himself. It's just not fair. I'm not having it.'

It was FA chairman David Bernstein who finally released a statement.

'We all have a duty to respect our referees. To question their integrity or imply anything other than total impartiality is reck-less and unfounded,' he said. 'It harms the perception and treatment of referees at every level of football, and we must not allow that climate to exist.'

The FA Cup fifth-round tie between Tottenham Hotspur and Bolton Wanderers, broadcast live by ESPN, took place at 5.30 p.m. on Saturday 17 March 2012. I was the man in the middle that evening – Mike Mullarkey and Peter Kirkup were my assis-tants – and a chilly White Hart Lane was buzzing with cup fever.

The visitors took an early lead courtesy of a Gareth Bale own goal – the ball had hit his shoulder and flown past Carlo Cudicini – but, on the 11-minute mark, Spurs clawed back an equaliser through a Kyle Walker header. A lively half-hour ensued, with Harry Redknapp's boys dominating the play while Bolton did their damnedest to hang on until the interval.

Around the 40-minute mark I awarded a throw-in to Bolton, on the far side from the technical area, near the corner flag. As I turned to make the signal I looked to my left, and saw, towards the halfway line, Bolton defender Fabrice Muamba lying face down on the pitch. My first impulse – I'll be honest – was to look for signs that he'd been hit by another player. The nearest person to him, Spurs' Luka Modrić, was a good five yards away though, and appeared as bemused as I did.

Then I saw Muamba's body starting to convulse, and my blood ran cold. I sprinted towards him and, as I signalled furiously to the medical team, Bolton physio Andy Mitchell was already tearing on to the pitch, closely followed by the club doctor, Jonathan Tobin.

For a minute or so there were a few random jeers from the home fans – the usual reaction when a player goes down – but when the doctor suddenly kneeled over Muamba, turned him on to his back and ripped open his shirt, everyone in the stadium realised that something was dreadfully wrong. As the doc meshed his hands together and began to pump his chest, White Hart Lane was stunned into silence.

As a copper I'd attended many emergencies, and had often witnessed paramedics giving CPR to people who'd collapsed in the street. Indeed, you fully expected to see such incidents when you worked on the front line of the police force. This, however, was completely different. This was totally unforeseen. This was a young, healthy professional athlete who appeared to be losing his life on a football pitch, before our very eyes.

The Spurs medical team soon entered the fray, sharing the CPR duties and helping to administer the defibrillator shocks. I also noticed a guy in normal clothing running on from the far side of the ground who, as luck would have it, was a Spurs-supporting cardiologist, Dr Andrew Deaner. A distraught Owen Coyle wandered on to the pitch, too, asking if he could monitor the situation.

'Of course, Owen, he's your player,' I said, ushering him forward.

Muamba's life was clearly in the hands of the medics who, for the next seven minutes – and under extreme pressure – continued their life-saving procedures in front of 40,000 stunned football fans. Within the stadium you could sense an upsurge of collective willpower to get the poor lad's heart beating again.

'Come on, Fabrice, come on ...' yelled anxious voices from the stands. The Bolton supporters also started up a rousing chant of 'Fabrice Muamba, Fabrice Muamba', which rippled through to the Spurs fans and, within moments, was loudly ringing around the entire ground.

As the match official I had a duty of care for the other players on the field, so I made a point of checking that they were OK. Some were standing within yards of Muamba, keeping a nervous eye on proceedings. Others were sitting on the perimeter fence, looking subdued, quietly chatting with teammates. A few were crouching down on the turf, averting their eyes, visibly upset.

The general consensus from the players was that they wanted to stay on the pitch rather than head for the dressing room. I completely understood; had it been a member of my team whose life was in danger, I'd have certainly preferred to have been in the vicinity.

The doctors were still frantically working on Fabrice while they carried him off the field, through the tunnel and towards a waiting ambulance. The White Hart Lane crowd gave them a standing ovation as they left the stadium. Thanks to the intervention of Dr Deaner, the player was whisked to a specialist heart centre – the London Chest Hospital in Bethnal Green – in the hope that he'd be able to receive the best possible care.

'What's going to happen now, H?' a red-eyed Scott Parker

asked as the players and coaching staff amassed near the dugout. 'Shall we call it half-time?'

I explained to the Spurs captain that the laws didn't allow me to shorten the half as such, but that we should all to go back to the dressing rooms, gather ourselves together, and assess the situation.

'We'll try and get a prognosis regarding Fabrice, Scott, and then maybe we can make some kind of decision.'

I then took Owen Coyle and Harry Redknapp to one side, suggesting that they took a brief time-out with their players before returning to my room so we could work out what to do next. Within two minutes, however, Harry was tapping on the door.

'There's no way we can restart this game, Howard,' he said. 'My players are distraught, and half of them are already getting showered. They don't want to play any more football today.'

Owen agreed, and the match was abandoned. The subsequent stadium announcement was met with nervy, muted applause from the Spurs and Bolton fans.

I was sitting in the dressing room, reflecting on these alarming events with my assistants, when in walked Dad. He was with the match assessor, Ian Blanchard, and had been overcome with emotion during Muamba's ordeal. He'd got himself into a bit of a state, by all accounts, and was in need of some comfort.

'That poor lad,' he said, gulping down sobs as I gave him a hug. 'I hope to God he pulls through.'

For a good hour or so, no one really knew the extent of Fabrice's condition – at one point rumours circulated that he'd actually died – and Dad and I left White Hart Lane none the wiser.

We listened to BBC 5 Live as we drove home – I remember Rotherham United manager Andy Scott being interviewed about his own heart-related problems – and it all felt very surreal. Midway through our journey we stopped at a service station on the M1, chatting with some tearful Bolton fans and watching a TV news bulletin summarising Muamba's fight for life.

Deep down, I honestly didn't expect him to pull through. He'd lain unconscious for so long on the pitch – and had spent 78 minutes without a natural heartbeat, I later discovered – and I just had a grim feeling about it all. So, when I awoke the next morning to find that he was still clinging on to life, and discovered the next day that he'd regained consciousness, I felt absolutely elated.

Fabrice Muamba's miraculous recovery was lauded throughout the sporting world although, following medical advice, he had no option but to retire from the game he loved. Football, however, had effectively saved his life. With the presence of highly qualified medical staff, with ambulances on standby and with a specialist hospital in the vicinity, White Hart Lane had turned out to be one of the safest places for Muamba to have suffered his cardiac arrest. Had he passed out in a restaurant, for example, or a shopping centre, he may not have survived.

The whole experience had a profound effect on me as a person, and it changed the way I reffed, too. If I ever saw a player lying on the deck – even if I suspected he was conning me – I never took a chance, and always stopped the game. If any opponents gave me stick for doing so, I'd soon put them straight.

'I was at White Hart Lane when Fabrice Muamba collapsed,' I'd hiss, which usually shut them up.

A few months later, Dr Jonathan Tobin and I attended a FIFA medical congress in Budapest to discuss our own experiences of sudden cardiac arrest on a football pitch. My advice to the attending coaches and club representatives was to be ever-aware that serious, life-threatening events could happen on the field of play, at any time, with any footballer. They needed to be vigilant and know what signs to look out for, whether it was during a training session or on a match day.

I then went on to outline how players who persistently feigned injury could be particularly worrisome in this context, and needed to curb their actions.

'A lad who often cries wolf may find he's ignored when he genuinely needs help, and that could be catastrophic,' I explained. 'As we saw ourselves with Fabrice Muamba, getting swift medical attention in those first moments can be the difference between life and death.'

The Premier League title race was nearing a fascinating climax in May 2012. It had become a straight battle between the reigning champions and the noisy neighbours, with Sir Alex Ferguson's Manchester United and Roberto Mancini's Manchester City both vying for the top honour.

I was appointed to the Blues' away fixture at Newcastle United on Sunday 6 May. It had been at St James' Park, in May 1968, that City had sealed their last league title, beating the Magpies 4-3. Fast-forward 44 years, and another victory would allow them to steal a march on their cross-town rivals and bring them closer to the prize that had eluded them for so long.

I felt the pressure mounting as the match loomed. It was such a pivotal fixture – an absolute must-win for City – and any mistake on my part would potentially have huge consequences for the title. Add into the mix some press speculation that the visitors weren't happy with my involvement – yep, the usual 'United fan' crap – and I was feeling more jittery than usual.

My nerves faded as I crossed the white line, though, and I was determined to do a good job for both sides. The game started briskly, with City dominating much of the play, but it wasn't until

Mancini's inspired 62nd-minute substitution that they were able to finally break the deadlock. Nigel de Jong – my karate-kicking nemesis from the 2010 World Cup – came on to replace Samir Nasri, allowing Yaya Touré to push up into a more advanced position. The Ivorian proceeded to steal the show, scoring two crucial goals and keeping City's title hopes alive. As the Blues' fans went crazy in the away end, I walked towards the tunnel, thoroughly relieved that there'd been no controversy to mar such an important game.

The following Sunday – the final match of the campaign – saw me in the thick of it once again, as I'd been designated to referee Sunderland v Manchester United at the Stadium of Light. The permutations were simple. Although both sides were level on 86 points, City's superior goal difference meant that, if they were to defeat relegation-threatened QPR at the Etihad – a foregone conclusion for many – they'd be Premier League champions. If United happened to win or draw, and City lost, the Reds would snatch the trophy from under their neighbours' noses.

Wayne Rooney grabbed an early goal to get United on to the scoresheet and, as play continued, fourth official Lee Probert was relaying snippets of news from the Etihad. These earpiece updates had limited bearing on the game we were officiating – it was win, draw or bust for United – but, like every other football fan in the country, we were gripped by the unfolding drama and wanted to be kept in the loop.

First, we heard that City had taken a one-goal lead. Then QPR equalised and, 20 minutes later, had nicked a second. Joey Barton got himself sent off for the visitors, and Edin Džeko had pulled one back for City. Proper roller-coaster stuff.

The United bench was passing on similar information to their players too but, with minutes to go, Ryan Giggs jogged past me.

'Is it still 2–2?' he asked.

'Think so,' I replied, 'although Barton's been sent off.'

If looks could kill I'd have been a goner.

'Fucking Barton,' growled Giggs, his eyes blazing. 'He's going to cost us the title.'

Moments later I blew the full-time whistle and, unaware of the final score at the Etihad, the Manchester United players anxiously loitered near the dugout, unsure what to do with themselves. There were some muted celebrations among the United fans, but no one dared conga through the aisles until their rivals' result had been confirmed.

Then, suddenly, MANCHESTER CITY 3, QPR 2 flashed up on the big screen at the Stadium of Light followed, ten seconds later, by the words MANCHESTER CITY CHAMPIONS. A last-gasp goal from Sergio Agüero had clinched the title for City in the most dramatic fashion imaginable. The despair among the Reds' fans and players was palpable; you could hear the collective gasp radiating from the away end. The Sunderland supporters, on the other hand, were celebrating like they'd won the title themselves, singing, dancing and partying in the stands.

'Astonishing,' I said to Darren as we walked off the pitch, passing a disconsolate United team as they wearily applauded the shell-shocked travelling support.

In truth, I was happy enough that Manchester City had won the title. They'd played the most exciting football that season, in my opinion, and had fully deserved the top honours. I'm sure there were many other neutrals who were pleased to see a different set of ribbons dangling from the Premier League trophy that May.

Happily, my 2011–12 season ended on a high. I was appointed to referee the Championship play-off final between Blackpool and West Ham, otherwise known as The Most Expensive Game In The World. The match – which West Ham won 2-1 – completed my domestic refereeing grand slam, adding to my League

Cup, FA Cup and Community Shield appointments. The officials and our families celebrated a hassle-free performance with a slap-up Italian meal at the Ristorante Belvedere in Ealing, a favoured post-Wembley eaterie.

After dessert we gathered round the TV to watch the Champions League final between Chelsea and Bayern Munich, Roberto Di Matteo's Blues winning the nail-biting penalty shoot-out courtesy of Didier Drogba's decisive spot-kick.

I sat in the restaurant, beer in hand, feeling pleased with the way my campaign had ended. I hoped that the good times would continue to roll through to June, when the 2012 European Championships were due to take place.

# CHAPTER 10

# If Anyone Can, Darren Cann

It goes without saying that top refs rely on great wingmen, and for that reason I'd always counted myself lucky that my career collided with Darren Cann's and Mike Mullarkey's. They were simply the best assistant referees in the business, and I'd never have achieved my ambitions without their presence on the touchline. To put their expertise in context, in six games spanning two World Cups, Darren and Mike didn't get a single decision wrong. Not one. Their judgement was impeccable.

When I was in the Select Group, Mike was well on his way to becoming the most decorated UK match official of all time (he'd attended more top tournaments than any of his colleagues) and Darren, as many refs would testify, was probably the finest specialist linesman in Europe, if not the world.

Over a seven-year period I worked with Darren on over 200 occasions, and he rarely made a bad call. He had a great understanding of the game – he'd been on Crystal Palace's books as a young player – and I always valued his opinion above anyone else's. Along with his prowess on the line, he had this instinctive understanding of a footballer's psyche, too; he just seemed to know how they ticked, what they thought and why they reacted.

I relished working with assistants whose judgement you could trust implicitly, and whose degree of certainty was so high. It was Darren who gave me the impetus to send off Emmanuel Adebayor in a 2012 north London derby, ordering me to flash the red card instead of dithering over the extent of contact.

During a Champions League game between AC Milan and Ajax, it was Canny's brilliant awareness, not mine, that pinpointed a leg-breaker of a challenge from Ricardo Montolivo that led to his rightful dismissal. Prior to my assistant's timely intervention, I wouldn't have even been reaching for the yellow.

It was also Darren who alerted me to the fact that I'd forgotten to dismiss Manchester United's Nemanja Vidić after two cautions, the kind of catastrophic mistake that would not only get you laughed off a football pitch, but could also have serious consequences for your career.

'Second yellow, second yellow, Howard, GET HIM OFF!' he yelled in his Norfolk twang, saving my bacon for the umpteenth time. While he panicked down the radio, I maintained a poker face, feigned an air of control, and brandished the red as if I knew exactly what I was doing.

I used to compare our working relationship to the old 1970s cartoon, *Hong Kong Phooey*. The canine lead character would often get the credit for solving a crime when, in reality, it was his trusty sidekick, Spot the Cat, who'd actually cracked the case.

Darren wasn't everybody's cup of tea, though. He could be a very intense, single-minded person – both on and off the pitch – and wasn't afraid of intervening when he felt his input would help. No matter which referee he worked with, he liked to play his part, speaking over the communication system where necessary, alerting his team to hazards and assisting in their decisions.

To some, like me, this was a huge bonus, but to others it was seen as interference. The more orthodox referees frowned upon this level of intervention. They liked to take full control of their games, preferring their linesmen to be seen and not heard. 'Assist, don't insist,' one former ref would often say. However, I took a different view. When top quality assistants like Darren or Mike had seen with certainty what needed to be done, I'd be quite happy for them to insist I make a particular decision, as this would often save my skin.

In fact, the newer breed of officials took the view that modern-day refereeing required a full team effort. Most were delighted to have Darren by their side: 'If anyone can, Darren Cann!' Mike Dean would grin when yet another razor-sharp offside decision was flagged up during a Select Group video session.

However, for reasons which I still find hard to fathom, senior figures took umbrage with Darren and did their utmost to undermine him. He'd be strategically placed at the far end of our annual international match officials team photo, for instance, whereas Mike and I would be afforded prime spots near the centre. At FA lunches, Darren would be shoved towards the end of the table with the more junior officials, while we'd be placed among the VIPs. All this blatant sidelining – verging on bullying, if you ask me – must have left Darren feeling hurt and humiliated, although he retained his professionalism throughout and continued to deliver consistently brilliant performances both domestically and internationally.

Things came to a dramatic head in December 2011, when Darren was abruptly withdrawn from my team for the 2012 European Championships. Despite his high level of performance the FA had opted to replace him with Peter 'Rev' Kirkup, who was to join Mike as my assistant, alongside Mark Clattenburg and Martin Atkinson as my goal-line additional assistant referees.

Darren was devastated – we spoke for hours on the phone afterwards – and I suddenly found myself in a quandary. Pete was a great bloke, and an excellent assistant, and had every right to be assigned to a prestigious tournament. However, my long-time pal and confidant – and a key member of my officiating team – had been unfairly dumped on.

Stuck between a rock and a hard place, I didn't know whether to kick up a stink and demand Darren's reinstatement, or to let things stand and allow Pete his day in the sun. After giving it some serious thought, I decided to go with the flow.

In hindsight, I made the wrong call. My loyalties should have lain with Darren, who'd helped propel my career to the top and who'd covered my backside on so many occasions. I should have stuck my head above the parapet and confronted the FA, delivering an 'all for one, and one for all' ultimatum. But, fearful that they'd see me as a troublemaker and make things difficult for me, I selfishly kept my trap shut. In the world of refereeing, you were very much in the hands of others in terms of appointments and opportunities, and I was acutely aware of that.

Looking back, it was an odd state of affairs. Here was I, an elite referee with a World Cup final medal to my name, yet I still lacked the confidence and conviction to challenge the big cheeses and stick up for my mate. It was something I'd always regret.

Jointly hosted by Poland and Ukraine, the 2012 European Championships proved to be one of the least controversial and most enjoyable tournaments of my career. No racism claims. No death threats. No armed guards. No bomb scares. And no karate kicks.

Also, of the twelve referees who'd been selected for Euro 2008, I was the only one making a return, as all the others had all since retired. In the space of four years I'd gone from inexperienced rookie to elder statesman.

Mindful of my controversy-mired experience at the previous Championships, I was pretty apprehensive about showing my face in Poland again. Unsure as to whether Howard 'English Bastard' Webb was still Wanted, Dead or Alive, I donned a cap-and-shades disguise when I paid my first visit to Warsaw city centre. I soon realised it was unwarranted, though, since the Polish supporters who recognised me were charming and magnanimous. The grudges had faded away, the water had passed under the bridge, and I was able to breathe a huge sigh of relief.

Mike, Pete and I were delighted to be handed a high-profile game on the opening day of the tournament. Russia v Czech Republic, in Wrocław's Stadion Miejski, turned out to be an even-tempered, trouble-free match without a single caution. UEFA's top dogs were delighted, apparently. Our game had come hot on the heels of a fiery Poland v Greece curtain-raiser which, following two red cards, had made everyone a bit twitchy.

I received some nice texts from friends and family back home, too, including one from former Glasgow Rangers and Birmingham City boss Alex McLeish.

'Now that's the way to referee a game, big man,' he said.

Our next appointment, Italy v Croatia in Poznań, wasn't so mellow. A volatile game, played in a full-blooded, southern European style, eventually finished one apiece. Martin Atkinson and Mark Clattenburg were fantastic behind the goals that day, and I remember feeling so lucky to have two such amazingly experienced officials in my corner.

Naysayers often moaned that these wand-bearing 'additionals' were surplus to requirements ('they're just freeloaders on city breaks', I once overheard), but I personally found them invaluable. Their extra support gave me an added safety net and allowed my officiating team to share the responsibility, particularly in and around the penalty area.

'Don't watch the ball; leave that to your additional,' UEFA referee coaches would implore. 'You can't afford to miss a push or an elbow if you're all ball-watching. Utilise your team. Spread your eyes around.'

Clattenburg's performance that day was so good – he'd made an excellent call for a defensive free kick – that UEFA would use the video footage to highlight the value of these newly created but much-maligned roles.

In contrast, however, Pete's performance on the touchline hadn't been without error. Back in the dressing room, I'd noticed him checking his phone, whispering to Mike and looking downcast. Later that evening, when we reviewed the game, the reasons behind Pete's demeanour became apparent. In the space of ten minutes, he'd mistakenly flagged for three offsides, all of which had gone against the Italians. They were tight, and they were marginal, but they were wrong.

Our collective spirit sagged as we watched all this unfold. UEFA weren't going to be impressed and, as a result, the likelihood of us being sent home early had probably increased.

'Mate, it happens to us all,' I assured my dejected linesman. As much as I liked and respected Pete, though, I couldn't help but think that Darren wouldn't have slipped up in that manner.

On the morning of the quarter-final announcement – which coincided with the first round of referee eliminations – I was summoned to see David Elleray in his guise as a UEFA committee member. I'd braced myself for the old heave-ho, so was utterly taken aback when he instead shook my hand and congratulated me on being retained.

'You've been allocated to Portugal versus Czech Republic in Warsaw, Howard, so well done,' he smiled. 'But it's not all good news, I'm afraid,' he continued. 'Unfortunately, Peter won't be working with you. After what happened in Poznań, we've decided it would be best to send him home.'

*Shit.*

I sprinted back to my hotel room, whereupon Mike and I discussed how we were going to tell our colleague. The officials' appointments were due to be announced within the hour, and we knew we had to inform him personally before UEFA did so publicly. I broke the news to him as gently as I could, but he was completely distraught. I felt awful. We'd all made mistakes in our careers – me more than most, perhaps – and maybe I should have argued Rev's case more forcefully with David. That said, I knew it was a foregone conclusion, and I knew that nothing I'd have said would have changed matters. And, unpalatable though it may sound, I was desperate for our team to remain in the tournament. In years gone by, one false move and we'd have all been going home so, as sad as it was to see him leave, the rest of us had been given a reprieve.

Pete departed for the airport shortly after the announcement, in such an emotional state that he could barely say goodbye as he clambered into the taxi. I felt for him, I really did. Here was a thoroughly decent guy and a top-quality assistant paying the price for some marginal errors.

But the show went on. Joining us for the game in Warsaw's state-of-the-art National Stadium was Pete's replacement, Dutchman Sander van Roekel. Apart from the intensely humid conditions (the retractable roof had been closed following a slight drizzle) everything went like clockwork. The game ended in a 1-0 Portugal victory – Cristiano Ronaldo had popped up with a late winner – and I was chuffed to bits with my makeshift team's performance.

Three days later we were sitting in a local bistro, gazing up at the big-screen TV, as Italy booted England out of the tournament via the dreaded penalty shoot-out. While I was crestfallen – my heart sank when Andrea Pirlo audaciously chipped Joe Hart – at the back of my mind I also knew that England's exit might boost our chances of progression.

As things panned out, we weren't assigned to either of the Spain v Portugal or Italy v Germany semi-finals. However, shortly before they'd taken place I'd been called into a meeting with Pierluigi Collina (whose good books I appeared to be firmly back in) along with two other refs: Pedro Proença from Portugal and the Italian Nicola Rizzoli.

'One of you three will be given the final,' he declared, before explaining that certain permutations would favour each one of us.

'Pedro, Nicola, you can't referee your own countries, naturally. And Howard, we won't appoint you if Spain get through, because of all the negativity after the World Cup final.'

Cheers for the reminder, Pierluigi.

It transpired that Portugal would be key to my progression; if they were to overcome their neighbours, it looked like I'd have a good chance of overseeing the final. On the night of their semi, I left the hotel restaurant to head back to my room where I'd watch the match, purposely passing Pedro and Nicola on my way out.

'Just off to watch the game, guys,' I grinned, before whipping off my FIFA tracksuit top to reveal a pristine Portugal shirt, which had been gifted to me by their football federation following the quarter-final.

As I witnessed the game going to penalties I remember thinking *wow, this could affect my life so much*. If things were to go my way, I'd become the first ref to officiate the triumvirate of the Champions League final, the World Cup final *and* the European Championships final.

My hopes were soon dashed, sadly. Portugal made a total dog's breakfast of the shoot-out, so much so that Ronaldo didn't even get the chance to take a fifth, grandstanding spot-kick.

I had one more slice of match action to go, though. The next evening, in Warsaw, I was Stéphane Lannoy's fourth official for the semi-final between Germany v Italy, a tie in which two-goal hero Mario Balotelli gave the performance of his life, enacting his famous shirtless, musclebound pose. The Italians would go on to be crushed 4-0 by Spain in the final, however, a game refereed beautifully by my friend Pedro.

All things considered, Poland-Ukraine 2012 proved to be a roaring success, not just for me, but for officiating in general. Only three red cards were issued during a tournament vaunted as much for its high standards of refereeing as for its exemplary player behaviour.

I flew out of Warsaw on cloud nine. I think I'd managed to restore some of the reputation that had been tarnished in 2010, and I dearly hoped my career was firmly back on track.

With much of my confidence salvaged, I approached the 2012–13 Premier League season feeling upbeat and positive. It would, in fact, become the smoothest campaign of my entire domestic career. The autumn months went particularly well; games at Anfield, Upton Park and the Madjeski Stadium heralded a string of decent assessments as well as a sizeable post-match handshake quota (always a telltale sign that I'd done OK).

My first significant flashpoint occurred in late September, when I sent off Wigan Athletic's Jordi Gomez for what I'd judged to be a dangerous tackle on Danny Rose (the card would later get rescinded, which really pissed me off – it was the only red card overturned in my whole career). Latics' boss Roberto Martínez was fizzing with rage and, at full-time, stomped up the tunnel to confront me as I entered my dressing room.

'You were bought, that's your problem,' I heard him shout.

I swung round, furious. Suggesting you're corrupt is possibly the worst thing a manager can level at a referee.

'I was *bought*?' I replied, bristling with anger. 'You'd better be careful what you say, Roberto. Sounds like you're questioning my integrity.'

He looked at me, alarmed, and then the penny dropped.

'Ah, no, I didn't say you were *bought*, Howard. I said you were *bored*. This game was too boring for you. You were not focused.'

It had all gone a bit *Two Ronnies'* 'Fork Handles', but he was suggesting, I think, that this fixture was beneath me, that I'd deemed it too low profile, and that I'd lost concentration. I liked Roberto very much – he was one of the Premier League's more amiable managers – but on this occasion he was talking nonsense. I prided myself on giving every game 100 per cent and, as a passionate supporter of a smaller club, I appreciated the importance of every single game.

A few days later I jetted off to Florida for a family holiday. It was the first mid-season break I'd ever taken and, as soon as I glimpsed Orlando's azure skies and tree-lined boulevards, I knew I'd made a wise decision.

It was while wandering around the Epcot Centre one Sunday afternoon that I was accosted by a bloke clad in a Stoke City shirt.

'Hey, your mate's fucked up, hasn't he?'

I didn't have a clue what he was talking about.

'Clattenburg,' he continued. 'Been accused of racism at Chelsea.'

When we returned to the villa I went online, scrolling down reports alleging that Mark had verbally abused Jon Obi Mikel at Stamford Bridge during the Blues' game against Manchester United. Shortly afterwards the club had issued a public statement reiterating their player's claims.

'No way is Clatts guilty of that,' I said to Kay, shaking my head. 'Not in a million years.'

Following an FA-led inquiry – and having been withdrawn from the refereeing roster for four weeks – Mark was exonerated as there was simply no case to answer. A month later, a clear-the-air meeting was convened between the Select Group and the Chelsea chairman, Bruce Buck, along with Mike Riley and Premier League boss Richard Scudamore. As a group – and with the backing of our union, Prospect – we'd requested the opportunity to air our grievances. Mark and his family had gone through hell, in the full glare of the media, and we were keen to have our say.

'These were career-threatening, reputation-damaging allegations,' I levelled at Buck, 'so why did your club publicly air them before any investigation had taken place?'

A fairly lively dialogue ensued, the upshot being that Chelsea had accepted the FA's verdict, and that Mark would be rightfully restored to the referees' list later that week.

A joint statement, released after the meeting, agreed that it was 'time to draw a line under this incident', adding that Chelsea FC had regretted not giving 'more consideration before issuing a statement'.

I think Mark appreciated the support he received from his Select Group colleagues. Indeed, following the departure of some of the older refs, and the arrival of a newer, younger breed, the mood in our camp had improved markedly. Among the influx of more laid-back and easy-going referees were the likes of Michael Oliver, Anthony Taylor and Craig Pawson.

Helping to keep our spirits high was Lee Mason, our resident class joker, who entertained us with his brilliantly observed impressions of players, managers and officials. In cahoots with Jon Moss – another lively addition to our troupe – Lee would also organise the annual Christmas party at our new base at St George's Park in Staffordshire. He'd choose a different theme each year, usually opting for a quiz show format so that he could mimic Bruce *Play Your Cards Right* Forsyth or Leslie *Price Is Right* Crowther.

'Er, g-g-good game, Howard, g-g-good game,' he'd say, jutting out his chin, wielding his over-sized playing cards and reducing us all to hysterics.

My 2013-14 season got off to an interesting start, even before I'd blown a whistle in anger. At 2 p.m. on Saturday 17 August – my first game of the campaign – there came a knock on the door of the Upton Park dressing room.

Standing there were Sam Allardyce and Malky Mackay, with skippers Kevin Nolan and Craig Bellamy, ready and waiting for the West Ham-Cardiff team-sheet exchange. Bellamy looked me up and down, his expression contemptuous.

'Oh, for fuck's sake, it's Celebrity Ref.'

Such a nice turn of phrase for a Premier League captain.

'Nice to see you too, Craig,' I replied. 'Shall we start again, but this time with a little more respect?'

Bellamy had previous with me, as it happened. I'm not sure what I'd done to rile him – and I don't care, really – but, not long after the World Cup, I was acting as fourth official at Anfield and was sitting quietly on my own at the back of the technical area. Bellamy was on the bench for Liverpool that day and, midway through the first half, happened to catch sight of me sitting behind him.

'Oi you, fuckin' shithouse,' he yelled, in full earshot of everyone in both technical areas. 'You fucked up that World Cup good and proper, didn't you, eh?'

Now he may well have had a good point, but I just thought it was a pretty nasty thing to say. Not wishing to lower myself to his level with a similarly snide retort, I pretended I hadn't heard. However, I remember thinking at the time that there weren't many more obnoxious players around than Craig Bellamy.

To be honest, I was becoming increasingly weary of the flak that kept coming my way. A few weeks later I reffed Swansea v Newcastle at the Liberty Stadium. When I blew for full time I received dogs' abuse from the Magpies' coach, John Carver, because a penalty decision hadn't gone their way. I've got to know him since and like him a lot, but the stick he gave me that evening was pretty vitriolic. And then his mucker Alan Pardew came storming into the dressing room to wipe the floor with me and I remember thinking *you know what, I really don't need this*.

Later that season David Moyes, by then at Manchester United, labelled me 'a fucking disgrace' in the tunnel because I hadn't awarded Ashley Young a penalty. Moyes wasn't my favourite manager at the best of times – he appeared to have a deep loathing for refs, and would often send in his assistants to harangue us on his behalf – and if there was one insult I hated being hurled at me, it was 'disgrace'. It really got my back up. I was just a referee who tried do an honest job and who occasionally made genuine mistakes. I may have been far from perfect, but I didn't think I was a disgrace.

On the eve of a game at Stamford Bridge, in October 2013, I asked to meet up with Mike Riley at my hotel. I needed to discuss an important matter with him, something that had been playing on my mind for a number of weeks.

'As you know, mate, I'm hoping to get the nod for next year's World Cup,' I said.

'Yeah, of course,' Mike nodded, 'and there's no reason why you won't get it, Howard.'

I took a deep breath, feeling slightly nervous about what I was going to reveal.

'But if I do happen to get selected for Brazil, I think it might be my swansong. I've had enough, Mike. I want to call it a day.'

'OK,' he replied, as if he'd half-expected it. 'Can't say I'm totally surprised. Let's talk.'

Reaching this decision hadn't been easy, of course, and had been prompted by many soul-searching heart-to-hearts with my wife and my parents. But I'd come to the conclusion that I'd run my course, and that it was time for me to bow out.

Life as an elite referee had been like the proverbial roller coaster, with exhilarating highs and plummeting lows. After nearly a quarter-of-a-century in the middle, however, those dips had started to take their toll. I'd had my fill of the pressures and stresses – the grief on the pitch, the name-calling in the tunnel, the ruined weekends at home – and, deep down, I'd realised that that my passion and energy for the job was waning.

'You always promised you'd stop when you lost the love for it, son,' said Dad when we'd sat down for a chat one evening. 'All things considered, your decision's probably a sensible one.'

Wise words indeed, but his expression told me that he was saddened that my refereeing journey was nearing its end.

Age had undoubtedly been a factor, too. Technically I could have carried on officiating for another five or six seasons in the Premier League (unlike FIFA and UEFA, whose age cap was forty-five), but I didn't want to be an old man in the middle. I'd seen too many ageing referees dragging out their careers for years – perhaps beholden to their £100,000+ salary – and that had never been my intention. Finishing at the top, and choosing my own destiny and departure time, was what appealed to me.

By unburdening myself of this emotional weight, I hoped I'd be able to relax into the final stretch of my Premier League career. Sadly, I was mistaken. Desperate to end on a high, I piled the pressure on myself and almost lost the plot. Before I knew it, the domestic season began to unravel before my eyes, the catalyst being a calamitous game between Chelsea and Liverpool on Sunday 29 December 2013.

In the opening minute I'd missed a red-card tackle by Samuel Eto'o on Jordan Henderson, which had been really difficult to detect at full speed. Everything then seemed to spiral downwards. In the second half, Eto'o clipped the heels of Luis Suárez, bringing him down in the 18-yard box. Since the incident had taken place off the ball (and in my peripheral vision) I couldn't be sure how Suárez had hit the deck – or whether he was exaggerating, which he certainly had previous for – so I waved away the penalty appeal. I was wrong – very wrong – and got rightly hammered for it afterwards.

That night I went to the PDC World Darts Championships with Darren and Mike, and what was intended as a festive jaunt to Alexandra Palace became anything but. Instead of cheering on Phil Taylor and Raymond van Barneveld on the oche, I spent the night staring into the contents of my pint glass and mulling over my dismal display.

Contrary to the opinion of many Liverpool fans, I had nothing whatsoever against their club – I truly respected its supporters, its players and its heritage – but it seemed the harder I tried to referee them well, the more I failed.

'It just gets worse, Darren,' I moaned.

In February 2014 I officiated over Arsenal and Liverpool in the FA Cup fifth round. In hindsight, I should have closed that date off in my diary. I'd been in Gran Canaria for a week-long FIFA seminar and, following a long flight delay, I was completely knackered by the time I arrived at the Emirates Stadium.

I went on to have a horror show of a game, my woes culminating in the 64th minute when, with Arsenal 2-1 up, I awarded Liverpool a free kick. Having been blasted into the wall, the loose ball was picked up by Luis Suárez, only for him and Alex

Oxlade-Chamberlain to collide into each other. Well, that's how I saw it anyway. I dismissed all the penalty appeals and sanctioned a goal kick instead, much to the disgust of the Liverpool camp.

Within minutes of the final whistle, I'd received a text message from an old Rotherham refereeing colleague, Steve Pickervance, whose love for the Reds knew no bounds.

'Howard, I know you're a mate, but how you didn't give us that penalty is BEYOND BELIEF,' he stated.

*That doesn't look good,* I thought, *but he's sporting his red-tinted glasses, obviously, and he's miffed that Arsenal are through to the next round.*

The next incoming text, however, was from ITV Sport commentator Clive Tyldesley, a fair-minded bloke whose opinion I greatly respected.

'One bad decision doesn't make you a bad ref,' it said, and I thought *shit*, I've definitely cocked it up.

I went and had a shower, and I remember closing my eyes, resting my head against the wall, and not wanting to come out. *What crap am I going to face when I get outside? How badly has my reputation been damaged? Who's going to be slagging me off now?*

It was, of course, the clearest penalty I'd seen for a long time – Suárez had been fouled, no question – and prompted yet another weekend of crawling into my shell and shunning all media. I spent the next few days replaying my error over and over again in my head, wondering how I'd misread things, what I could have done differently, and why I was getting things so catastrophically wrong.

In contrast with my woeful Premier League displays, I found myself performing fantastically well on the international circuit. In the autumn of 2012, after some lobbying on my part, Darren had been reinstated as my chosen assistant referee, and the

following June our usual trio had flown over to the Confederations Cup in Brazil, a tournament often seen as the precursor to
the World Cup.

Despite temperatures hitting the mid-30s – and me suffering a
severe attack of the runs – our two games went brilliantly, including the Italy v Spain semi-final. It may have been an evening
game, but it was still swelteringly hot in Fortaleza's Estadio
Castelão. I remember Fernando Torres coming off the pitch at
half-time, mopping his brow and wearily dragging his feet.

'This heat is terrible, ref. I can hardly move,' he moaned.

'Fernando,' I replied, as the sweat oozed from every pore,
'you're from bleedin' Madrid. You should be used to this. Imagine
coming from Rotherham!'

Somehow I doubt that Fernando Torres had ever imagined
coming from Rotherham.

I performed well in Europe, too. Being away from the Premier
League bear-pit, where familiarity often bred contempt, probably
helped in this respect.

In March 2014, I was appointed to a Europa League tie
between Fiorentina and Juventus. To my surprise, as I warmed up
on the far side of the lovely old Artemio Franchi stadium in
Florence, a section of the crowd broke out into a spontaneous
round of applause.

'*Bravo, arbitro inglese, bravo!*' they yelled.

While I was aware that English refs were revered in Italy, I was
really taken aback by all these happy-clappy supporters. All the
crap that I'd been experiencing back home had left me feeling
slightly wounded, and I found it strangely touching.

The following month, I absolutely nailed the Champions
League quarter-final between Atlético Madrid and Barcelona at
the Vicente Calderón stadium. The contrast between my conti-
nental and domestic mindsets was striking.

'Don't question me; I'm good at my job,' I remember barking at Xavi, who'd sprinted across the pitch to challenge a penalty decision. No doubt he thought I was an arrogant swine, but that's how I often felt when I was on foreign soil; in the zone, in total control, and not to be messed with.

The Real Madrid v Bayern Munich semi-final, on Wednesday 23 April, witnessed another first-rate performance from me and my team. However, after flying home I received a concerned email from Pierluigi Collina, who'd been my assessor that night. During our post-match chat, he'd sensed that I was contemplating retirement.

'I know that this kind of decision is a very personal issue and I don't want to be impolite writing to you about it,' he said. 'Nevertheless, it is my responsibility to guarantee UEFA competitions the best referees and I cannot imagine the next season without Howard Webb.'

Just a week after being praised to the hilt by the great Collina, I was being pelted with abuse at Selhurst Park.

'Fuck off, Webb, you fuckin' wanker. Hope you're better than last time, you tosser,' yelled the Palace fans as I warmed up before their game against Manchester City.

Ten minutes later I trudged back to the dressing room, my head down, my shoulders sagging.

While UEFA were happy to assign me to Europe's finest, the Premier League had clearly lost all confidence in my refereeing abilities. Following the Arsenal v Liverpool debacle, they were unwilling to trust me with the key matches and, to be brutally honest, I didn't blame them. Each Monday, when the PGMOL email arrived, I became accustomed to seeing my name tagged against a lower profile tie, whereas the big games would be tackled by in-form refs like Martin Atkinson and Michael Oliver.

With my final domestic match looming on Sunday 11 May, Mike Riley gave me two or three fixtures to choose from. For a long list of reasons, I plumped for Hull v Everton. I'd run my last ever Football League line at the old Boothferry Park stadium, I'd refereed the first ever game at the new KC Stadium, my sister Claire had attended university in the city, and I liked the place and its people. But, most importantly of all, it was the closest fixture to my Rotherham home, meaning that my family could travel over to witness my final game.

So at 4.45 p.m., having notched up a grand total of 298 Premier League fixtures, I blew the whistle and brought my domestic career to a close. It was all very low-key; I'd not wanted any kind of fuss or fanfare and, other than Mike Riley, had only told my relatives and my officials that I'd decided to quit. As I walked off the pitch I felt a slight pang of sadness, but also felt sure I'd made the right decision. Refereeing had treated me well – and had taken me on the most incredible journey – but it was time to say thank you and goodbye.

Darren, Mike and I shared a bottle of champagne in the dressing room.

'Here's to you, Howard,' said Darren, raising his glass. 'The end of an era, mate.'

'Not quite the end though, is it?' I replied, thinking ahead to our next adventure.

'Hull this week, Rio the next.'

My 2014 World Cup selection had finally been sealed on a cold November night in Stockholm, on the occasion of the second leg of the Sweden v Portugal play-off. I'd been very nervous during the run-in; such decisive, do-or-die contests demanded exemplary, error-free refereeing, and this tie was probably the highest profile of the lot.

The sports media had billed it as a battle between Zlatan Ibrahimović and Cristiano Ronaldo; depending on the game's outcome, only one of these footballing superstars would have the chance to shine in Brazil. The margins were tight – the first leg had finished 1-0 to Portugal – and as both teams kicked off, the pressure felt intense.

Following a goalless first half both teams sprang into action in the second. Ronaldo's left-footed strike opened the scoring five minutes after the interval, but an Ibrahimović header pulled one back to make it 1-2 on aggregate. Then, with about 20 minutes remaining, the ball pinged into the Portuguese penalty box, whereupon Kim Källström took a touch, went past the defender and fell to the ground.

From my vantage point it appeared like a dive, not a trip. I wasn't 100 per cent sure, though – neither were Darren or Mike – but my strong gut feeling suggested no penalty, and almost immediately I blew the whistle on instinct. Sixty thousand Swedes were doubtless expecting me to point to the spot but, instead, I yellow-carded Källström for simulation before signalling a Portugal free kick.

All hell broke loose. The decibel level in the Friends Arena hit new heights, and I found myself being surrounded by a pack of livid Swedes, all railing at my decision. In order to ward them off I used every inch of my 6 foot 2 frame, extended my arm at a 70-degree angle, and gave them the sternest look I could muster. All the while I was thinking *fucking hell, I really hope that was a dive*.

It was a huge call, not just regarding Sweden's progression to Brazil, but regarding mine, too. An incorrect penalty decision would almost certainly scupper my team's World Cup chances; I'd seen what had happened to my friend Martin Hansson after the Thierry Henry incident four years previously.

Ibrahimović scored again to make it 2-1 on the night, the

Swedes just needing one more goal to secure their place. The irrepressible Ronaldo saw what was happening, however, and grabbed the game by the balls, whipping in two more goals to send him and his ecstatic team-mates to Brazil. It was by far the best individual performance I'd ever seen from a footballer.

Mercifully, the texts I received straight after the game suggested that my Källström call had been spot-on.

'YESSSS,' I shouted, punching the air with glee.

Moments later, the Swedish coach Erik Hamrén, along with striker Johan Elmander, popped their heads into the dressing room.

'Congratulations on a great game, ref,' said Hamrén. 'We've watched the footage back, and it was a dive. There was no contact at all. Well done, and enjoy Brazil.'

How noble of them, considering their World Cup journey had just ended. It proved to me that there were still some nice guys in football.

I departed for the World Cup in June 2014, with the Duke of Cambridge's kind words ringing in my ears. I'd met him some six months earlier – I'd refereed the FA's 150th centenary match at Buckingham Palace – and his passion for football was evident.

'Best of luck to Howard Webb and his team,' he said as part of his official good luck message to the England lads. 'They remind us that we are up there with the best when it comes to refereeing.' I thought that was a really nice touch from the Prince.

As things turned out, we weren't awarded a match in Brazil for a good two weeks. During that fortnight we lived in a football bubble, spending most our time working out on the training pitches or watching the games, either in the Maracanã Stadium itself or stationed in local bars. Unlike our isolated World Cup base in rural Pretoria, our Rio HQ was located within a stone's throw of Barra Beach, which wasn't without its attractions. This low-profile start prompted a raft of jokey messages from the UK.

'Eh, pal, are you really in Brazil or what?' texted one mate of mine.

'Enjoying your holiday, Webby? How's Copacabana looking?' emailed another.

We were eventually appointed to Match 21, Colombia v Ivory Coast, in the sprawling capital of Brasília. Assembling in the tunnel on Thursday 19 June was a full complement of Premier League Ivorians: Didier Drogba, Wilfried Bony, Didier Zokora, Cheick Tioté, Gervinho and the two Touré brothers.

Like most players, they'd probably not paid too much attention to that day's referee appointment, but when they eventually clocked me, their eyes lit up in recognition. Here was a familiar face from the UK, someone they knew and hopefully trusted.

'Ah, Webb, good to see you,' smiled Drogba, giving me a hug before his compatriots lined up to do the same.

Out of the corner of my eye I could see the Colombians suspiciously eyeing this cosy-looking love-in. So, once Yaya had given me a rib-splintering pat on the back, I pointedly approached the South Americans, too, embracing and high-fiving as many of them as possible, regardless of the fact that – apart from West Ham's Pablo Armero – I didn't know any of them personally.

Colombia won 2-1, the game went well, and we finally felt part of the tournament. Our adrenalin rush was tempered a few hours later, however, when we watched England's World Cup hopes fade at the hands of Uruguay. A double-whammy from Luis Suárez had left Hodgson's boys standing on the brink of an early exit.

We flew back to our base in Rio and, following another long-ish wait, FIFA informed us that, for the second major tournament in succession, we'd be taking charge of Brazil v Chile in the round of 16.

'Couldn't they have given us something more high profile?' I said to Darren and Mike, smiling and rolling my eyes.

This was going to be huge, of course. The host nation playing a near-neighbour. The opening last-16 knockout match of the tournament. The hopes of a football-obsessed nation pinned on to their yellow-shirted idols.

I found myself embroiled in some pre-match controversy, too, Chile's Alexis Sánchez having insinuated that FIFA's match officials had felt impelled to keep Brazil in the tournament. I hadn't been put under any pressure whatsoever, and was planning to ref it like any other game. Sánchez's comments had predictably incensed the Brazilian camp, who accused their opponents of disrespecting both their country and their national team.

'We are Brazil. We don't need the referee's help,' responded an angry Phil Scolari.

The heat was turned up to the max at the Estàdio Mineirão, Belo Horizonte, on the afternoon of Saturday 28 June. By the 50-minute mark the game was delicately poised at 1-1, David Luiz and Alexis Sánchez having scored at either end. In the 51st minute, however, I'd had to make one of the hardest decisions of my refereeing life.

Having latched on to a decent cross from Luiz Gustavo, Brazilian striker Hulk had controlled the ball, which had promptly dropped dead like a stone. From my perspective, about 25 yards from the action, the dynamics looked unusual. The ball appeared to have thudded on to the pitch after hitting a right angle; an outstretched arm, maybe. Not feeling entirely convinced, I didn't whistle.

From his angle, Mike hadn't seen anything untoward, either, which further reduced my level of certainty. *I'll let play go on*, I thought. *Hulk will probably put the ball wide, and I'll be able to give a goal kick.* But he went and shinned it, and it bobbled into the bottom corner.

As the stadium erupted, and three or four Chilean players hurtled over to remonstrate, time seemed to stand still. *FUCK*, I thought. Do I disallow this goal because my instincts say handball, or do I let it stand because I haven't seen anything concrete? It was a coin-toss of a decision in a game of huge consequence.

With the clock ticking, I knew I'd have to make one of those stomach-churning, sixth-sense judgements. It wasn't about making a wild guess; it was about trusting my instincts, my knowledge and my understanding, and realising that some of the best decisions were often reached in that way.

The reaction from the trio of Chileans ultimately swayed it for me. They'd occupied better vantage points than mine, undoubtedly, and the strength of their appeal – which was immediate, independent from one another and not at all contrived – suggested I hadn't been the only person on the pitch to have suspected handball. So I inhaled deeply, blew my whistle, and disallowed the goal.

I couldn't gauge much reaction from Hulk, who stormed off with a dismissive wave of the arm. However, Fred – his fellow attacker – said 'for handball, ref?', before nodding knowingly. And while that indicated that I'd perhaps made the right call, the incident followed me round, like a black cloud, for the remainder of the game.

The match was decided by a penalty shoot-out, Brazil triumphing after Gonzalo Jara's spot-kick had hit the post for Chile. While I didn't care who won, I realised that my passage in life was probably going to be easier with Brazil as victors. Had they lost, my pivotal decision might have made me chief scapegoat, with ramifications of Euro 2008-sized proportions.

'Webb, you're still the best!' beamed Scolari as I exited the pitch, the fireworks ricocheting round the stadium. *You wouldn't have bloody said that if you'd lost*, I thought.

More telling, in my mind perhaps, was a post-match comment from Brazil's head of media, who'd been sent to the stands at half-time for picking a fight with a Chilean substitute.

'Can you imagine?' he said, his eyebrows raised, as I passed him in the tunnel. I feared what he was getting at. Can you imagine, ref, if you'd have disallowed a perfectly good goal for us? Can you imagine if Brazil had been unfairly knocked out in our own country? Can you imagine how despised you'd have been?

I needn't have worried. My decision to trust my instincts had been a lifesaver. As I lay on the dressing room bench, mentally and physically exhausted, I scanned the congratulatory messages pulsing through to my phone.

'Astounding call, H, well done,' texted Martin Atkinson.

'Balls of steel,' texted Mike Riley.

'Congrats to Mike Mullarkey for spotting that one,' texted one cheeky so-and-so.

The video replay revealed that Hulk had discreetly used his upper arm to control the ball, and that to have allowed the goal would have been a major injustice to the Chileans.

A few days later, I learned that FIFA had provisionally allocated our team the Argentina v Holland semi-final in São Paolo and, as was the drill, had run this past both countries. It transpired that the Dutch were more than happy to accept our appointment – regardless of the events of South Africa 2010 – but it was the Argentinians who'd protested, citing political issues relating to the Falkland Islands dispute. FIFA decided to play safe, and the tie was awarded instead to Turkish referee Cüneyt Çakir and his team.

My linesmen and I watched both semi-finals from a Barra Beach bar and – like the shell-shocked locals – were in a state of utter disbelief as we witnessed Germany's 7-1 annihilation of the host nation on the evening of Tuesday 8 July. The aftermath was like a mass bereavement. All the wonderful hotel workers and FIFA drivers that we'd befriended over the past six weeks were so embarrassed and devastated that they could hardly look us in the eye.

I'd never been in with a shout of officiating the final – FIFA protocol dictated that the same ref couldn't oversee it more than once, and there were so many excellent candidates for the job at the tournament – but I was delighted when Match 64, Germany v Argentina, was awarded to Nicola Rizzoli. I was the only man in the room who knew exactly how he was feeling when the announcement was made, and that evening both our teams had dinner together.

'This appointment will change your life, Nic,' I smiled. 'Don't forget that you've got here on merit, though, and don't forget to enjoy it.'

Following the announcement, FIFA had invited the remaining officials to stay in Brazil to watch the final at the Maracanã, all expenses paid, but Mike and I declined their kind offer. Now that our mission was complete, we didn't feel the need to hang around and just wanted to get back to our families. Darren stayed on, but we caught the next day's flight home to the UK.

As our Boeing 777 soared over the Atlantic, and as Mike snoozed beside me, I gazed out of the window and pondered my Brazil 2014 experience. Ideally I'd have liked to have reffed more than two games, of course, but I was hardly going to complain. After all, there weren't many referees who could cite Brazil v Chile at Belo Horizonte, in the 2014 World Cup, as their final ever match.

# CHAPTER 11

# A Whole New Chapter

On the morning of Wednesday 6 August 2014, at the FA's St George's Park HQ, I announced I was blowing full-time on my career. After a 25-year stint in the middle, spanning nearly 300 Premier League games and nine major international tournaments, it was time to reveal the news that I'd kept under wraps for months.

Following early-bird BBC interviews with *Breakfast*'s Sally Nugent and 5 Live's Nicky Campbell, I sat down with a clutch of sports reporters in the press centre to explain the reasons behind my decision, and to elaborate upon my brand new position with the PGMOL.

'Today marks the end of my reffing, but it's the beginning of a fresh challenge,' I said, outlining the chain of events that had led to my announcement.

Shortly after the World Cup, following a series of conversations with Mike Riley, I'd decided to accept the role of Technical Director with the PGMOL. He'd made it clear that he wanted to keep me on board ('I don't want to lose you, Howard, you've got too much to offer,' was the general gist) and went above and beyond to accommodate me by creating a bespoke position.

According to Mike, the job's remit would involve overseeing the coaching and training of my former Select Group and National List colleagues, as well as developing a programme to provide a career pathway, ensuring that the two complemented each other strategically. I'd also be tasked with a media relations role, liaising closely with various broadcasters to inform and educate them regarding officiating matters.

It seemed like the ideal option for me; not only would I still be involved in the world of football on a day-to-day basis, I'd also be promoting and supporting my Select Group ex-colleagues. I was particularly looking forward to speaking up on their behalf, filling the void that was all too often occupied by ill-informed pundits.

'I'm really excited about my new position,' I told the assembled journalists. 'Refereeing has been good to me over the years, but it's time to give something back now, and time to pass on my knowledge and expertise to others.'

I then stuck around for a few minutes to take some questions.

'This may come as a surprise to some people, Howard,' piped up a reporter. 'You're only forty-three. Did you not think you had a couple more seasons left in you?'

'No, I don't reckon so,' I replied, adding that it was the right time to bow out, that I'd had a career most refs could only dream of, and that I'd always wanted to finish at the top.

As the news of my retirement filtered out, I received a steady stream of good luck messages. FA chairman Greg Dyke paid tribute to my 'magnificent and unrivalled refereeing career' and FIFA's referee committee chairman, Jim Boyce, thanked me for my contribution, stating I was 'highly thought of both at FIFA and UEFA'. Prince William and Michel Platini made contact, too, and a number of football clubs sent me nice letters.

Coming as no major surprise, though, were the sarky responses that cropped up on social media.

'All at MCFC wish Howard Webb the best in his new role after bringing an end to 25 years of officiating,' tweeted Manchester City, cheekily tagging on a photo of me red-carding Sun Jihai.

'Great news folks, we won't be Webbed again. He's retired. Happy days,' posted ex-Liverpool striker John Aldridge.

'Farewell, Howard Webb,' tweeted former *Daily Mirror* editor Piers Morgan. 'The least incompetent referee in British football.'

The internet photoshoppers got in on the act, too, dredging up the usual Manchester United-related images; one picture featured a group of tear-stained, red-shirted fans, with the caption 'Lads, Howard Webb's retired ...'

My announcement at St George's Park had happened to coincide with the Select Group's annual pre-season get-together. Since I hadn't confided in any of the refs beforehand, most were taken aback when I bumped into them following the media briefing.

'Bloody hell, mate, you kept that one quiet,' said Mike Dean.

'Don't know what to say, Howard. It'll be weird not having you in the group,' remarked Michael Oliver.

'I'll still be around, guys, just in a different capacity,' I replied.

Later that afternoon, Mike Riley and I made our way to the training pitches to watch the lads being put through their paces by the resident sports scientists. Anthony Taylor, Andre Marriner et al. were sprinting and stretching in the summer sunshine, like I'd done myself on so many occasions.

Suddenly, like a thunderbolt, it hit me that my reffing career was over. I'd known for months that I was calling it a day, and must have run the consequences through my mind a million times. However, at that moment, it was as if I'd only just grasped the concept. My retirement finally felt real, and I unexpectedly found myself overcome with fear and doubt.

*What the hell am I doing here?* I thought as I hovered near the touchline in my black PGMOL tracksuit, my instincts telling me to ditch the clipboard and dash on to the pitch.

*The Premier League season starts next week*, said a voice in my head. *You should be out there, with the others, preparing for the new campaign* ...

Only a few hours had passed since my announcement, yet already I'd begun to question the huge decision that I'd made. It all seemed very ominous.

Just six days' earlier I'd resigned from South Yorkshire police, too. My long-term sabbatical had come to an end in April 2013, and for the next 18 months I'd reported to the force's Attercliffe district HQ to undertake part-time ambassadorial and community work.

My bosses were particularly keen for me to trade on my football links in order to facilitate some sport-related projects for local youngsters. As with many other parts of the country, inter-racial tension had become a problem in pockets of South Yorkshire – including the deprived Fir Vale area of Sheffield – and it was felt that football might help to promote understanding and integration among the area's many ethnic groups.

With the assistance of a wonderfully dedicated PCSO, Craig Butcher – and a very proactive communications officer, Samantha Mawson – I accessed funds from the FA's Football Mash-Up scheme and channelled them through an existing local project, Sport FX. Together with excellent support from Sheffield and Hallamshire County Football Association, we were able to train up PCSOs to work as football coaches, who then laid on sessions for disadvantaged kids on 4G pitches across the county.

Within a matter of weeks we'd secured fifteen venues – mostly after-school facilities – and were engaging with over a thousand local children. We even extended the project to include boxing and dance, too.

'My kids love coming here, Howard,' I remember a woman telling me outside one of our hubs. 'It's so great to see them being part of something. Just make sure it keeps going.'

Many of the project's beneficiaries were youngsters with behavioural or discipline issues, who'd often sought confronta-tion with our PCSOs. However, out on the football pitch these kids would see my colleagues in tracksuits, not uniforms, and would be encouraged to address them by their first name. Bridges were built and relationships were fostered, leading to more mutual respect and less 'them-and-us' when both parties encountered each other on a Barnsley estate or a Doncaster street corner.

By advocating mixed teams, Sport FX also gave kids from differ-ent communities a rare chance to integrate. Sides would comprise boys and girls of Pakistani, Polish, Afro-Caribbean and Roma her-itage, for example, and it was heart-warming for us to see them playing happily together and forming lasting friendships.

Just prior to Brazil 2014, we held our own alternative World Cup finals day at Sheffield Hallam University's sports ground in Tinsley. The event happened to be featured on a Radio 4 broad-cast called *Howard's Way*.

'Sport engages young people, irrespective of their background or culture. It's the common ground for these children,' I told pre-senter Peter White, as the sound of giddy young kids booting footballs floated over.

I loved my community policing – and was incredibly proud to be associated with Sport FX – but when I was offered the PGMOL role I realised I'd be unable to combine the two.

'You'll be missed, but what a great opportunity for you,' said Chief Constable David Crompton when I handed in my notice. I was deeply honoured to receive an exemplary service award from him, which I duly framed and hung up on my kitchen wall.

So, within the space of six days, I'd left the police and had quit refereeing, closing the door on two vocations that had shaped, defined and motivated me for more than 20 years. *So who am I now, then?* I thought to myself as I drove home from St George's Park on that August afternoon, worried that my decision had triggered some kind of identity crisis.

'It's not going to be easy, Howard,' said Dad when I stopped by my parents' house for a quick cup of tea. 'This is a whole new chapter, son. It's bound to take time to adapt.'

Each weekend, my new role would take me to the TV match centre at Salford's Media City. There, together with ex-referee Dermot Gallagher, I'd monitor live feeds of every game, pinpointing and recording any significant refereeing incidents.

We did this for two reasons. Primarily, we were on hand to advise the Premier League's broadcasting rights holders about officiating decisions and points of law. At half-time I'd receive a call from BT Sport's football researcher, Joel Miller ('what's your take on that double touch from Joe Hart, Howard?') and would promptly relay my opinion and interpretation. Two minutes later, presenter Jake Humphrey would offer up this insight to the BT Sport viewers, namechecking PGMOL 'experts' in the process. A similar service was also offered to the Sky Sports and talkSPORT teams, plus a range of others.

Dermot and I advised *Match of the Day*'s producers and pundits, too, providing them with pointers and feedback to add weight to their Premier League highlights. Since they were also based at Media City, at 7.30 p.m. we'd hold an informal debrief with the likes of Gary Lineker, Mark Lawrenson and Alan Shearer, replaying and reviewing a compilation of noteworthy clips.

They were all nice enough blokes, but I had a feeling that the latter had still not quite forgiven me for the events of Saturday 16 May 2009. That particular day I'd overseen the Newcastle v Fulham game – Shearer hadn't long taken the managerial reins at St James' Park to try to fend off relegation – and I hadn't exactly covered myself in glory. Throughout the match I'd been aware of Magpies midfielder Kevin Nolan constantly harassing goalie Mark Schwarzer, blocking him one minute and stepping on his toes the next (something that Nolan was renowned for). Eventually I lost my patience and ended up doling out some words of advice.

'You'd better be careful, Kevin, I'm watching you,' I warned.

'Yeah, yeah, whatever ...' came the reply.

When the next corner came in, I spotted Nolan buffeting Schwarzer in the penalty box. *Right, that's it*, I thought, and immediately blew my whistle for a free kick. As I did so, however, Newcastle striker Mark Viduka powered a majestic header into the top corner of the net. I had no option but to disallow the goal, as I'd already blown. The home fans were enraged, even more so when Fulham went on to win this crucial six-pointer 1-0.

A furious Alan Shearer barged into my dressing room after the game.

'There was nothing fuckin' wrong with that goal,' he roared. 'That point could have meant everything to us.'

As it happened, he had every right to be fuming. Replays had shown that Nolan's contact hadn't been substantial enough for me to whistle, and that I'd probably been guilty of tracking him too closely and almost pre-empting a foul (occasionally, you're so desperate not to miss something you almost end up seeing too much). Top match officials, when reffing confidently, will give themselves time, and will use that time well. In this instance, though, my assessment was flawed and I should've given the goal. The fact that Newcastle were eventually relegated didn't make me feel any better about the situation.

Bearing all this in mind, I felt slightly awkward when, six years down the line, I met Shearer again in the *Match of the Day* studio. I offered him my apologies, which he duly accepted, shaking my hand. However, I noticed that while his mouth was smiling, his eyes were not.

The other element of my Media City work involved distributing match-day video clips to Select Group referees. I'd initially done this as a quick favour to them – it was all a bit unauthorised, really – but it soon became an integral part of their weekend schedule.

As I knew only too well from my own reffing days, the post-match uncertainty attached to key decisions could be torturous. On countless occasions I'd found myself trying to get a steer via Twitter after the final whistle, or banking on reassuring texts from friends who'd seen the game.

In the Salford studio I'd compile bespoke montages of refereeing decisions from the match feeds, before uploading them on to a file-sharing site for each official to access afterwards. Most of them found it invaluable. Instead of fretting about that borderline red card during the long drive home to Wiltshire or Northumberland, they could put their mind at rest (or psych themselves up for the shit-storm) by just looking at their devices as they left the stadium or when they stopped off at a service station.

'Congrats pal, you did really well, here's a couple of clips you might want to look at,' I'd say, tapping out an email to one of my ex-colleagues or – when the news wasn't so good – 'Mate, probably not what you want to hear, but that tenth-minute yellow looked like a red to us. Check out the footage and see what you think.'

My PGMOL remit had supposedly included some PR work, effectively giving a human face to what many people saw as quite a serious, staid organisation. I was told that my new role would allow me to become the Select Group's chief spokesman and advocate, commenting publicly on their behalf to clarify certain laws, decisions and actions.

The reality was different, however, and it all became very frustrating. While I'd worked hard to foster a good relationship with the broadcasting fraternity, for whatever reason my bosses weren't keen for me to become the organisation's mouthpiece. I appreciated that it was a difficult balancing act to get right – on the one hand the PGMOL didn't want to appear like a closed shop, yet on the other hand didn't want to bang the drum too loudly – but I thought they were swerving a great opportunity to raise awareness of the methods and mechanics of officiating.

Take Premier League assistant referee Andy Garrett, for instance. In September 2014, he'd made a great call at Old Trafford, sticking his neck out to disallow a West Ham goal for offside. It was a complicated judgement, but he'd got it absolutely spot-on.

Hammers boss Sam Allardyce was infuriated – he'd claimed it had cost his team a point – and gave the linesman a proper slagging on *Match of the Day*, questioning his ability and moaning about the injustice of it all. Yet Andy – who'd used great skill and judgement to arrive at the correct decision – had no right of reply, as the powers-that-be had dissuaded officials from making any post-match comments.

I messaged the PGMOL management the following day, outlining my concerns and suggesting that, as their employers, we ought to be staunchly defending our officials, whether it was via a statement, an interview, or on social media. My email was pooh-poohed, though, the reasoning being 'if we do that for the good calls, we'll have to do it for the bad calls too.'

I didn't agree. Pundits and journos were always more likely to focus on the dodgy decisions, and we needed to redress the balance by drawing attention to the decent ones, too, by giving our refs and linesmen a voice. PGMOL statistics confirmed that Select Group officials made considerably more accurate judgements than inaccurate and, as far as I was concerned, overlooking this fact was a mistake.

There was a conflict of interest at play, however. Due to its close, inextricable links with the Premier League, the PGMOL was always going to find itself constrained and compromised. Any attempt to defend a referee from criticism by a stakeholder club was bound to cause friction, especially when the person responsible for PGMOL communications, Phil Dorward, was employed by the Premier League, and therefore represented both organisations. I got on well with Phil, and he was excellent at his job, but he was in an impossible position. As time went by, therefore, I became increasingly hacked off that officials were seen – and often verbally battered – but were never heard.

In November 2014, Sky Sports invited me on to their *Monday Night Football* show to take part in a general discussion about refereeing issues. The PGMOL agreed – somewhat reluctantly, I sensed – but packed me off to the Isleworth studios with a four-page briefing document about how I should respond on certain issues. Immediately I felt restricted.

It proved to be a tough hour. Before and after that night's live offering, Ed Chamberlin, Gary Neville and Jamie Carragher grilled me about a variety of refereeing matters – with topical footage to spark debate – and posed some searching questions, which I answered as best I could within my tight PGMOL boundaries. Gary Neville was particularly keen to discuss the whys and wherefores of simulation on the field of play, asking me how prevalent I thought the problem was.

I explained that, while I didn't think it had worsened over the years, I understood the injustice and frustration felt by those supporters who witnessed a cheat going scot-free.

'As refs we feel pretty bad about being conned by somebody who dives,' I replied. 'We care about what we do, Gary, and want to be as accurate as we can.'

The reaction to the programme was mixed, with positive feedback from viewers who'd enjoyed some rare TV insight from an ex-referee, and negative responses from those who just saw me as a PGMOL puppet.

'The opportunity to educate and clarify was wasted,' commented Graham Poll in his *Daily Mail* column. 'PGMOL personnel feel duty bound to support their colleagues, their mates ... working in live TV isn't easy but well within Webb's ability if his hands were not tied.'

My role as Technical Director also reunited me with a certain Mr Mourinho. Towards the end of his second Premier League stint José had begun to stir up some referee conspiracy theories, lamenting the number of incorrect decisions that Chelsea FC had apparently suffered at the hands of the Select Group. It was all bullshit, of course. To claim that top-flight officials had an agenda against particular clubs was both laughable and insulting. When I was a ref, performing the role to the best of my ability – and for the benefit of both teams – was always paramount. When I was on the pitch it genuinely became red versus blue, white versus yellow; I neither had the time nor inclination to favour one side over another.

As regards Mourinho, things came to a dramatic head following Chelsea's home match against Burnley in March 2015, in which Martin Atkinson had awarded a series of controversial decisions against the Blues. José went on the warpath in the post-match press conference, detailing the 'four important mistakes,' that he'd felt had impeded his team. Martin was also savaged by the panel on that night's *Match of the Day*.

In an attempt to smooth things over, Mike Riley and I held a private clear-the-air meeting with Mourinho. Contrary to press reports, this didn't end up with José throwing a tantrum and ejecting us from Chelsea's training ground. As it happened, we had a pretty fruitful and constructive discussion.

Mourinho had initially gone on the offensive, testily reeling off a dossier that listed all the decisions he'd felt had gone against his team, and wiping the floor with the Premier League representative who'd accompanied us. But I'd come equally well prepared, counter-claiming with my own spreadsheet of good calls that had actually worked in his favour. By the end we'd almost cancelled each other out, and the mood was conciliatory rather than inflammatory.

'You know I respect you, Howard, but I just think too much has gone against us,' said Mourinho. 'The FA, the media, the referees … it's just too much.'

This meeting had again highlighted the lack of redress for embattled Select Group referees, though. The bee in my bonnet was buzzing progressively louder, and I decided to air my views in an authorised interview with *The Times'* Matthew Syed. *WEBB TAKES A FIRM STAND IN REFEREES ROW*, proclaimed the back page headline a few days later.

'The one thing that sometimes got to me as a referee was the idea that I was not impartial,' I told Syed. 'It's one thing to have your professional ability questioned, but when people start to insinuate that you are part of a conspiracy, well that's just crazy.'

My ex-colleagues loved the article; finally, someone was fighting their corner and vouching for their integrity. Others, however, were less impressed. A few days later Mike Riley called me into a meeting at St George's Park, informing me that Premier League boss Richard Scudamore had been angry when he'd read the feature, because I'd obliquely criticised a member club and its manager. Via Mike, he'd relayed the message that it mustn't happen again.

For me, this finger-wagging reprimand was the final straw. I didn't need this level of control and this lack of support, and knew I'd ultimately have to walk away. It was the beginning of the end of my PGMOL career. I soldiered on as best I could, but my heart was no longer in it.

Mike Riley, sensing that I was deeply unhappy, even redefined my role as 'Performance Director' to include more hands-on coaching, but things didn't improve, sadly.

Having lost all sense of purpose and relevance, I guess I'd reached something of a crisis point. My job had become too vague and ill-defined, to such an extent that I'd wake up in the morning unsure of what was on the agenda, and would spend the rest of the day mooching around like a spare part. Sitting in PGMOL meetings I'd feel awkward and embarrassed, paranoid that other colleagues were thinking, *What exactly is Howard Webb doing here? Jobs for the boys, eh. It's all right for some …*

Having spent so many years operating in the strictly regimented worlds of policing and refereeing, my life felt weirdly out of focus. And, with hindsight, coming straight off the training pitch into a strait-laced corporate role had been the wrong move for me. Being so close to the Select Group of referees – lads who'd been my peers and colleagues for ten years – had only served to remind me what I was missing.

I didn't blame Mike Riley – he'd been a great friend and ally over the years, and had done everything to accommodate me – but my mind had been made up. I'd had enough. In May I drove to his home in Roundhay to put us both out of our misery.

'I'm so sorry it's not worked out, Howard, but I understand your reasons,' he said as we sat at his kitchen table. 'You'll be successful in whatever you choose to do, mate, but it's just a shame that it won't be with us.'

'Cheers, Mike.'

He smiled, got up from his chair and flicked on the kettle.

'C'mon, let's have a coffee.'


There was a time, believe it or not, when I could have gone into politics. I've twice been asked to stand as a Labour MP, firstly for Barnsley Central in 2010 (a seat now held by Dan Jarvis MP, often touted as a future party leader) and then for Rotherham, following the resignation of Denis MacShane in 2012.

While I'd never been a card-carrying member of the Labour Party I'd always held socialist values, believing that society was obliged to take care of the less fortunate, as opposed to an 'every man for himself' state of affairs. As a copper I was barred from being party political, although I do remember sitting in the West Bar canteen on the morning of Friday 2 May 1997, feeling thrilled that Tony Blair's New Labour had seized power from John Major's Conservatives. In contrast, most of my blue-tinted colleagues were crying into their cooked breakfasts.

'What a fuckin' disaster,' said one.

'Loony bloody lefties,' said another.

It was no secret, however, that the Webb family had left-wing leanings – my ex-miner father had been a paid-up member of the NUM and a huge supporter of party leader Neil Kinnock – and this was no doubt picked up in local Labour circles.

It was Barnsley East MP Michael Dugher who'd made the initial overtures, informing me that central office was seeking a Yorkshire born-and-bred candidate; someone, he said, with status and integrity. While it was flattering to be asked to stand for two local constituencies, after giving it some thought I politely declined both offers. Being a Member of Parliament would have consumed my whole life – my reffing would have fallen by the wayside, obviously – and I was concerned that nailing my political colours to the mast would have alienated half my friends and colleagues.

'Shame, really,' said Mum. 'Howard Webb MP's got a nice ring to it, hasn't it?'

My interest in politics didn't wane, though. I attended an anti-discrimination summit at Downing Street with Prime Minister David Cameron and an assortment of football delegates, I supported Andy Burnham's campaign for the Labour Party leadership, and I also addressed the All-Party Parliamentary Football Group over a very boozy House of Commons dinner. I even did a favour for a Tory, offering advice and guidance to Culture Secretary Jeremy Hunt – a nice enough fella, incidentally – who'd decided to train as a referee. But I've no plans to enter the House of Commons just yet.

One post I had no qualms in accepting, though, was the role of Honorary Ambassador for Rotherham United FC. Shortly after the 2010 World Cup, chairman Tony Stewart had invited me to take up the position, its premise being to help with the club's PR and make some public appearances. I gladly accepted, once I'd received final clearance from my PGMOL bosses.

'We may have to reassess this if Rotherham get promoted to the Premier League, though,' they said, which made me guffaw.

One of my first duties was to officially announce the name of our brand new stadium which, by late 2011, was well on the way to being completed. My good mate, *Sheffield Star* journalist Les

Payne, had come up with the idea of the 'New York Stadium'. This was neither a gimmicky nod to our American cousins nor a high-and-mighty delusion of grandeur. The name, in fact, harked back to a bygone part of town near the site of the old Rotherham foundry, next to which the new ground was being built. It was a lost community of back-to-back terraces that had been razed to the ground in the 1930s; indeed, I have vague childhood memories of my grandma referring to her 'old friends in New York'.

The construction of the stadium heralded a new era for my beloved club, which had suffered a decade of hardship and heartache. Ongoing disputes between the former chairman and his successor had forced us to decamp from Millmoor in 2008 and move to a temporary home at Sheffield's Don Valley Stadium. Not only that, our descent into administration had triggered a 37-point deduction over the space of three years. We memorably began the 2008-09 season with a 17-point deficit, Mark Robins' lads slowly but surely climbing the league table to finish a remarkable tenth.

My honorary role saw me promoting Rotherham United in a variety of ways, whether it was after-dinner speaking at a fundraiser, hosting a sponsor's table on a match day, or giving out prizes on behalf of the club's excellent Community Sports Trust. I once took part in a charity match on a freezing cold February afternoon, performing refereeing duties while the legendary Chuckle Brothers – both diehard Millers fans and great mates of mine – acted as physios. In the very first minute Paul and Barry mischievously toddled over with a bucketful of water.

'To me, to you, to me, to you, to HOWARD!!!' they shouted, before dousing me from head to toe.

The cheeky Chuckles had quite literally wet my whistle which, in the sub-zero temperatures, totally froze up.

\*

Around the time that my PGMOL role was in freefall, I heard that BT Sport were seeking a new referee match-day analyst, someone to bolster their Premier League and European coverage.

Together with my good friend Mick McGuire, Head of Sport for the James Grant Group, I attended a fact-finding meeting with the programme editor, a talented creator of sports broadcasts called Dylan Jane. I was concerned that the role wasn't just designed to pinpoint refereeing cock-ups and controversies, and sought reassurances that I'd be allowed to give genuine insight to a wide range of situations.

'It's not about praising or slating referees, Howard,' Dylan explained.

'It's about giving our viewers a real understanding of what you guys do. They want to know why a ref has got something right or wrong, and how he's reached that decision. As you said, it's insight that we're after.' Dylan could also see the way the game was going with regards to video replays. He outlined how BT Sport wanted to pre-empt how video technology could work within the game, and wanted to show how quickly somebody could look at all the angles and make the correct decision. 'We want to almost be ahead of the game,' he said. 'Video technology is likely to happen at some point, and we can show how it can be done with the hi-tech equipment at our disposal in the trucks.' I held similar views.

I went home to mull everything over. On the one hand, a job with BT Sport would present me with a fresh challenge in a dynamic new environment, enabling me to work alongside ex-pros like Michael Owen, Ian Wright and Steven Gerrard. On the other hand, if I accepted the role, I'd have to don my tin hat to withstand the flak that would inevitably come my way. The refereeing community largely frowned upon old boys joining forces with the media, the perception being that you'd defected to the dark side and sold your soul to the devil; you were seen as a grass, a turncoat.

But I weighed everything up, wrestled with my conscience, and concluded that it would provide a great platform for me to speak on behalf of the referees. It might even make up for the lost opportunity with the PGMOL. *Sod it*, I thought. *I'm going for it.*

A couple of weeks later, having had that difficult conversation in Mike Riley's kitchen, I'd had to visit the Premier League's London HQ to sort out some admin. As I approached the office I happened to bump into Richard Scudamore in the corridor.

'Ah, star of TV now, are we?' he said as I passed by.

Now, had I been Steven Gerrard in that corridor he'd have no doubt warmly shaken my hand and congratulated me on my new media role. But I wasn't an ex-player, I was just an ex-ref. One of those blokes with a whistle who others thought they were entitled to take a pop at, whether it was from the football terraces or in the corridors of power.

I began my BT Sport career on Saturday 8 August 2015, assuming my seat in the broadcast truck for Manchester United v Tottenham Hotspur. Like any new job, it took a few weeks for me to get into the swing of things and for the nerves to settle. The set-up was straightforward enough; whenever there were any notable or contentious decisions the match director would cut across to me, and I'd either speak to camera or provide some audio. If I thought the ref had made a good, strong call I'd happily sing his praises but, by the same token, if he'd committed a blunder I'd provide constructive criticism.

I'd try to back up any comments with reason and rationale, explaining how and why the official had come to his decision. The most problematic scenarios were those ambiguous, borderline calls where you could make a strong case either way. However, as a pundit, there were only so many times you could say 'It's one of those marginal calls,' without appearing to be firmly impaled on the fence. I did my best but – like my own reffing career, I suppose – I didn't always get everything right, even with the benefit of several replays at various speeds. I tried not to get too het up about it, though, reminding myself that football was seldom black and white, and was full of grey areas. Often there was never a right or wrong answer to be given, just an opinion to express.

This forensic examination of former colleagues didn't always rest easy with me. My natural, default position was as chief cheerleader – I knew first-hand how supremely talented these guys were, and how tough the job could be – and I had to learn to take a deep breath, take a step back and comment objectively. As expected, a few referees were unhappy with my on-screen presence, though, believing that my role existed solely to highlight their mistakes.

'It's all right for you, with your slo-mo replays and your multiple camera angles,' carped one.

I sympathised to an extent – perhaps I wouldn't have liked an old colleague critiquing my own performance – but their grievances were largely misplaced. I knew just how difficult it was to make split-second decisions and to recall complex points of law and, if anything, I was there to champion their role to the viewing public. I'd blown that whistle. I'd shown those cards. I knew exactly how they felt.

Some Select Group members were more accepting than others. Early in the 2015–16 season, I was on BT duty for the Newcastle United v Arsenal game when Andre Marriner had failed to award a rightful penalty to Arsenal. He'd missed it, I reckoned, because Florian Thauvin's trip on Héctor Bellerín had been as a result of a clip of the heel, and Andre – from his vantage point – had probably been focusing on upper body contact.

He got in touch with me after the game.

'That's exactly what I'd have wanted you to say,' he texted. 'Yes, I made a mistake, but you explained the reason behind it.'

Other referees weren't so magnanimous, however. A former

colleague sent me a terse text one Saturday evening ('Thanks for your support. Not.') after I'd suggested he'd been naïve to play an unnecessarily long amount of stoppage time at the end of a first half during which a team had scored. The same official also sent me an outraged message after I'd mildly criticised him during a key game, informing me that my number had since been deleted from his phone and that I shouldn't bother contacting him again. This really was the exception to the norm, though; luckily, I was able to remain on friendly terms with most referees.

Working with BT Sport quickly taught me that life in broadcasting could be challenging and unforgiving. Make a wrong call, stumble over a word or sport a lilac shirt and within seconds you'd receive a slagging on social media. I heeded the constructive criticism, though, learning to change my intonation (some keyboard warriors claimed my voiced droned on a bit), trying to be as succinct and concise as possible, and updating my wardrobe with a few new tops.

I also learned to think carefully before I opened my mouth, backing up any contentious opinions with genuine evidence and, when necessary, obtaining clearance from the powers-that-be. A case in point was the March 2016 Europa League tie between Manchester United and Liverpool. I'd been so incensed with Marouane Fellaini's behaviour – the big Belgian had yet again been reckless with his elbows – that I'd felt the need to speak my mind.

I knew exactly what I wanted to say after the game, but had an inkling that it might be a bit controversial. So, to cover my back, I ran it past BT Sport's assistant producer.

'Would I be OK to describe Fellaini as a thug?' I asked.

'It's strong, Howard,' he replied, 'but I think you'll be all right.'

So, having been given the green light, a few minutes later I was saying my piece.

'It's one thing imposing yourself on the game, but another thing being a thug on the pitch,' I said, speaking directly to camera. 'We know what Fellaini's about when we're refereeing, and we've seen it all throughout his career, but he seems to be getting worse and worse. He can't get through a game without violently throwing his arm into people's faces. He gets away with it week in, week out, and I think people are getting a little bit fed up of it.'

The media quickly seized upon my remarks, culminating in a *Football Focus* interview with Fellaini himself a few days later in which he was asked directly to respond to my comments.

'I like to win my challenge,' he said. 'If you want to win the game, you have to be aggressive. I never want to injure a player. I'm not like that. I just defend myself.'

A few months later, I was in a Madrid restaurant having a bite to eat with Steve McManaman before the Real Madrid v Manchester City Champions League semi-final. Also joining us was a pal of Steve's, who was introduced to me as one of Marouane Fellaini's advisors.

*Here we go*, I thought, as I stood up to shake his hand. *I bet this fella's going to have a right pop at me here …*

He didn't, as it happened, and just laughed the whole thing off.

'It was one of those things, Howard,' he said, tucking into his steak. 'Everyone's entitled to their opinion. It's really not a problem.'

Much to my relief, BT Sport's resident pundits made me feel really welcome when I first came on board. I was a bit worried that I'd feel excluded from the posse of ex-players and ex-managers – I was the big bad wolf referee coming back to haunt them – but, like the directors and the production team, they couldn't have been more friendly.

Glenn Hoddle, for example, is a gem. For someone who was once an outstanding, world-famous footballer – and an ex-England manager to boot – he's ridiculously friendly, humble and down to earth. Ian Wright's similar. He has to be among the nicest people in sport, one of those grounded ex-pros who, on the way to the studio, will acknowledge every doorman, every cleaner and every receptionist. A top, top fella.

I've spent lots of European travelling time with Michael Owen, Rio Ferdinand, Steve McManaman and Owen Hargreaves – with a few drinks in between – and their company is much easier than I ever thought it would be. I've got to know the commentators and presenters well, too, Darren Fletcher and James Richardson in particular. And while I'm conscious that this may read like a BT Sport love-in, there's really nobody in the organisation who's difficult to work with. Even Robbie Savage, believe it or not.

I've had the pleasure of Robbie's company on numerous occasions and can report that, behind all the bluster and bravado, the lad's got a very big heart. He's developed a genuine interest in refereeing (get yourself trained up, Rob!) and I'd like to think that he's acquired a deeper understanding of the world of officiating, courtesy of our little chats-cum-debates on the *Fletch & Sav* show.

I even rang his BBC 5 Live *606* show following Rotherham United's amazing, relegation-dodging spell towards the end of the 2015–16 season, expertly masterminded by my old adversary Neil Warnock. Robbie had sent me a mocking 'HAHAHAHAHA' text when Derby County had gone 3-0 up against the Millers, only to go strangely silent once we'd dramatically drawn level.

'And we've got Howard from Rotherham on the line,' said Darren Fletcher, presenting me with the perfect opportunity to give Savage some much-deserved hammer.

*

Around the same time that I joined forces with BT Sport, I took on a new consultancy role in Saudi Arabia. The country's football federation – masterminded by Prince Abdullah, the Minister of Sport and co-owner of Sheffield United FC – were looking for someone to develop their officials and head up their referee programme. After meeting me in London, they decided I was the right man for the job, and offered me a three-year deal as a consultant director. This would comprise at least 12 days of working and coaching in Riyadh each month, meaning that I'd be able to combine it with my TV work.

Financially, it was a decent move for me – I had a family to provide for, when all's said and done – and it presented me with the fresh new challenge that I craved. After the disappointment of my PGMOL role, I'd thought it sensible to distance myself from my ex-Premier League colleagues for a while and, for the next few years, forge an alternative career away from the UK.

I arrived in Saudi in August 2015, having spent the summer working as a FIFA referee instructor at the Under-20s World Cup finals in New Zealand. The first thing that struck me about Saudi (apart from the blistering 40-degree heat) was its unbridled passion for football. The locals devour the sport – both domestically and internationally – and their knowledge of Premier League clubs, players and managers was enormous.

'Why did you always give bad decisions against my team Liverpool?' complained a guy on passport control when I'd landed at Riyadh's King Khaled Airport.

After a couple of weeks of observing games and officials, it became evident that the standard of football in Saudi's fourteen-team professional league was pretty decent. Jeddah-based Al Ahli FC – managed by ex-Spurs boss Christian Gross – were the league's top outfit and, boasting a hybrid team of talented locals and overseas players, were probably on a par with an English

Championship side. Top-flight matches regularly attracted crowds of 60,000-plus, too.

There was also a massive interest in refereeing over there. Well-known international match officials were lauded and revered – I couldn't believe how many people accosted me in the shops or on the street ('Mister Howard! Mister Howard!') – and, for some reason, the national newspapers were full of referee-related features.

Since arriving in Saudi, my overarching remit has been to improve the nation's standards of officiating, and to instil their home-grown referees with more confidence and know-how. The Federation still relies on international refs to some extent – league clubs can request foreign officials for up to five home games per season and, in 2016, a Spaniard was chosen to ref their version of the FA Cup – and my goal has been to reduce this dependence.

To that end, I've helped to apply Western methods to their systems, building the infrastructure required for an effective modern-day refereeing department and developing its training and recruitment programme. There are some really talented refs in that part of the world with a lot of potential; I'm simply aiming to inject more professionalism.

I've formed a good team around me, including ex-FIFA referee Herbie Barr, a Northern Irishman who acts as my eyes and ears in Saudi when I'm not around. The role has had its own challenges, of course – I'm away from home a lot, the extreme temperatures take some getting used to, and the Saudi culture is totally different to ours – but, from a work perspective, things have gone well. I think I've started to make a real difference and, once I've completed my three-year stint, I'm hoping that I'll have made my mark and left a legacy.

Maybe I'll have also built a bridge or two. When I first reported to work at the Football Federation I learned that the office down the corridor was occupied by a certain Bert van Marwijk. Bert had been appointed manager of the national team in 2015, arriving in Riyadh just before me, and I admit to feeling a little wary when I first clocked the nameplate on his office door. We'd not exactly parted on good terms when we'd last met; bad memories still lingered of the Dutchman berating me on the Soccer City pitch in the aftermath of his team's World Cup final defeat in 2010.

*Bet he won't be happy to learn I'm in the same building,* I thought.

Shortly after my arrival, however, I'd received a message via a member of his coaching team.

'Bert sends his regards, Howard, and looks forward to catching up with you at some point.'

'Cheers,' I replied. 'Send him my best wishes, too.'

Things had moved on for both of us, I hoped. Maybe it was time to let bygones be bygones and to look forward.

# CHAPTER 12

# Extraordinary Things Can Happen

Speak to an ex-referee, and most of them will tell you they don't regret giving up refereeing. Not one jot. While they're able to look back fondly on their careers, they'll be the first to admit that life is pretty good these days; no stress, no hassle, no hostility.

I can't agree. I've found it tough. I've struggled a lot. While I haven't suffered with depression, I've found the transition to the big wide world – and the pursuit of a brand new identity – harder than I'd ever imagined. I spent 25 years as a football official, playing an important and relevant part on the biggest sporting stage. I worked my bollocks off for nearly three decades, reaching the summit of my chosen profession. But suddenly, with one stroke of the pen and with one announcement to the media, I brought it all to a dramatic halt.

It's amazing how many people still think I'm a referee, though.

'Who've you got tomorrow, Howard?' some bloke will holler as I walk through Sheffield city centre on a Friday afternoon. I'll stop, I'll smile, and I'll tell him that I've actually been retired for some time now.

'Retired? What did you wanna do that for?' he'll reply.

So sometimes, just sometimes, I'll find myself yearning for my old life in the middle. Often it's when I'm stationed in the BT Sport broadcast truck, on one of those big Champions League nights. I'll be watching the TV screens as the officials are warming up, and I'll suddenly feel a pang for bygone days.

*This time, a few years ago, it would have been me out there on the pitch,* I'll think to myself. *It would have been me doing those shuttle runs, those ankle circles, those sidesteps, those hamstring stretches ...*

I guess there's lots about the old routine that I still miss. Like driving over to a ground on a frosty morning, with Dad in the passenger seat, chatting about that day's fixtures, Radio 5 Live blaring from the car radio. A few hours' later, I'd pull in to an iconic, history-steeped stadium – White Hart Lane, Villa Park, Anfield – feeling ready to play my part in a small slice of football history.

I miss hooking up with Darren and Mike before a game, and following our usual pre-match routine: the pitch inspections, the security briefings, the 'c'mon lads, let's be the best!' rallying cries. I even miss those fleeting team sheet exchanges with preoccupied captains, both lads limbering up and nodding absent-mindedly while I'd run through my pep talk.

I miss that special five-to-three buzz, that spine-tingling thrill when I'd lead both teams out of the tunnel, swipe the ball off its plinth, and face a stadium swathed in colour and pulsing with anticipation. I miss the drama of a play-off, the grandeur of a cup final, the excitement and expectation of the season's opening and closing games. Those 'pinch-me-now' occasions that would make you feel so lucky, so fortunate, to be at the sharp end of this beautiful game.

'Look around, soak it up,' I'd say to Darren and Mike as we'd emerge from the tunnel, prior to a top-of-the-table clash. 'We'll not be doing this forever.'

I miss that exhilarating feeling following a smooth, trouble-free game, when I had a full complement of player handshakes, when I got smiles – not snarls – from their managers, and when Sky's Steadicam focused on a face other than mine. And then in the dressing room, there'd be no anxious inquests, no hurried scrolling on Twitter, no burning ears during a post-match press conference.

I miss Dad driving me back after a match, motoring up the M1 as it cut through Bedfordshire, Leicestershire and Derbyshire. I'd stretch out my aching limbs in the passenger seat, feeling that warm, Ready Brek glow, knowing that I'd done a proficient and professional job for both teams. Then there'd be that huge sense of relief when I arrived back home and walked through the front door, to be greeted by a smiling Kay wearing a 'thank-God-it-went-well' expression. I'd be able to relax for the rest of the night, sinking into the settee with my cans and my Chinese takeaway, daring to look forward to *Match of the Day*.

I miss the glamour of overseas tournaments and contests, and the allure of foreign travel. From Canada to Brazil, from Spain to South Africa, from Turin to Tokyo, UEFA and FIFA despatched my assistants and me to majestic stadiums around the globe, allowing us VIP status and entrusting us with prestigious games and superstar players.

I miss the spirit and camaraderie that existed among the various officials' teams. We'd train together, we'd socialise together, we'd sightsee together. We'd explore new cities and would experience different cultures, visiting churches, cathedrals, museums, vineyards and game reserves. And we'd want for nothing when we returned to our luxury bases: meals cooked, rooms cleaned, beds made, kits laundered.

We worked hard, and occasionally played hard; if a match had gone well, we'd reward ourselves by piling back to someone's room, cracking open the beers, rigging up the iPod and chatting until the early hours. Happy days indeed.

It was a charmed life – a self-centred life, I suppose – and I'd often experience a huge sense of anti-climax when I returned home. It was always great to be reunited with Kay and the kids but, after a few days, reality would take a grip and I'd come crashing down to earth.

'Just because you're a World Cup ref doesn't mean you can't clean the dog mess off the patio, love,' Kay would say, chucking me the pooper-scooper.

There's a lot about my former job that I don't miss, though. That fairly important section between coin toss and final whistle, for starters. Bizarre though it may sound, while I loved being part of the refereeing fraternity, I sometimes dreaded the actual stints on the pitch and, certainly towards the end of my career, often spent that 90-minute period wavering between fear and loathing. The 'before' and 'after' was far easier to bear, and I'd try and get through that crucial bit in the middle with minimal fuss and maximum damage limitation. For me, too many games would be endured, not enjoyed.

On occasion I'd be lucky enough to breeze through a match relatively painlessly, but the vast majority wore me out, mentally and sometimes physically. The need to focus, to evaluate and to legislate for two halves of football – your every action being watched over by thousands in the stand, and millions on TV – would make your brain hurt and your head pound. And then there was the added uncertainty and unpredictability of a football match to deal with; even the most prepared and professional referee couldn't predict what lay round the corner, and couldn't foresee if he was about to make the best or worst decision of his life.

Unsurprisingly, I don't miss the flak and the fallout from a bad decision or a poor performance. The mobbing by the players. The taunting from the terraces. The intimidation by a manager. The pasting in the media. Your long sulks. Your low mood. Your lost sleep.

Neither did I like the fact that, when something went badly on the pitch, it could affect my family off it. While I'd willingly chosen to enter the world of officialdom, my wife and children hadn't, yet they regularly needed to be shielded from some football-related storm or other. The events of Euro 2008 proved to be particularly distressing, but whenever I was embroiled in any kind of controversy – Ryan Babel's tweet, or de Jong's karate kick – Kay and the kids would have to brace themselves for the odd comment or two, whether it was in the playground or at the school gates. That used to really upset me.

Refereeing drained so much of my spare time, too, and often took me far away from the family home. If I wasn't on the road or in a plane, I'd be running round a pitch, immersing myself in training or attending a conference. Between 2006 and 2014, I never spent the month of June at home and, for three-quarters of the year, Fridays and Saturdays were all but wiped off my social calendar. I'm not trawling for sympathy – I'd known exactly what to expect when I'd signed up – but being absent for school concerts, friends' weddings and children's birthdays wasn't ideal. I had to sacrifice a lot for refereeing, and it was often my family who suffered.

'Who the hell arranges a kids' party for three o'clock on a Saturday, anyway?' I remember once grumbling to Kay, who was rightly unhappy at having to traipse to another Wacky Warehouse, essentially a single parent.

'Normal people who've got a life outside football, Howard, that's who,' came her weary but truthful response.

The benefits of refereeing far outweighed the drawbacks, though. As I plied my trade in the finest grounds in the land, I don't think I ever lost sight of its many paybacks and privileges. For someone whose childhood had revolved around playing and watching sport, and who'd been reared on a TV diet of *The Big Match*, *Saint & Greavsie* and *World Cup Grandstand*, mine was a job to die for.

While I was never able to truly 'watch' a match that I officiated – my need to focus and concentrate put paid to that – sometimes I witnessed some stand-alone moments of genius that made me feel like I had the best seat in the house.

Take Gareth Bale's goal for Tottenham against West Ham in February 2013, for instance. In the last minute, under the glare of Upton Park's floodlights, the Welshman had been upended with the ball at his feet. Poised to give Spurs a free kick, I noticed Bale scrambling back up, so waved play on (expertly so, if you don't mind me saying). He retrieved the ball from Gylfi Sigurdsson, took a couple of deft touches and then curled a superb match-winner into the top right corner from 25 yards out. A corker of a strike, and a pleasure to behold.

But the best goal I saw with my own eyes, without question, was scored on Saturday 24 March 2012, at the Britannia Stadium. Stoke City's Peter Crouch, lurking between the corner of the 18-yard box and the right-hand touchline, had latched on to Asmir Begović's goal kick before nodding the ball on to Jermaine Pennant. His teammate headed it back, only for the beanpole forward to control it with his left instep and volley it from long range, straight past Manchester City's Joe Hart.

It was one of those 'I was there' moments. Every man, woman and child in the Britannia was utterly gobsmacked – I could even hear the gasps from linesmen Jake Collin and Andy Halliday over the radio – and the buzz around the stands continued until the final blow of the whistle.

As well as Bale and Crouch, my job brought me into contact with many other impressive characters on the pitch. The vast majority of footballers I met, I'm pleased to say, were decent people and model professionals. Most player-referee relationships were extremely positive and respectful, in my experience; they did their job, I did mine, and we tried to work together as best we could.

While I was never in the business of cosying up to players – I didn't count any of them as my friends, as such – there were some that I hugely admired. My favourites were those enthusiastic, glass-half-full individuals who seemed to revel in their football and appeared to savour every moment.

Gianluigi Buffon, captain of both Italy and Juventus, was a perfect example. The guy sported a permanent grin and had tons of charisma and, despite being one of the most exalted goalies in Europe, was without edge or ego.

'Ciao, Howard,' he'd say, patting me on the back. 'Good to see you over in Italy again. I wish you well with the game, my friend.'

I wasn't the only match official who tended to form stronger bonds with goalies than outfield players. We just seemed to have more in common. Like us, they had a more isolated role on the field of play. Like us, they could deliver an exemplary display for 89 minutes, but their entire performance could be defined by a last gasp cock-up. This would often be in direct contrast with their striker buddies, who could have a shocking game – perhaps fluffing several sitters in the process – before nicking a final-minute winner and riding out as instant heroes.

I found that goalies had a greater affinity with the officials' roles, too. Their detached position often gave them a more objective view of the action, enabling them to see the bigger picture as moves and incidents developed, and as refs' decisions and measures were taken.

Level-headed, undemanding keepers like Tim Howard, Paul Robinson, Brad Friedel and Petr Čech were easy to referee, as were most of the lads between the sticks. In my experience there were only one or two exceptions, most notably Arsenal's charmless Jens Lehmann. In 2005, when Bundesliga referee Robert Hoyzer was convicted of match-fixing in Germany, Lehmann strongly hinted in the media that something similar could happen in the UK.

He'd made his comments after the Arsenal v Bolton Wanderers match in which I'd failed to send off Abdoulaye Faye for his awful challenge on José Reyes. Granted, I'd made a mistake, but Lehmann's post-match insinuations really pissed me off. He was bang out of order, and any remaining respect I'd had for him quickly evaporated that day.

Some officials didn't share my beef with Lehmann, however. Indeed, it was always fascinating to see how certain Premier League players polarised opinion among referees. Now and again, during our fortnightly get-togethers, my Select Group colleagues would carry out a 'Pick Five' exercise. This would entail listing a few footballers that we liked and disliked reffing, before comparing notes and exploring player-management techniques. Without fail, you'd find the same names cropping up on the Good list of one referee, and the Bad list of another.

I tended to hit it off with the characterful players who engaged and interacted – I didn't mind a bit of opinion and attitude – so would often plump for lads like Joey Barton, Robbie Savage, Mark Noble, Danny Mills and Kevin Nolan. Conversely, the other category would be made up of those players I found aloof and disdainful, who'd refuse to engage in dialogue, and who'd infuriate me with their dirty looks and dismissive gestures. Lehmann and Craig Bellamy were mainstays – no shock there, then – but regularly joining them on the naughty step would be Cesc Fàbregas, Ryan Shawcross and Fernando Torres. Curiously, the latter's behaviour seemed to correlate with his form on the pitch; the Spaniard was a dream to ref when he was flying at Liverpool, but became more difficult when he was bombing at Chelsea.

These 'Pick Five' sessions would invariably throw up some fierce debate. We'd spend ages questioning and challenging each other's choices, with my own selections attracting a fair amount of scorn and scepticism.

'Barton, for Chrissakes? He's the most difficult player I've ever reffed, Howard. He's virtually uncontrollable.'

'What on earth is Fàbregas doing there, pal? He's as good as gold with me. Never once had an issue with him.'

If memory serves, I think Cristiano Ronaldo – with whom I enjoyed a patchy relationship – featured on both my hero and villain lists over the years. We had a few run-ins, did Cristiano and I, not least during the November 2008 Manchester derby at the Etihad Stadium, shortly after the FA had launched its Respect programme, and the Premier League its Get On With The Game initiative.

Players and managers, from grass roots to top flight, had been asked to honour a code of respectful conduct, with officials being actively encouraged to penalise incidents of dissent and contempt. It prompted the introduction of the Fair Play handshake – as well as the captains-and-managers-only team sheet exchange – and emphasised the need for courteous player-referee relations.

During that particular game, I'd cautioned Ronaldo for scything down Shaun Wright-Phillips.

'Why you hate me? Why always me? I've done nothing wrong,' he'd moaned after I'd blown my whistle.

When I'd cautioned him, United's number 7 had smirked and sarcastically applauded which, under Respect's auspices, could have – and should have – justified a dismissal for a second yellow card offence.

I remember being in two minds about my course of action. On the one hand, I'd have been well within my rights to send him off for undermining me. On the other hand, however, an instant red card would have changed the whole tenor of such a high-profile game, for what was essentially a non-football reason. Rightly or wrongly, I chose the latter – admittedly easier – option. As it transpired, Ronaldo would eventually be sent off in the second half for handling the ball.

In the aftermath, a number of grass-roots officials condemned me for not taking a stand, and for not making myself a potential martyr to the Respect cause.

'An opportunity missed, Howard,' griped one emailer. 'Here was a high-profile player, playing on a worldwide stage, that you could have made an example of. A red card would have shown everyone that we meant business.'

While I could see their point, these detractors had never walked a mile in the shoes of an elite level referee. They hadn't taken charge of huge games with enormous rewards, watched on TV by millions of fee-paying fans at home, and thousands more in the stadium who'd parted with hard-earned cash to witness eleven-versus-eleven of the country's best players. They hadn't experienced the pressure of having to weigh up whether a decision would be endorsed and supported by the FA and the Premier League, or would be perceived as a poorly managed over-reaction. Had they put themselves in my position, perhaps these emailers might have had more empathy.

Fast-forward five years, and Ronaldo's attitude towards me had totally transformed. I was as surprised as anyone when he made a beeline for me following the Sweden v Portugal World Cup play-off in Stockholm, handing me the damp red shirt that he'd worn as he'd scored his memorable hat-trick.

'You reffed great. I want you to have this,' he said simply, before wandering off to join his teammates.

Thankfully, during my Premier League career the good guys outnumbered the bad eggs. Ever-obliging players like Patrice Evra, Per Mertesacker and Phil Jagielka were always great to have around, expertly corralling and cajoling their teammates and therefore making our jobs considerably easier.

Scott Parker, formerly of Spurs and West Ham, was an absolute gem to ref. He was a superb captain whose peace-making skills had a hugely positive effect on both his colleagues and the game itself.

'I'll sort him out for you, ref,' he'd say, before sprinting off to placate an overly boisterous teammate.

Scott was no angel, though, and would often find himself in my book for mistimed tackles that, while rarely malicious, could be excessively forceful.

'Bang out of order, that,' I'd say, reaching for my yellow card after he'd upended an opponent in added time.

'Aw, H, do you have to?' he'd say, eyebrows raised and arms outstretched. At the end of the day, I still had a job to do.

Chelsea's Frank Lampard was a player I had a lot of time for, too. In February 2012, I took part in a special Sport Relief episode of *Outnumbered* featuring most of the sitcom's cast, with the little girl who plays Karen acting as Frank's mascot. Earlier that week I'd had a torrid time at Stamford Bridge, awarding two (albeit rightful) penalties to Manchester United which, together with a late equaliser by Javier Hernández, had enabled a dramatic Reds comeback. The match had finished 3–3, and I'd exited the field to a chorus of boos.

The filming was due to take place at Chelsea two days later, and I was dreading showing my face at the stadium again, especially to the Blues' talisman. Having read the script, I knew that I'd been given a couple of lines to say when Frank and Karen lined up in the tunnel, and I was expecting an extremely frosty reception.

I couldn't have been more wrong. Lampard was charming – so chatty, warm and friendly – as was his girlfriend, Christine Bleakley, who was also taking part.

'Gutted that United got the point, Howard, but we'll just have to try and make up ground next week,' he said.

It turned out to be quite a funny sketch – I believe it's still on YouTube – although Frank and Christine's acting skills and comedy timing put mine to shame.

Another footballer whom I held in great esteem was Gary Speed, who I refereed on many occasions. He was so cool, calm and collected; the sort of lad who I'd often turn to for sanity and sanctuary during a tough, testing match. Referees as well as players sometimes needed the metaphorical arm round the shoulder when things were going pear-shaped, and Gary was a thoughtful, kind-hearted player who'd always oblige with a consoling word or two.

'Keep going, mate, not long to go now …' he'd say, flashing me a big smile as he ran past.

Like everyone else in the world of football, I was shocked and saddened to learn of his untimely death. In February 2012, I was honoured to be asked to referee his memorial game – Wales v Costa Rica at the Cardiff City stadium – which proved to be an incredibly moving and poignant occasion. RIP Gary; you are so missed.

*

I've been lucky (or not so lucky) to have met a procession of football managers during my career, from tough-talking taskmasters like Mick McCarthy and Diego Simeone to mild-mannered strategists like Carlo Ancelotti and Roberto Martínez.

Some bosses were trickier to deal with than others, of course. In my era, the bane of many a ref's life was the loud and lairy (although strangely charismatic) Steve Evans – formerly of Rotherham United and Leeds United – closely followed by rant-master general (and latterly Rotherham United saviour) Neil Warnock. Both bosses took a great interest in the world of officiating, which had its benefits and drawbacks. On the plus side, their knowledge was so broad that you rarely needed to explain a regulation or directive. On the negative side, however, they'd persist in haranguing you from the technical area, almost enacting a running commentary of your performance.

I had to remain incredibly focused when these vociferous managers bawled from the dugout. On the one hand, I had to be careful not to subconsciously lean towards their team in order to ease the constant earache from the touchline. On the other hand, I had to avoid unwittingly veering the other way in order to prove to the opposition that I was strong and unyielding. It was a real balancing act; one of those 50-50 scenarios in refereeing that you just had to manage to the best of your ability.

Football's upper echelons contained legions of stats-obsessed managers who, prior to each game, would do their research and work with analysts to gain the upper hand over their rivals. Former Bolton boss Sam Allardyce was a prime example, as was his predecessor, Gary Megson. Once, a couple of hours before a match at the Reebok, fourth official Peter Walton and I visited the dressing rooms to double-check the kit for colour clashes, one of our many match-day duties.

As I entered the home dressing room, I clocked a whiteboard, on which a PowerPoint slide featuring a huge image of me had been projected. It featured all my season's match stats, together with phrases like 'doesn't show many red cards for tackles' and 'allows the first one', the implication being that it was their chance to try to get stuck in. I afforded myself a little smile; even us refs were part of the match preparation at some clubs.

Another Bolton manager, Owen Coyle, was an interesting character. A few of my colleagues weren't enamoured with him – he could have a pretty sharp tongue sometimes – but I quite liked the guy. What amused me about Owen, though, was the way that, after a game, he'd come on to the pitch and smile and shake your hand, knowing that the TV cameras were likely to be trained on him. What viewers didn't realise, though, was that behind the grinning façade he'd be giving you the mother of all bollockings, hissing at you behind gritted teeth like a ventriloquist.

While to all the world it looked like was saying 'Jolly good game, ref, hope to see you at the Reebok again soon, old chum,' in reality it was more likely to be 'That was a penalty you blind bastard, now piss off home and don't come back.'

I never shied away from confrontation with managers – I'd faced far worse as an inner-city cop – and I could deal with them having a pop if they did it to my face and with a bit of personality. It was the sneaks that slated me behind my back that I couldn't stand, the ones who'd hide in their offices, sending one of their lackeys to my dressing room to give me a post-match pasting. Thankfully they were few and far between.

Brian Horton, who managed Manchester City and Macclesfield Town among others, was a member of the up-front and even-handed brigade. He'd regularly storm into the post-match dressing room to bombard me with an expletive-fuelled rant but, without fail, would re-enter five minutes later with four beer bottles clanking in his hand.

'D'you wanna Bud?' he'd beam, as if his outburst had never happened, before chatting amicably to me and my linesmen.

Ex-Stoke City boss Tony Pulis could be a firebrand, too, but I couldn't help but admire the passion he had for the game. Our relationship was affable enough, although this cordiality could well have been jeopardised one particular Saturday night.

I'd been watching *Match of the Day* when Pulis had appeared on my TV screen, sporting his trademark baseball cap, mercilessly slagging off a referee colleague in his post-match interview. I was far from impressed, and composed a text to my mate Martin Atkinson who I knew would be watching too.

'Pulis? What a fucking wanker,' I typed. 'Unbelievable!'

It was only when I pressed the Send button, and heard the tell-tale whoosh of its despatch, that I realised I'd mistakenly sent the message to Pulis himself. With one eye on the telly, I'd absent-mindedly selected his name from my contacts. I desperately tried to delete it, hammering the red button until my forefinger ached, but it was too late.

'X' came his reply, two minutes later.

No further reference was ever made to that episode on the subsequent occasions that I encountered Tony; I can only assume that he didn't have my name recorded against my number.

The tables were turned some time later, however, when I was at the receiving end of some stick from a Premier League manager, via his mobile. I'd been sharing a room with a fellow referee at our Select Group HQ, and one afternoon had walked in to find him reclining on the bed, clad only in his Sloggi undies, talking to someone on speaker phone. The person on the other line was loudly slagging me off in a broad Glaswegian accent; fuckin' Webb this, fuckin' Webb that.

My room-mate pointed at his phone and started laughing.

'Kenny Dalglish,' he mouthed.

I'd reffed Dalglish's Liverpool side the week before, and it hadn't gone well, hence his spiky rant. Why my colleague was speaking to him in the first place is anyone's guess – lying in your pants having leisurely chats with Premier League bosses wasn't entirely ethical – but he often gloried in his football connections.

I just sighed, shook my head, closed the door and walked out. I didn't want to hear any more.

Getting all pally-pally with managers just wasn't my style; I had enough mates in Rotherham, thanks very much, and didn't need any more. The friendliest I got was sending congratulatory texts to various bosses I respected, whether it was Roberto Martínez triumphing in the FA Cup or Manuel Pellegrini prevailing in the Premier League. I either obtained their numbers from obliging club secretaries, or saved them in my contacts whenever they'd sent me a 'well done' text (I received a few after the 2010 Champions League and World Cup finals, the managers having probably got my number from the same administrators).

Pellegrini was one of the more enigmatic managers I came across. In 2014, I'd reffed the game at Stamford Bridge between Chelsea and Manchester City, the two title favourites. A last-minute mix-up between Joe Hart and Matija Nastasić had led to a dramatic Fernando Torres winner and, following the final whistle, the visitors had dejectedly traipsed off the pitch.

I was getting showered after the game when I heard a steward's voice echoing across the room.

'Sorry to disturb you, Howard, but Mr Pellegrini has asked to see you before he leaves,' he said. My heart sank. This was nearly always a bad sign. What had I missed now? Perhaps the Chilean had an axe to grind because his side had dropped three valuable points.

'Don't always look on the bad side, H,' winked Darren as I towelled myself down.

'He probably wants to congratulate you on the game and wish you a safe journey home.'

When I was all suited and booted, Pellegrini strode in.

'Mr Referee,' he said, smiling broadly and extending his hand. 'I just want to say well done, good game, and have a safe journey home ...'

Even after my retirement, refereeing still plays a huge role in my life, whether it's discussing it on the TV, coaching new recruits in Saudi or giving teamwork talks to business leaders. I continue to be baffled – and flattered – that people still recognise me and I often find myself getting waylaid in pubs, airports and shopping malls. The football fans I meet are pretty friendly and respectful, which is nice, and these days are more likely to request a selfie than give me some stick. From time to time I'll receive the odd dig, though.

'Oi, why didn't you red card de Jong?' some fella will yell out of his car window, or 'How the hell did you miss that Suárez penalty?'

I suppose that's to be expected, though. It's human nature for people to focus on your flaws not your fortés and – whether I like it or not – there are some incidents that will always define me more than others.

For the vast majority of the great British public, refereeing is probably the last job in the world they'd want to do. Many still perceive it as an unglamorous profession, a thankless career, a role for control freaks. No doubt people see the way we're treated, and hear the abuse that's flung our way, and think 'nah, not for me, thanks; not in a million years.' It's a skewed opinion, I think – I'll continue to champion top-flight refereeing as a worthwhile vocation – but I can see why some may have misgivings.

That being said, there are plenty of brilliant people who still choose to join the ranks of officials; thousands of men and women throughout the UK who devote their spare time to patrolling the middle or pacing the sidelines. I'm often asked to speak to these local heroes at Referee Association dinners and meetings – as well as other grass-roots events – and I'm always more than happy to oblige.

As I stand on the stage, I'll tell these fledgling refs about the amazing journey that I embarked upon one winter's afternoon. A long and winding road that began with the Under-11s at Orgreave, that ended with the Brazilians at Belo Horizonte, and that had some entertaining stops in between: Warsaw, Cardiff, Wembley, Milan, Madrid, Johannesburg.

I'll give mention to all the different people that I've met during my career, from princes to politicians, from footballing superstars to refereeing idols, from hopping-mad chairmen to life-saving doctors, from miserable managers to the Chuckle Brothers.

And then I'll speak from the heart, encouraging them to follow their dreams, and revealing how I fulfilled mine. I'll tell them how self-belief and mental resilience underpinned everything I did. How hard work, patience and perseverance propelled me to the top. How I put my ambitions above the fear of failure and allowed myself to believe, to achieve, and to succeed.

'Once upon a time, there was a lad from Rotherham who thought he'd give this refereeing lark a go,' I'll say, bringing things to a close. 'And that same lad's standing here today, a World Cup final ref, proof that extraordinary things can happen to ordinary people.'

There's one area of my life that I've yet to address at the various dinners and functions I attend, though. Given time – and with a little bit of inner strength and Dutch courage – I'm sure that, at some stage, I'll be ready to talk publicly about my OCD. I'm aware that there are thousands of fellow sufferers out there who may identify with my situation, and I think I'd like to help raise awareness of what can be a much-misunderstood and much-maligned condition. After all, I spent years believing I was a crazy weirdo, and I'd hate to think that others with similar symptoms are feeling the same.

Until writing this book I'd never opened up about my issues to anyone; I felt awkward, I felt embarrassed, and I just bottled things up and coped alone. I agonised about tackling the subject within these pages – I was fearful of people's reactions, scared that their perceptions of me would alter – but by not doing so I'd have been overlooking an intrinsic part of my personality.

Bringing 'Howard's habits' to the fore, and talking things through, has turned out to be a hugely helpful and cathartic process. Not only has it enabled me to recognise, rationalise and understand my condition, it has also made me realise that sufferers can not only function on a day-to-day basis, but can also excel in all areas of life. I'm now able to freely discuss my OCD with my loved ones, and this has helped me more than I'd ever imagined.

Admittedly, my compulsions have eased somewhat since I quit refereeing – perhaps there's less acute stress in my life to act as a trigger – and they no longer govern me as much as before. Now and again my little behaviours will surface, though, and I'll find myself going through the motions of covertly touching walls and tapping doors until that positive thought offsets a negative thought. But the older I become, the more I'm able to accept my traits and quirks. The shame has gone. The stigma has faded. OCD, I've come to realise, is just part of who I am.

My refereeing days may be behind me, but I still like to keep in touch with a few of my old Select Group colleagues. Martin Atkinson, Michael Oliver and Jon Moss continue to be great pals and confidants of mine, and I'll occasionally touch base with Graham Poll, Mike Riley and Keren Barratt.

I also remain close with Darren Cann and Mike Mullarkey, my assistants extraordinaire; Darren's been a fantastic friend to me for over ten years, and I was proud to be in the crowd in December 2014 to witness his final Champions League game, at Barcelona's Nou Camp (he'd by then reached the UEFA age limit of forty-five). I remember watching him as he exited the international stage, at one of the most iconic stadiums in the world, taking in all the sights and sounds for one last time. His outpouring of emotion when I unexpectedly entered the dressing room – he had no idea I'd made the trip – is something that will live with me forever.

Darren, in my opinion, remains the finest assistant referee to have ever graced the Premier League – he's still running the line with aplomb – and I'll continue to enjoy our weekly, hour-long, putting-the-refereeing-world-to-rights phone calls.

Mike ended his career in style at the 2016 European Championships in France – he'd been part of Martin Atkinson's excellent team of officials – and has now taken up a coaching role with the Premier League.

'A brilliant team player and one of the most decent, honest, kindest men I have the pleasure of knowing,' is how I texted him when I learned of his retirement. 'Take a breath now, Mike Mullarkey, but also take a bow.'

I also maintain close ties with many of my ex-copper mates, too, some of whom I've known since my days at A1 sub-division in Doncaster. It's always great to catch up with the old crew; they recently dragged me along to a stag party in Ibiza, but were under strict orders to delete all photos featuring a sozzled former World Cup referee with his head slathered in glittery body paint. I also keep in touch with my former detective inspector, Dick Venables, a great friend and supporter who encouraged me to enter the world of public speaking following my 2010 World Cup exploits.

As for my family, I'm glad to say that football continues to govern our household, even after my retirement. Kay and the children are all Rotherham United season ticket-holders, and I attend as many games as I can when I'm in the UK. There's nothing the Webbs like more than taking our seats at the New York Stadium, cheering on the mighty Millers and giving the referee some stick (good naturedly, of course).

Some weekends I'll also go and watch my son turn out for his local team at Oakwood High School playing fields. Not long ago I was asked by his manager to step in as an emergency referee, which greatly amused everyone. Everyone apart from Jack, that is.

'Don't you DARE say a thing to me,' he'd scowled, mortified that his dad was galloping around the pitch, like the good old days.

'You're lucky I don't book you for dissent, son,' I'd grinned.

Naturally, the match went without a hitch. Not a single caution. I put it down to my superlative game management. It never leaves you. Once a ref, always a ref.

Hollie, Jack and Lucy are keen followers of the Premier League, too – especially if their dad's doing a stint on the telly – and are proud owners of a small collection of framed football shirts. In addition to Cristiano Ronaldo's (handed over after that game in Stockholm), they have a sky blue Sergio Agüero number (won by me at an auction, shortly after his famous 'Agueroooooooooooo' title-winner), as well as one of Gareth Bale's Real Madrid tops.

It was given to me by the player himself, following the Schalke v Real Madrid tie of February 2014, not long after the Welshman had signed from Spurs. I can't say I knew him that well, but he'd approached me in the car park in Gelsenkirchen, insisting that I accept his shirt. I remember wondering at the time if he was a little homesick, and had just wanted to pass it on to a familiar face from the UK.

'Thanks, Gareth, that's really kind,' I'd said, shaking his hand. 'Really hope everything works out for you in Madrid.'

'Yep, me too,' he'd replied.

Possessing the lion's share of my football-related memorabilia, however, are my parents. I'm not keen on displaying refereeing mementoes at home – I'd be a useless candidate for *Through the Keyhole* – but Billy and Sylvia Webb have no such qualms. Their house is adorned with souvenirs and keepsakes of their son's career: photographs in the lounge and kitchen, artists' portraits on the landing, match programmes on their bookshelves, balls and pennants in the spare bedroom. Any first-time visitor will always be given the full guided tour by my dad, who probably knows enough about my life and times for a *Mastermind* subject.

'... and this is the Champions League final medal, presented to Howard by Michel Platini on Saturday 22 May 2010,' he'll say, grinning from ear to ear.

Mum is also justly proud of her 'Webb's Bit of Fame' scrapbooks – all thirteen of them – that she's lovingly compiled over the last 25 years, and which chronicle my time in football from the junior leagues to the Premier League. They don't just feature me, though; Mum has included cuttings relating to the whole family, and is as rightly proud of my two sisters as she is of me.

While I'll sometimes feign embarrassment at all this fuss and attention, deep down I'm delighted that my career has brought so much joy and happiness to two such wonderful people. A few years ago, at a dinner laid on in my honour at the Rotherham Referees' Association, I presented Dad with the actual ball from the 2010 World Cup final as a token of my gratitude for all his love and support over the years. I gave Mum and Kay a gift, too, to recognise all the many sacrifices and allowances they'd also made. It was an emotional moment for the whole family; I think Dad even shed some tears, the soppy so-and-so.

'It's the very least I could do, Dad,' I said, giving him a big hug.

My life nowadays can be hectic – I divide my time between Riyadh and Rotherham, with my TV work in between – but I'll try and catch up with my parents whenever I can. It's always good to keep abreast of any family news via Mum, and to chat about the latest football goings-on with Dad. So, usually on a Sunday afternoon, I'll drive through the familiar streets of Brinsworth, past my former school and the old playing fields, past the Working Men's Club and the Three Magpies pub. I'll draw up outside Mum and Dad's neat semi, parking on the same road on which I played my boyhood games of kerby and keepy-uppy, convincing myself I was the next Kevin Keegan. I'll walk up the driveway, peeking over to the back garden where, all those years ago, on a warm summer's day, Billy Webb told his teenage son to take up refereeing.

And then I'll step up to the front door, and I'll ring the bell.

*DING-DONG-DING-DONG-DIIIIIIING-DONNNNNNG*, it goes.

# ACKNOWLEDGEMENTS

When the idea of writing a book was first suggested I was excited at the prospect of sharing some of the amazing football-related occasions that I've been privileged enough to experience around the world. However, the thought of converting these events into a memoir was somewhat daunting. Step forward the incredibly talented Joanne Lake, who not only brought my story to life, but also became a great friend in the process. I also want to thank her lovely husband Paul and their kids Edward and Hannah for allowing Jo to dedicate so much time to this project.

Creating this memoir was made so much easier by my mum's meticulous recording of my career via cuttings that she saved in her many family scrapbooks. Mums are brilliant and I love mine dearly.

My publishers, Simon & Schuster, have been so supportive from day one – particularly Ian Marshall – and I'd also like to thank Gary Smith from the James Grant Group and Rory Scarfe from Furniss Lawton for their excellent advice and assistance. My good friend Dick Venables also deserves a special mention for encouraging me to pen my memoirs in the first place.

The many positive experiences outlined in the book wouldn't

have happened without the help of so many individuals who – thanks to their coaching, guidance and belief – have shaped and developed me as a referee, both domestically and internationally. I'm therefore indebted to people like Ron Skidmore, Trevor Simpson, Keith Hackett, Keren Barratt and Hugh Dallas and – above all – my dad Bill.

My success as a referee also relied on the support of some wonderful colleagues. Undoubtedly the single biggest factor was the good fortune I had when my career coincided with that of two of the most talented assistant referees of all time, who also became close friends of mine. To Darren Cann and Mike Mullarkey, no words can fully express my gratitude and admiration for you guys.

To achieve your dreams in any walk of life takes strength, determination and single-mindedness, which can equally – and accurately – be described as selfishness. It also requires the presence of special people in your life who are prepared to buy into your dreams and accept that self-interest. Without the wonderful support of Kay and our children Hollie, Jack and Lucy, my successes would have been almost impossible to achieve. My family were patient with me when things went wrong and tolerated my subsequent mood swings. They accepted the many days spent away from home and understood when I had to miss important family events. They also helped me to celebrate my career high-points – what's the point of success if you have nobody to share it with? – and I hope I've made them proud.

But success also comes at a price and can change people and circumstances, as Kay and I have both come to realise. Whatever the future holds, I want her to know that I'll be eternally grateful for the huge part she played in my life both personally and professionally in the time chronicled within the pages of this book.

# INDEX

# INDEX